THE
REFERENCE
SHELF

THE

REFERENCE

SHELF

THE WELFARE DEBATE

edited by ROBERT EMMET LONG

THE REFERENCE SHELF
Volume 61 Number 3

THE H. W. WILSON COMPANY

New York   1989

THE REFERENCE SHELF

The books in this series contain reprints of articles, excerpts from books, and addresses on current issues and social trends in the United States and other countries. There are six separately bound numbers in each volume, all of which are generally published in the same calendar year. One number is a collection of recent speeches; each of the others is devoted to a single subject and gives background information and discussion from various points of view, concluding with a comprehensive bibliography that contains books and pamphlets and abstracts of additional articles on the subject. Books in the series may be purchased individually or on subscription.

Library of Congress Cataloging-in-Publication Data

Main entry under title:

The Welfare debate.
  (The Reference shelf ; v. 61, no. 3)
  Bibliography: p.
  Summary: Examines the effectiveness of the current welfare system and possible reforms.
  1. Public welfare—United States. 2. United States—
Social policy—1980-   . [1. Public welfare.
2. United States—Social policy—1980-   ] I. Long,
Robert Emmet.   II. Series.
HV95.W445   1989   361.973   89-16536
ISBN 0-8242-0782-3

Cover: Want in the midst of plenty—a homeless man, bundled against the cold, solicits money on Fifth Avenue in front of a window display from one of the high-priced shops which line New York's fashionable shopping street selling Christmas goods that he has no possible use for.
Photo: AP/Wide World Photos

Printed in the United States of America

CONTENTS

Preface 5

I. Background: Welfare and the Reagan Presidency

Editor's Introduction 7
Lawrence D. Maloney. Welfare in America: Is It a Flop?
.... U. S. News & World Report   8
Tom Joe. Forgotten Americans: The "Working Poor" ..
.... USA Today   22
David Whitman. The Key to Welfare Reform ..Atlantic   27
Susan B. Garland. A Return to Compassion? ....
.... Business Week   37

II. Welfare Reform: Welfare vs. Workfare

Editor's Introduction 42
Jacob V. Lamar, Jr. From Welfare to Workfare ... Time   43
Laurie Udesky. Workfare .... Progressive   47
Michael S. Dukakis. The Greatest Welfare Reform:
    REAL JOBS .... USA Today   56
Susan B. Garland. Welfare Reform May Finally Be in the
    Works .... Business Week   61
Mickey Kaus. Is It Hype or True Reform? ...Newsweek   66
Mimi Abramovitz. Why Welfare Reform Is a Sham .....
.... Nation 69
Andrew Hacker. Getting Rough on the Poor ....
.... New York Review of Books   76

III. Child Welfare

Editor's Introduction 95
Michael Robin. A Right to the Tree of Life .....Nation   96

Marian Wright Edelman. Who Will Protect the Chil-
    dren? .... USA Today   99
Dinitia Smith. Children of the Night .... New York   106
Andrew Stein. Children of Poverty ....
    .... New York Times Magazine   122
David Whitman. The Hollow Promise ....
    .... U. S. News & World Report   131

IV. Homelessness

Editor's Introduction   139
Marjorie Hope and James Young. Sinking into Home-
    lessness .... Commonweal   140
Richard J. Margolis. "Is the Next Step Penn Station?" ...
    .... New Leader 147
Ellen L. Bassuk. The Homelessness Problem ....
    .... Scientific American 151
Jonathan Kozol. Distancing the Homeless .. Yale Review 161
Thomas J. Main. What We Know about the Homeless ..
    .... Commentary 174
Mickey Leland. Toward a National Policy to End Home-
    lessness .... America   188

Bibliography

Books and Pamphlets   193
Additional Periodical Articles with Abstracts 197

PREFACE

The increasing social and financial costs of welfare in the 1980s have provoked a national debate. Some Conservative politicians blame the high cost of welfare on Liberal spending programs that must be curbed. Their proposals reflect the sentiments of many middle-class Americans who feel that their tax dollars are being used to support a class of people who do not do enough to find employment, and who live without toil—sometimes even for generations—at a level of affluence nearly equal to their own. To many Liberals, however, the welfare system in America is not doing enough to assist the needy, the helpless, and the disadvantaged. They stress compassion and humane social ideals, and deplore the fact that America provides for its needy on a scale well below that of the industrialized nations of Europe.

In the late 1980s the welfare debate has come to a head as costs of social programs continue to rise. Attention has been called to long-term welfare recipients who are in many cases single mothers, bearing child after child out of wedlock and adding to welfare dependency indefinitely. In recent years a new "welfare consensus" has come about in which many Liberals have joined with Conservatives in calling for reform in the system intended to help these single parent mothers. Under the new "workfare" program recently enacted in Congress, single mothers will be given job training and expected to find employment. The program, however, is modestly budgeted and many critics charge that it will have no appreciable effect on the welfare rolls. Will this be a "revolution" in welfare that will break the cycle of poverty or is it merely a symbolic gesture of social planners who have found the welfare problem essentially intractable? This question and many others on various aspects of the welfare system are posed in this volume.

The first section concerns the welfare policies of the Reagan administration. It indicates what initiatives were introduced, what retrenchments were made, and how these actions were regarded. The second section turns to the most widely discussed development in current welfare reform, the workfare program. The evolution of the workfare concept in the states, introduction of the act in Congress by Senator Daniel Patrick Moynihan, and its eventual passage, are treated in a series of articles. Also included are several articles that consider the chances for success of the workfare concept, and its larger implications, particularly in regards to the "feminization of poverty." Section three deals with child welfare and the formidable problems of assisting the children of poverty, abuse, and neglect. The final section takes up the important question of the homeless in America, whose numbers have grown swiftly during the Reagan years.

The editor is indebted to the authors and publishers who have granted permission to reprint the materials in this compilation. Special thanks are due to Joyce Cook and the Fulton Public Library staff, and to the staff of Penfield Library, State University of New York at Oswego.

ROBERT EMMET LONG

June 1989

I. BACKGROUND: WELFARE AND THE REAGAN PRESIDENCY

EDITOR'S INTRODUCTION

During the 1980s the welfare system has been the subject of prolonged controversy. The Reagan administration spent lavishly on defense but cut expenditure for welfare. Many were dropped from the welfare rolls, programs were curtailed, and federal funding for low-income housing was slashed. President Reagan's attitude toward those on welfare was at best unsympathetic; he spoke of "welfare queens" who arrived in Cadillacs to pick up their welfare checks, and referred to the homeless as "homeless, you might say, by choice." Yet despite his cutbacks, the number of those on welfare actually rose during his administration, and homelessness rose dramatically. To his opponents, Reagan's neglect of welfare created a crisis for America's poor that called for new thinking about the welfare system. These events provide the essential background for the discussion of the welfare system since the mid 1980s.

The articles in Section One survey the social policies of the Reagan years. The opening article by Lawrence Maloney from *U. S. News & World Report* reviews Reagan's policies at the end of his first term. Ironically, as Maloney points out, although the Reagan administration initiated the Job Training Partnership Act (JTPA), costing $10 billion a year, the number of those on relief has continued to climb. Another article of the same year, by Tom Joe in the magazine *USA Today*, focuses on the effect of policy changes on the "working poor." The administration's Omnibus Budget Reconciliation Act (OBRA) of 1981 increased the tax rate on this group significantly, while denying it Medicaid funding. As Joe notes, the act merely made it more profitable for low-income workers to become welfare recipients.

Two following articles, written at the end of President Reagan's second term, examine the cumulative effect of his approach to public assistance. David Whitman's article in the *Atlantic* surveys the legislative acts of the administration, all of which failed

7

to reduce the welfare burden. Neither the Omnibus Budget Reconciliation Act (OBRA) nor the Job Training Partnership Act (JTPA), Whitman claims, has had any practical effect. Nor did the program known as GROW (Greater Opportunities through Work) result in any significant reduction of the welfare rolls. In the final article, reprinted from *Business Week*, Susan B. Garland contends that poverty has increased during the Reagan years, a trend that will be difficult to reverse in a time of deficits.

WELFARE IN AMERICA: IS IT A FLOP?[1]

A 20-year crusade to wipe out poverty in America has cost government at all levels hundreds of billions of dollars, but a rising chorus of critics is asking some hard questions—Could it be that this money has been wasted and that the poor are actually worse off? Indeed, have millions of people become more deeply mired in poverty because of the very programs designed to help them?

The answers hold more than mere academic interest. At a time when federal budget cutters are desperately searching for ways to trim a 200-billion-dollar yearly deficit, poverty programs once again loom as inviting targets—just as they were in 1981 when the Reagan administration took its first slash at federal spending.

Among the leaders in this new assessment of the welfare system is social scientist Charles Murray of the Manhattan Institute for Policy Research. His controversial new book *Losing Ground* has stirred sharp debate by insisting that ever increasing amounts of government aid to the poor have destroyed individual initiative, undermined family life and created an army of people dependent on the dole.

"We tried to provide more for the poor and produced more poor instead," writes Murray. "We tried to remove the barriers to escape from poverty and inadvertently built a trap." He adds

[1]Reprint of an article by Lawrence D. Maloney, *U. S. News & World Report* staffwriter. Reprinted by permission from *U. S. News & World Report*, December 24, 1984. Copyright © 1984, *U. S. News & World Report*.

that the percentage of Americans now in poverty—15.2 percent—is higher than when Lyndon Johnson left office, despite the huge outpouring of aid.

Murray's bold solution: Scrap all the major welfare programs—Aid to Families With Dependent Children (AFDC), medicaid, food stamps, subsidized housing, disability insurance, compensatory education—as well as affirmative-action programs that give special breaks to minorities.

While others may not recommend such draconian measures, Murray has many supporters among leading social-program thinkers, such as former White House domestic expert Martin Anderson, Nobel Prize–winning economist Milton Friedman, black economists Thomas Sowell of the Hoover Institution and Walter Williams of George Mason University, and George Gilder, the author of *Wealth and Poverty*.

"The Murray book is an accurate description of what has been happening," says Professor Williams. "Because welfare pays more than the minimum wage, there is no incentive to enter the work force. What we need is a withdrawal program to wean welfare recipients away from their dependency."

Such thinking is music to the ears of the White House, whose philosophy is to rely on economic growth to move the able-bodied members of the nation's 35 million poor into jobs while retaining a "safety net" of benefits for the disadvantaged elderly and disabled.

Yet for every expert who lines up behind Murray in his condemnation of a welfare system that now costs the federal government 80 billion dollars a year, there is another who argues that programs for the needy have indeed lifted millions out of want and that it is both callous and simplistic to call the war on poverty a flop.

"Murray says the programs have failed, but he is 90 percent wrong," declares Sar Levitan, a George Washington University economist and author of *Beyond the Safety Net*. "His thinking fits with the tenor of the times, which is that many problems associated with poverty are intractable, so let's just give up."

Who is right in this debate over one of the most vital issues of domestic policy? What have been the successes and the failures of all those Great Society programs set in motion by Johnson two decades ago? Is spending for the poor really busting the budget, or is it modest compared with outlays for defense, Social Security and other needs?

For the answers, editors and economists of *U.S. News & World Report* talked with dozens of experts and combed reports and statistics dealing with poverty and the welfare system. What follows is a fresh assessment of the war on poverty—a generation after its launching in March of 1964.

What Those Billions Buy

With the exception of AFDC and public housing, which date to Depression days, most of today's major welfare programs are the children of a single President, Lyndon Johnson. Among his creations: Food stamps, medicaid, "Head Start," Job Corps and medicare.

But if Johnson gave birth to these programs, his successors, with coaxing from Congress, nurtured them and added a few of their own, including expanded housing-subsidy programs, home-energy assistance, and Supplemental Security Income (SSI) for the blind, disabled and low-income aged.

Altogether, federal poverty programs have grown from 4.4 billion dollars in 1965 to more than 150 billion when medicare—the health program for the elderly—is included. Who benefits most from these efforts? On this, experts are nearly unanimous: The elderly. Combined with the 1972 provision to give annual increases in Social Security benefits based on the cost of living, programs for the poor and medicare have lifted hundreds of thousands of elderly people out of poverty. In 1966, there were 5.1 million elderly poor—17.9 percent of all poor Americans. Today, the elderly poor number 3.7 million, or 10.5 percent of the poor. A Census Bureau study shows that when noncash benefits such as food stamps and subsidized housing are counted, only 1 elderly person in 30 is poor.

"To a great extent, the aged owe their relative well-being to government transfers," report analysts at the University of Wisconsin's Institute for Research on Poverty. In fact, some now argue that government has done too good a job of helping the elderly at a time of strained federal resources.

Beyond programs for the elderly, however, agreement over the effectiveness of government welfare programs begins to break down. Each month brings some new report of fraud or waste, and rising administrative costs siphon still more dollars. In the fiscal year ended September 30, administrative costs associated with eight major antipoverty programs exceeded 4 billion dollars—about half the cost of the entire AFDC budget.

Housing Vouchers. Expensive programs to create public-service jobs, many researchers say, did little to enhance the future earnings of participants and often replaced jobs that states and cities would have funded. Similarly, construction of subsidized housing is criticized not only for its high costs but for shunting the poor into isolated ghettos where crime runs rampant. The Reagan administration has virtually halted all subsidized-housing construction, except for the elderly, and is instead providing housing vouchers to about 100,000 new families each year.

Yet certain programs are yielding good results. A General Accounting Office report on the special supplemental food program for Women, Infants and Children (WIC) found that "the proportion of infants at risk at birth because of low weight decreased by as much as 20 percent" because of the program. This fall, a report by a Michigan research foundation gave high marks to Head Start, a 1-billion-dollar program that offers education and nutritional help to about 440,000 needy preschoolers. Other compensatory-education programs for older children are credited with helping to boost the number of blacks attending college from 227,000 in 1960 to about 1.2 million today. For example, about 60 percent of Upward Bound high-school students go on to college.

More controversial is the Job Corps, which takes disadvantaged youngsters age 16 to 22 out of their neighborhoods and puts them in residential centers for counseling, remedial education and job training. The cost per trainee, say critics, can equal a year's tuition at Harvard University. Yet defenders say taxpayers should look at the long-term costs of *not* reaching such youths. Says Marc Bendick, a researcher at the Urban Institute in Washington: "For every $1 spent on Job Corps, the government gets back $1.48 from income taxes paid by graduates, plus savings from reduced costs resulting from crime, welfare benefits and unemployment insurance. Job Corps really ought to be expanded."

The program, which costs 610 million annually, reaches 88,000 youngsters, a relatively small number considering an unemployment rate of 40 percent among black teenagers, who make up the bulk of trainees.

Welfare Trap: The Murray View

It is not these special programs for needy children or youths
that anger a new generation of welfare critics. Rather, it is the
whole mosaic of programs such as cash benefits, food stamps,
housing and health subsidies that together have made welfare an
inviting alternative to work, particularly for individuals with few
or no job skills.

In *Losing Ground*, Murray traces the fortunes of a mythical
low-income couple—Harold and Phyllis—living in Pennsylvania.
They have no special job skills, and Phyllis is pregnant. As Murray sees it, in 1960 common sense would dictate that the two mar-
ry and avoid going on welfare because of three major factors:
AFDC benefits were meager, welfare benefits would be reduced
on a dollar-for-dollar basis if Phyllis took a part-time job, and
Harold would not be allowed to live with the family without their
losing benefits. Harold thus takes an entry-level job at a laundry
to support his new family and hopes for the best.

By 1970, however, the situation has changed dramatically.
Not only have AFDC benefits been raised but the Great Society
has brought in medicaid, food stamps and housing subsidies. Regulations have been changed to allow Phyllis to work at a part-time
job and keep the first $30 she makes. After that, her AFDC bene-
fits are reduced by $2 for every $3 of earned income. Because of
a 1968 Supreme Court ruling, Harold can stay in the house without the family's losing benefits. Also, as long as he is not legally
responsible for the child, his income will not count against the
family's AFDC benefits. As Murray explains it: "The old-
fashioned solution of getting married and living off their earned
income has become markedly inferior. The bottom line is that
Harold can get married and work 40 hours a week in a hot, tire-
some job; or he can live with Phyllis and their baby without getting married, not work and have more disposable income."

While some critics fault Murray for picking Pennsylvania, a
relatively generous state for welfare benefits, many agree with his
basic argument that burgeoning government benefits have severely damaged incentives to work and have undermined the
family. "Poor people may be poor, but they aren't stupid," says
Williams of George Mason. "If you make it easier for them to live
without working, many of them will, just as those in other income
groups would."

The factors that have created a throng of dependent families, says Murray, go beyond expanded welfare benefits. He points to slumping educational standards in the 1960s and 1970s that reduced the ability of low-income individuals to get jobs and a more lenient legal system that made crime, at least for some, a real alternative to work. Meanwhile, with the surge in advocacy groups for the poor and the influence of the media, social planners and other "intelligentsia," welfare began to be described as a "right," not a "privilege." No longer was poverty the fault of the poor, but of society, and those who chose to work at low-level jobs instead of taking the dole were perceived as fools. Such changes in attitudes, says Murray, are a far cry from the 1950s when "it was seen as a truism that a welfare system was perpetually in danger of tilting the balance in favor of the easy way out."

Murray's interpretation draws plenty of criticism. A prime target is his view that growth of the welfare state blocked the progress that economic growth had been making in reducing the poverty rate by an average of 1 percentage point a year until the late 1960s.

"He ignores the fact that the unemployment rate in the 1980s is much higher than in the 1960s, and economic growth is slower, too," says Robert Greenstein, director of the Center on Budget and Policy Priorities in Washington, D.C. "When unemployment goes up, the poor and minorities are hurt more than most."

Still others blame much of today's poverty on the decline of well-paying but low-skill factory jobs, such as those in autos and steel, that were once the door to opportunity for many families. Divorce, more lenient sexual mores and rising numbers of illegitimate births also are cited as big factors in putting more women and their dependent children on the welfare rolls.

A Dependent Underclass?

While they may debate whether rising welfare rolls are caused more by government programs or by a troubled economy, many experts are worried about the growth of a hard-core, impoverished population with bleak prospects of ever moving into the middle class.

A study of welfare recipients by David Ellwood and Mary Jo Bane of Harvard University found that about 60 percent were in the midst of a poverty spell lasting eight or more years. Estimates of the long-term-poor population—the so-called underclass—range from as few as 5 million to as many as 18 million.

Those most likely to depend on welfare for long periods, say Ellwood and Bane, include high-school dropouts, nonwhites, unwed mothers, mothers with many children and women who had not earned any income before going on AFDC. Other analysts add households headed by the disabled and the very old to this category.

The "feminization" of the poor, however, may well be the biggest generator of persistent poverty. There are now 3.6 million poor families with a female head of household—up 82 percent from 1960. Such households comprise nearly half of all poor families, and they dominate the relief rolls in areas ranging from Los Angeles County to Detroit to rural West Virginia. John Burdette, commissioner of human services in West Virginia, notes: "We have seen a gradual shift away from the traditional family to households with a single parent, usually female."

Among minorities, the situation is particularly serious. Blacks and Hispanics account for almost 80 percent of the 477,000 single-parent AFDC families in Los Angeles County. Nearly all these households are headed by females. A report by the National Urban League on the state of black America notes that 70 percent of all poor black children live in female-headed households and that more than 80 percent of babies born to black teenagers are illegitimate.

Says the report: "This is a prescription for disaster. A child growing up in such circumstances has two strikes on him or her from the start, and may well grow into adulthood as a member of a growing sector of our society perpetually without gainful employment or any hope of ever escaping the clutches of poverty."

The degree to which welfare dependency or a "culture of poverty" is passed on to children has been debated for years, but few experts deny that the phenomenon exists. In his studies of inner-city youths in Philadelphia, Boston and Chicago, economist Robert Lerman of Brandeis University found that 70 percent of those who came from families on welfare neither attended school nor had a job. Says Lerman: "The existence of another person in the family who works definitely raises the chances that young people will stay in school or get a job."

Lerman also found a strong link between female-headed households and diminished opportunity for young people. So did

Sara McLanahan of the Institute for Research on Poverty, who concludes that regardless of place of residence, parent's education or race, young people who lived with single mothers were more likely to have dropped out of school than those living in two-parent households.

The Many Faces of Want

Just as it is a mistake to dismiss the idea of a culture of poverty, it is also wrong to view poverty as a homogeneous mass of welfare mothers and dependent children.

Based on his studies of 5,000 American families over a 15-year period, sociologist Greg Duncan of the University of Michigan estimates that one quarter of the U.S. population fell below the poverty line at one time or another during the 1970s, even though the official poverty rate in any one year was never more than 12.6 percent. For many, the brush with hard times was brought on by temporary setbacks—illness, divorce, unemployment—that were overcome after a short period.

This trend has been even more evident in the last five years amid the mass layoffs in factory jobs brought on by recession and the drive by companies to cut costs through automation. Particularly in the Midwestern "rust bowl," local poverty agencies have been deluged with requests for emergency help from people who had never before sought welfare benefits—the so-called new poor.

Others in this group fled to the sun belt in the hope of finding jobs, sometimes setting up tent cities while they waited in vain for employment. "This is a group of people dropping into poverty through no fault of their own," says David Johnson, Louisiana State University research director, one of many who are calling for bigger retraining programs for laid-off industrial workers.

Still others among the poor are the products of another type of shutdown—not of factories but of mental hospitals. In the last 20 years, a nationwide shift toward community mental-health care has resulted in the release of tens of thousands of patients from state hospitals into cities that often are unprepared to provide services. The result, says a recent report by the American Psychiatric Association, has been to create a new class of "society's untouchables."

The association estimates that from 25 to 50 percent of the nation's homeless population, which studies peg at 250,000 to 3 million, suffer serious mental illness. Says the report: "Hardly a section of the country, urban or rural, has escaped the ubiquitous presence of ragged, ill and hallucinating human beings, wandering through city streets, huddled in alleyways or sleeping over vents."

Millions more of the nation's needy labor at low-paying jobs that keep them in poverty—or just a notch above it. A worker holding down a full-time job at the minimum wage of $3.35 an hour would receive a gross income of $7,000, well below the average poverty threshold for a family of four of $10,178. The minimum wage has not been raised since January of 1981, while living costs during that time have risen 21 percent.

Progress or Backsliding?

Whether labeled "underclass" or "new poor," the ranks of the needy—at least by the official poverty definition—have swelled during the Reagan years. From 1960, when the poverty rate stood at 22.2 percent of the population, the rate dropped steadily to a low of 11.1 percent in 1973 but has since moved upward to the current 15.2 percent.

Still, the recent setbacks hide what many see as considerable progress. Although 35 million people today are classified as poor—out of a population of 232 million—40 million were poor in 1960 out of a population of 180 million.

The official definition of poverty does not count the noncash benefits the poor receive, such as food stamps, housing subsidies and medicaid. When these are considered, the poverty rate drops to the range of 10 to 14 percent, the Census Bureau reports.

Clearly, federal aid has lifted millions out of poverty and has reduced the deprivation of millions of others. According to congressional studies, 1 American in 4 would fall below the poverty level without government support. David Stockman, the President's budget director, claims that more than half of the elderly would be impoverished without federal assistance.

Then why the recent uptick in the poverty rate? Among factors cited by Greenstein of the Center on Budget and Policy Priorities:

• Economic troubles, including the steep inflation of recent years and high unemployment brought on by two recessions in the early '80s.

• Failure of AFDC benefits to keep up with inflation. The purchasing power of such aid fell by nearly a third between 1970 and 1984.

• The increasing feminization of poverty.

• Federal budget cuts affecting social programs. Greenstein estimates that 560,000 were added to the poverty ranks in 1982 because of tougher eligibility standards.

Whatever the reason for the increase, a flurry of reports from around the country point to a greater demand for services to aid the needy. In nearly every big city, authorities and charitable agencies are adding or expanding soup kitchens and temporary shelters.

In Washington, D.C., the Rev. John Steinbruck, who helped found a food program called Bread for the City, says: "Four years ago, we served about 400 people a month. Today, it is 3,400 and still going up."

New York City is spending more than 200 million dollars a year to shelter about 18,500 a night—up from the 3,500 sheltered on an average night three years ago at an annual cost of 12 million.

In Chicago, former Alderman Dick Simpson notes that there are as many as 25,000 homeless but only 1,400 emergency beds. The city is distributing 20,000 boxes of emergency food each month, up from 1,000 in 1982. "If funding doesn't come from the city, people will be dying this winter of hunger and pneumonia," says Simpson. "For the homeless, the city government is becoming the last resort when the safety net of the federal government has dropped out."

Helping the Poor: The Reagan Philosophy

Simpson is one of many who blame what they see as increased human suffering on budget cuts in social programs. While White House officials insist that the "truly needy" are being cared for, critics say thousands are slipping through the administration's self-described safety net.

Shortly after a presidential task force reported early this year that rampant hunger in the U.S. could not be documented, a New England commission, led by Larry Brown of Harvard University's School of Public Health, found hunger to be "widespread and increasing" and laid the blame on "clear and conscious actions taken by government leaders."

Figures show clearly that poverty programs did sustain major cuts, primarily in Reagan's first budget, for the fiscal year 1982. In that year, spending for AFDC and food programs declined in real terms by 11.2 percent, primarily because of tougher eligibility standards. For instance, the income of stepparents was included for the first time in determining AFDC benefits, and stricter limits were placed on the amount of income that could be earned without having benefits reduced. These and other changes removed about 450,000 families from the AFDC rolls. Other restrictions had the effect of removing 1 million from food-stamp benefits and 600,000 children from medicaid coverage. All told, spending on programs for the poor in 1984, after adjustment for inflation, is about 7 percent below what it was in 1981.

The net effect of budget cuts and tax reform during these years, according to the Urban Institute, has been to reduce the average real disposable income of the poorest fifth of U.S. families by about 8 percent. Yet the institute confirms the White House's view that the safety net for the poorest Americans remains largely intact.

The impact of these changes falls primarily on the able-bodied poor. This is consistent with the White House philosophy that jobs and an expanding economy, not welfare aid, are the best way to bring people out of poverty. That same view has led the administration to push workfare, a concept that requires welfare recipients to perform some sort of job in return for their benefits. Authorized by Congress in 1981 for both AFDC and food-stamp recipients, optional workfare experiments are being tried by some 40 states.

While proponents praise workfare as a way to introduce welfare recipients to the world of work, critics feel the administrative costs are still too high and that most programs are mainly "punitive" rather than steppingstones to good jobs. "Rarely do they provide a training component or day-care assistance for welfare mothers," says Morton Sklar, director of Catholic University's Jobs Watch program.

"**Don't Pay Enough.**" Researcher Demetra Nightingale of the Urban Institute adds: "The sorts of jobs that workfare prepares people for don't pay enough to be an incentive to go off welfare. At best, even with a training component, workfare might reduce the welfare case load by 2 percent." Currently, about 200,000 people are enrolled in workfare programs—a tiny fraction of the welfare population.

Also controversial is the Job Training Partnership Act (JTPA), the administration's successor to the much maligned Comprehensive Employment and Training Act, which in its heyday of 1979 funded 430,000 training slots and 725,000 public-service jobs at a cost of 10 billion dollars. JTPA instead uses private-industry councils that work with local governments to determine the sorts of jobs and training needed. Observers say, however, that the councils tend to pick the cream of the crop for training rather than try to rehabilitate the hard-core disadvantaged. Still, the Labor Department reports that more than 70 percent of those who completed the program in its first six months were able to find jobs, far exceeding expectations. The administration estimates that JTPA will train close to a million people in 1984 and 1985 at a cost of 3.6 billion dollars annually.

Yet another Reagan initiative for the poor—enterprise zones—remains bottled up in the House of Representatives. A measure passed by the Senate would create 75 of these zones in depressed areas, giving tax breaks and other advantages to employers who train and hire low-income workers.

Directions for the Future

While programs such as workfare and JTPA are still in their infancy, the course of America's treatment of its poor during the Reagan era is well established.

Virtually no expert expects to see massive reform of the welfare system during Reagan's second term, whether it be the wholesale scuttling of programs, as Murray suggests, or the substitution of a guaranteed minimum income or similar system in place of all the individual welfare programs.

"There is no drive to reform welfare now, certainly not from those who might want to liberalize it," says economist John Palmer of the Urban Institute. "They are fighting a defensive action."

"Reagan doesn't want to get involved with a cash-grant system or a negative income tax that supplements the income of poor families," adds economist John Weicher of the American Enterprise Institute. "This administration is saying, 'If you can work, you should get off welfare.'"

Experts believe the White House will keep nipping around the edges of welfare programs to squeeze more savings. "Everyone—Republicans and Democrats alike—knows that the poverty programs bore the brunt of cuts in 1981 and 1982," says economist Isabel Sawhill of the Urban Institute, "and they know that poverty has been going up."

Federal outlays for poverty programs now comprise about 17.5 percent of all social spending, down from 22 percent in 1978. While spending for nonpoverty social programs, such as Social Security, unemployment insurance and education aid, increased by 27.7 percent from 1981 to 1984, programs for the needy rose just 5.1 percent.

The general public, despite the popularity of the Murray book, does not appear to be up in arms over the level of welfare spending.

A CBS/*New York Times* exit poll on Election Day found that 79 percent of the respondents felt that government benefits for the poor were either too low or about right.

Californians in November also defeated a proposition that would have slashed 3 billion dollars from that state's relatively generous welfare system.

Following its New Federalism concept, the White House is expected to try to get states and cities, as well as private business and charities, to take on more responsibility for the poor. Resistance to that idea already is mounting. At a meeting of the National League of Cities in late November, leaders urged the federal government to double the funds for emergency shelters. League President George Latimer of St. Paul told fellow mayors that it was their job to become "watchdogs for the poor."

Major charity campaigns report steady increases in giving—but bigger demands for help, as well. Last year, the United Way collected a record 1.95 billion dollars. It expects another record this year.

Yet spokesman Stephen Delfin points to a "growing group of new poor who have lost their jobs and gone through their unemployment compensation." The Rev. Marvin Mottet, director of the Catholic Church's Campaign for Human Development, has a similar view: "We need a third more funds than we got last year to meet all the requests from good programs that meet our guidelines."

Officials with many such agencies also worry that giving could suffer if Congress goes along with measures that are now being proposed to reduce the tax advantages of charitable contributions.

The Toughest Challenge

After a generation of fighting poverty, the most difficult part of the battle lies ahead.

Those whose plight can be eased primarily with financial aid, such as the elderly, have to a large extent been helped. What is left is a population of younger, ill-educated poor—the AFDC mothers, the high-school dropouts—whose basic needs are being met by current programs but who face a hand-to-mouth future of dependency in a complex and sophisticated society.

"Twenty years ago, we looked around and asked what was needed to help the elderly poor, and we took steps to correct the situation," says poverty analyst Diana Pearce of Catholic University. "If we could do the same thing to address the feminization of poverty, we could go a long way toward solving the problem of poverty in America."

Yet programs for unskilled welfare mothers are expensive and time-consuming, often requiring job training, counseling, transportation and day care. The same is true in reaching inner-city youths, many of them illiterate. "You need to give them a tremendous amount of individual attention," says Yvonne Franklin of the Center for Employment Training in San Jose, Calif.

Beyond giving people the skills to move out of poverty, experts urge families, schools and communities to give more attention to the "intangibles," such as building values and character so youngsters will have the fortitude to stay in school and avoid the traps of crime and teenage pregnancy.

On the Move. Alarmed by the sharp increase in female heads of families and in illegitimate births, black groups such as the National Urban League and Delta Sigma Theta sorority this year launched studies and conducted meetings across the country aimed at shoring up the black family.

Others challenge their fellow Americans to take a more personal interest in the poor rather than to presume that welfare will take care of them. A recent report by a commission of prominent Catholic lay people, headed by former Treasury Secretary William Simon, noted: "Too many people want to entrust the problems of the poor to the government and then forget about them. Many will give large amounts of money, vote for higher government aid. The only thing they will *not* do is be seen among the poor, helping the poor, person to person, family to family."

All this is to say that poverty always was and always will be a complex problem that goes well beyond dollars and cents and into the realm of attitudes and aspirations. The Reagan administration may well be right in its prediction that the poverty rate will soon fall, but not even a booming economy can give jobs to those who have no skills or no desire to work. Nor can poverty be wiped out in such a diverse and ever changing nation by new infusions of federal aid, no matter how massive.

FORGOTTEN AMERICANS: THE "WORKING POOR"[2]

In the world according to the Reagan Administration, there are two significant groups in society—middle-income Americans and the "truly needy." The real world, however, is more complex; families and individuals are spread along an income continuum, not simply divided into two distinct groups. In basing its policies on a dual-society paradigm, the Reagan Administration has overlooked and penalized a crucial element of our community—a group known as the "working poor."

The "working poor" is a group not easily defined, in part because it is in no way homogenous. The name reflects all that its members have in common—they are working and they are poor. The working poor live in cities, suburbs, in the country; they are black, white, Hispanic; some have finished college, others only elementary school. The working poor are employable persons who,

[2]Reprint of an article by Tom Joe, director of the Center for the Study of Social Policy, Washington, D.C. Reprinted from *USA Today* Magazine, March 1984. Copyright 1984 by the Society for the Advancement of Education.

in today's tight labor market, have managed to find low-paying jobs, and barely scrape out a living on meager wages. They are all too familiar with the growing unemployment lines, as their attachment to the labor force is quite fragile.

Equally important is a negative definition. The working poor, according to the Administration, are not the "truly needy"; they are not wholly dependent on the government for support. The working poor are different and must be treated that way—something the Reagan Administration is just now beginning to realize.

How many people constitute this vague, but important, group is difficult to say. In 1982, when the poverty rate rose to 15%—a 17-year high—34,400,000 persons lived below the poverty standard. Forty per cent of these were children under 18. More than 9,000,000 of these poor—including more than 3,600,000 family heads—worked at some time in 1982. While 9,000,000 is a significant figure, it includes only those below the unscientific poverty line, which was a scant $7,693 for a family of three. If we consider those families with income less than 150% of the official poverty standard, the number of persons living in working poor families may jump to 35,000,000.

What is important is not precision in figures, but simply the recognition of the existence of this in-between group, working, living, and struggling somewhere between the caricatured non-working welfare recipient and the caricatured middle-American wage-earner. In many ways, these working poor families are economically the most vulnerable of all Americans. While the Reagan Administration has officially recognized the importance of a "safety net" of policies for the "truly needy," its policies toward economic recovery have seriously burdened the working poor. In his social policies, his revision of tax laws, and in his general economic theory, the President has placed a disproportionate burden on this neglected group.

In 1981, more than 500,000 of the working poor received partial Aid to Families with Dependent Children (AFDC) benefits, designed to encourage work and supplement their incomes. Under the Omnibus Budget Reconciliation Act of 1981 (OBRA), the "marginal tax rate" on earnings for these families increased to 99% (in 46 of the 50 states). This means that, for each dollar the average working AFDC recipient earns, he or she would lose at least 99 cents in Federal aid. Thus, in many cases, OBRA made it more profitable for low-income workers to become full-time welfare recipients.

When they lost their AFDC benefits, most of these families lost their Medicaid coverage as well. Both by tightening AFDC enrollment requirements and by additional cuts in Medicaid funding, OBRA has left millions of persons—two-thirds of whom are children—without medical care. This poses a particularly great threat to the working poor, for many low-wage jobs do not include health insurance. For these families, Medicaid had been a buffer against the high costs of essential medical care. Under OBRA, the financial survival of the working poor must now ride on their hopes for good health.

As if to tempt disaster, however, the Administration has stretched these hopes by orchestrating further cuts in nutrition assistance programs. Food stamps were reduced by nearly 20%, cutting a critical supplement from the food budgets of the working poor. As breakfasts and dinners on the tables of these families shrank, the Administration found more "savings" in the School Lunch Program. When subsidies for school lunches were reduced, more than 3,000,000 children were forced to leave the program.

Devastating Impact

The absolute impact of these cuts is devastating. From all directions—disposable incomes, medical care, nutrition—these changes threaten the well-being of the working poor. In relative terms, however, it is clear that these policies are not only hurtful, but grossly unfair as well. Through its policies, the Administration has demonstrated nothing but an absolute lack of recognition and even conscious disregard for these working members of American society.

A study by the *National Journal* shows that the average family in the bottom fifth of the income spread would lose $80 in Federal benefits, while a family in the top fifth would lose $50 from the budget cuts enacted in fiscal years 1981 and 1982. This difference is particularly disturbing when one recalls that the bottom quintile lacks the personal safety net of savings of the top fifth. Even if all income quintiles had lost equal shares, OBRA would still be seriously inequitable. Fairness does not mean treating everyone alike; it means treating like cases alike. Fairness requires distributing burdens in proportion to resources. The burden of diminished transfers should fall to those least reliant on such transfers, not on the poor. That the poorest Americans, including the working poor, must bear the brunt of the Administration's economic recovery plan is gravely unfair.

Nevertheless, a similar approach pervades the Administration's tax reforms. By cutting the tax burden of all income groups by the same percentage, the Economic Recovery Tax Act (ERTA) is effectively redistributing wealth to the more affluent members of society. A study by the Urban Institute found that, for a family of four whose income was half the median income, ERTA established a net increase in disposable income of $263. In contrast, a similar family whose income was twice the median would have a net increase of $2,630. Although the income of the latter is four times that of the former, the tax cut to the more affluent family is 10 times that of the less affluent family.

In sum, while the working poor are bearing disproportionately heavy shares of the budget cuts, they are also reaping disproportionately small gains from the tax cuts. If our country is in fact on the road to economic recovery, we are evidently riding there on the backs of low-income workers.

Throughout much of his term, Pres. Reagan has emphasized the needs of both middle Americans and the "truly needy." Precisely who constitutes this latter group has never been made clear, for fully 40% of the poor receive no Federal aid. Whether he has succeeded in protecting this group is debatable, but from what we have discussed here, it is clear that the Administration has shown little more than neglect for the in-between group we call the "working poor."

It is not difficult to understand the Administration's stark dual-society approach if one wades through documents authored by the Office of Management and Budget (OMB). OMB's report, "Means-Tested Individual Benefits," is an example. In its argument that the difference between poor and middle-income Americans is not very great—i.e., that even the poor are not that badly off—OMB states that "150% of the poverty level for a family of four was . . . equal to 92% of the median annual earnings of employed workers." OMB continues its argument with claims such as "Only . . . 17.7% of all Food Stamp household heads worked at all [in FY 1981]." This implies that there are few aid recipients who also work, suggesting a near dichotomy between workers

and welfare recipients. Taken together, these claims suggest that
the poor are divided into two classes—non-working welfare recipients and working persons whose incomes are not too far below the median.

Supplied with such information, it is not difficult to understand how the Reagan Administration assumed its rather simplistic dual-society approach. Unfortunately for the Administration
and millions of working Americans, the OMB report was rife with
errors—both statistical and logical. For example, the first claim
above compares 150% of the poverty level for a family of four
with the median income of individual workers, quite clearly mix-
ing apples and oranges. The more accurate comparison would be
between 150% of the poverty standard and the median income
for a family of four. Using these figures, 150% of poverty is only
about half the median income—which has very different implications than the above described claims.

OMB also erred in reporting the number of working aid recipients. While OMB claimed that only "17.7% of Food Stamp
household heads worked at all" in 1981, the correct number is
46.1%. Again, the actual numbers suggest a very different view
of the world than the OMB figures. The Administration's attempt to divide society into the truly needy and the self-sufficient
seems quite naive when the OMB errors are revealed.

Perhaps now that the dual-society illusion has begun to crack,
the significance of the working poor will become manifest. The
working poor are, in a way, the infrastructure of the American
economy. Low-wage workers perform the essential chores—
clerical, technical, and manual—of our society. Perhaps more importantly, while the working poor may not be truly needy according to the President, they are striving to climb out of poverty.
Even if the Administration did leave the safety net intact for
some, it sliced away a great deal of the ladder which rises out of
that net. By removing Federal aid, incentives, insurance, and
training programs, the Administration has virtually locked the
working poor into poverty. No matter how great their motivation
or how grand their aspirations, working poor families are being
pushed deeper into poverty and are being denied the resources
they need to lift themselves out of poverty. In this way, the Reagan worldview may be self-fulfilling, for it may force the in-
between group—the working poor—down into the tattered safety net with the "truly needy."

In spite of these adversities imposed by government, the working poor have, for the most part, chosen to continue working, rather than to rely solely on government aid. Despite the new disincentives to work, many of the working poor have continued to hold their jobs, showing that, if anywhere, the American work ethic still resides in the working poor. These are proud people who scratch out a living and save so that their children may scratch a bit less. These are the people, hard-working, but on the margin of the labor force, that work incentives, insurance, and training programs were designed to aid. These are the people whom the Reagan Administration has overlooked, and, in cutting the budget, it has also cut their hopes.

The costs of penalizing the working poor can be measured today both in terms of the human condition and in terms of fairness. However, we can only begin to estimate what the costs of such policies will be tomorrow. In saving a few dollars today, we are penalizing the next generation, hindering the advancement and mobility of millions of hard-working Americans.

For the most sympathetic among the liberals, it is possible to perhaps forgive Pres. Reagan, who, with his simplified dual-society worldview and misinformation, made this a dry, scraping time for millions of American families. However, the information has been set straight now and the working poor—if only through their plight—have stood up and been counted. To continue the Reagan experiment in light of this situation is unforgivable. The costs of such a continuation will be—both now and in the next generation—very severe.

THE KEY TO WELFARE REFORM[3]

Welfare is bad for you—on that proposition liberals and conservatives now seem to agree. President Ronald Reagan and Senator Edward Kennedy have both recently advanced proposals to cut the relief rolls, and Senator Daniel Patrick Moynihan sees

[3]Reprint of an article by David Whitman, senior editor, *U. S. News & World Report* and contributor to the *Atlantic*. Copyright © 1987 by David Whitman. Reprinted with permission from June 1987 *Atlantic*.

"one of those rare alignments that bring about genuine social change" in this new bipartisan consensus. Yet while the Hundredth Congress may well pass legislation affecting welfare, it's unlikely that any reform bill will do much to move welfare recipients from the rolls to the payroll. A look at the history of two key welfare reforms of the Reagan years—the welfare-eligibility restrictions of the 1981 Omnibus Budget Reconciliation Act (OBRA) and the creation of the Job Training Partnership Act in 1982—shows why the current proposals may promise more than they can deliver. Both of those reforms also seemed surefire ways to slash the welfare rolls, yet each ended up having little or no practical effect.

Today the relief rolls stand at near record levels despite six years of the Reagan presidency. Some 11 million Americans currently receive payments from Aid to Families with Dependent Children, the main cash-assistance program available to the nonelderly. Roughly 3.7 million families were on the rolls in 1986, near the 1981 all-time high of 3.9 million. Nor was the high number of welfare families last year unusual during the Reagan Administration. More families have been on AFDC in *each* of the past four years than at any previous time, with the exception of 1981. Correspondingly, federal expenditures on AFDC have edged upward, from $7.8 billion in fiscal year 1982 to $9 billion in fiscal year 1985. After adjustments for inflation, that amounts to a rise of three percent.

Those numbers don't square with the conventional wisdom about Reagan's cold-blooded budget cuts. In fact most of the President's domestic-program curtailments took place during his first year in office; since then few people have bothered to study their impact. Reagan's OBRA cutbacks are a case in point Democrats widely denounced them at the outset—yet recent, little-noticed assessments of the regulations' effects indicate that the gloomy prognostications have not come true.

At first the toughened eligibility guidelines appeared to make a real dent in welfare dependency. Generally, they reduced the amount of earned income that could be disregarded in determining AFDC benefits, thereby removing several hundred thousand "working poor" families from the welfare rolls. The General Accounting Office estimated that 442,000 families were cut off AFDC by mid-1984 because of the new rules.

Yet the welfare rolls started rising in 1983, and no one was quite sure why. Unemployment was high, but increases in unemployment have not been closely linked to AFDC caseload growth during the past two decades. The persistence, moreover, of bloated welfare rolls in 1984 and 1985—years when the economy was booming and an unprecedented number of jobs were created—subsequently cast further doubt on the unemployment hypothesis.Divorce, which often pushes women and their children onto relief, remained level, and illegitimacy did not climb more rapidly than it had in previous years.

One possible explanation for the recent increase in dependency is that the Administration's rule changes, which made it harder to mix welfare and work, ultimately enticed mothers with low-paying jobs to go back on welfare. A recent analysis by Robert Moffitt, of Brown University, concludes that women who were combining work and welfare stayed on the job after losing their benefits because of inertia—until a crisis hit. Then, once, say, a child became ill—an emergency that Medicaid typically covers if the mother is on AFDC—the mother reduced her working hours to restore her AFDC eligibility. Since crises of this sort occur only every now and then, Moffitt suggests, the dependency-inducing effect of the OBRA restrictions was delayed.

An equally critical and perhaps more disturbing shortcoming of the 1981 reforms is that they have failed even in the short term to curb the dependency of the hard-core welfare mothers—the women who stay on AFDC for a decade or more at a time. These chronic recipients have become the real source of public concern about welfare in recent years, and rightly so. "There is a difference," as Senator Moynihan puts it, "between people who have some trouble come into. their lives and those whose whole lives are in trouble." Few taxpayers are outraged by a mother who goes on welfare for eight months because she's been deserted by her husband or laid off. Many do object, however, to women whose kids grow up seeing that it isn't necessary to work for a living (or that it's necessary only rarely). Two million children, most of whom are black, now live in families that have survived on welfare checks for a decade or more.

It is extremely difficult, it turns out, to reduce the welfare budget without getting these chronic users off the rolls. "Any program which fails to help the long-term recipients cannot possibly save much welfare money," says David Ellwood, of Harvard University's Kennedy School of Government. Whereas chronic recipients currently make up only a quarter of those who use AFDC, they consume at least 60 percent of its budget. That's because as the short-termers go on and off the rolls over a period of years, the chronic recipients remain. Thus, at any one time long-term dependents actually constitute the majority of welfare recipients. Getting someone off the dole, in short, is not the crux of the problem—*whom* you get off is.

Unfortunately, OBRA cut off the wrong families. According to a 1984 study by The Urban Institute, it removed from the welfare rolls "those at and near the margin—those most likely to leave anyway . . . leaving behind a relatively 'hard core' group of recipients." A 1986 study by Vicky Albert and Michael Wiseman, of the University of California at Berkeley, found a marked lengthening of stays on AFDC in California. "OBRA effects appear to have been perverse," the authors conslude. "Because of OBRA, the state has been left with a more expensive and, in the long run, more dependent caseload." Ironically, President Reagan defended the cutbacks by saying that they were restricted to better-off recipients, leaving the "truly needy" unharmed in the social safety net. In fact the cutback primarily punished a small number of the most industrious welfare mothers. Left unaffected were those whom critics of welfare have always derided as "welfare dead-beats"—the able-bodied women who bear illegitimate children, drop out of high school, and live off relief checks for years at a time.

Just as the Administration's rewrite of the public-assistance rule book has failed to curb dependency, its efforts to reform work and training programs for welfare mothers have done little to get welfare mothers working. Work programs have never reached more than a small percentage of welfare recipients—and they appear today to be reaching even fewer families than they did when Reagna entered office. And though some small programs seem spectacularly successful—for example, the Reagan Administration's Job Training Partnership Act—much of that record turns out to be little more than statistical sleight-of-hand.

To date, Administration officials have essentially pursued two approaches to reforming job programs. They sought first to correct the abuses of previous job-training programs; then they created their own program to try to show how it should be done. Correcting perceived abuses led to eliminating funding for the Comprehensive Employment and Training Act (CETA)—which had a reputation for sloppy administration and placed participants in temporary public-service jobs, instead of moving them into permanent private positions. Overall, funding for work and training programs was cut 50 percent in real dollars from 1981 to 1986. The main program of job training and placement for welfare recipients—the Work Incentive Program, known as WIN—was reduced even more sharply, from $365 million in 1981 to $110 million in 1987. Nationwide the number of welfare recipients trained for jobs is minuscule: it is estimated that WIN moved 130,000 people off welfare in 1985, or about one percent of those on AFDC. Similarly, the much-touted, proliferating "workfare" programs, which require recipients to work off their welfare benefits in community jobs, are believed to cover about one percent of AFDC recipients.

Besides cutting back, the President sought to make job programs more efficient—WIN recipients should be hustled into jobs, instead of taking college courses that taxpayers' money pays for; welfare mothers should be induced to read want ads and look for a job, instead of simply sending in an application to city hall and calling it quits.

The no-frills solution developed by the Administration was the Job Training Partnership Act (JTPA), which established a program emphasizing quick placement in the private sector by teaching enrollees job-search techniques and offering them short-term training. Although the program is open to the members of various disadvantaged groups, it is clearly meant to reach AFDC mothers, since "reductions in welfare dependency" are a statutory goal of the program. Since the program began, in 1983, it had placed 61 percent of its participants in jobs, and the President has proudly boasted that it has "the highest job-placement record of any of the employment programs the government has ever tried." He's right—even though, paradoxically, the program is probably a waste of resources.

The hitch is that the Reagan Administration has never evaluated how similarly situated welfare recipients who did *not* go through the JTPA program fared in finding work, so no one really knows what difference the program makes. For example, JTPA may place 60 percent of its participants—but if 60 percent

of similarly situated welfare recipients who do not go through
JTPA also find jobs, the program is a waste of money. As conservatives have been quick to point out, the absence of a control
group has proved a critical stumbling block to evaluating other
job programs, such as Massachusetts's much-heralded ET initiative. Of course, not knowing whether JTPA made a difference is
not the same as knowing that it didn't—but there's good reason
to believe that it doesn't do much to reduce dependency. Study
after study of the program shows that it achieves its high placement rate by "creaming"—skimming the most talented few
off the top. In 1985 only 72,500 AFDC recipients "entered
employment" through JTPA (meaning they showed up for at
least one day of work). According to the best estimates of the Labor Department, JTPA participants were significantly better ed-
ucated than the rest of the AFDC population.

Creaming, it should be noted, is not limited to the JTPA program. It is endemic in job programs, because most administrators
prefer to help job-ready applicants. Such applicants are often
more eager to work, and it's easier to get them hired—enabling
the administrator, naturally, to show a high job-placement rate.
What the Reagan Administration did, though, was encourage
more creaming, by tilting federal incentives further away from
working with hard-core welfare mothers. For example, the Administration's performance standards offer financial incentives to
program managers who can quickly place applicants in private-
sector jobs at a low per-slot cost. Women who have been on welfare for a decade or more, however, need more than the shallow
but "efficient" support offered through JTPA—a few weeks of
training and a lecture about how to shape a résumé aren't
enough. Several recent studies of other programs (studies that do
use control groups) show that the most disadvantaged welfare recipients—mothers who dropped out of high school, have little or
no work experience, and stay on welfare for long periods—
benefit the most from employment and training programs. The
same studies show that AFDC recipients who are better prepared
for the job market—like those who go through the JTPA program—ultimately derive little benefit from work programs. The
job-ready candidates would have climbed off welfare without
government help.

In view of JTPA's shortcomings, diagnosing the ills of current job programs seems easy enough: they've failed to reach enough welfare mothers, and those they have reached have least needed the help. The prescription, consequently, seems equally clear: expand job programs and give priority to serving chronic welfare recipients. But neither the Administration's nor the Democrats' work program under debate in Congress this year would affect the welfare rolls more than marginally. The divide in this year's debate is between those who favor a targeted approach to work programs (generally Democrats) and those who favor a blanket approach (generally Republicans). The problem, it turns out, is that the targeted approach is not so carefully aimed and the blanket method is not so all-inclusive.

Targeting, whose champions are Ted Kennedy and Augustus Hawkins (the respective chairmen of the Senate and House labor committees), would give chronic welfare mothers priority over job-ready recipients. For example, Kennedy's Jobs for Employable Dependent Individuals (JEDI) program provides financial bonuses to states that train and place AFDC recipients who have been on welfare for at least two years or are young high school dropouts. JEDI passed the Senate last April, 99 to 0, and Kennedy says that it "could be the catalyst for real change in long-term dependency." Yet no one actually knows how to reach hard-core welfare mothers on a broad scale. The National Governors' Association favors the pre-emptive strike—that is, immediately going after welfare mothers who are candidates for long-term dependency. Suggested reforms include requiring teen mothers to stay in school, mandating immediate work for young unwed mothers, and requiring mothers to seek work as soon as their youngest child turns three.

Reagan's advisers dismiss targeting as the latest academic fad. Robert Carleson, a former Reagan aid now in the private sector, says, "Social scientists always try to categorize people, but you can't sit in your ivory tower in Washington and apply these kinds of demographic distinctions to millions of people around the country. It would be a disaster." Even David Ellwood—who with his colleague Mary Jo Bane has done most of the work analyzing how short-term and chronic recipients differ—is skeptical. "Targeting which is handled badly can make people feel isolated and stigmatized," he says. "You don't, moreover, want to offer help only to those with the greatest impediments, since that can

create the wrong impressions about what is rewarded." As Ellwood points out, setting aside resources for chronic welfare recipients could seem to penalize job-ready welfare recipients who
finished high school or have recent work experience.

The only real way to get welfare mothers working, Administration officials assert, is to have a broad, mandatory program.
For the past seven years Reagan has proposed, with little success,
a national version of a "workfare" program, but Congress is now
taking the work-requirement approach more seriously. The
Administration's current proposal—the Greater Opportunities
Through Work (GROW) program—is easily its most ambitious
to date. Previous Administration workfare plans allowed most
mothers to beg off if their youngest child was less than six years
old. GROW would require mothers with children of six months
or more to participate, roughly doubling the number of welfare
recipients who would be reached by the program. When the program was fully operational, 60 percent of those eligible would be
looking or training for work, finishing high school, or in a workfare slot.

GROW would cast a wider net than Kennedy's JEDI proposal,
but it still would reduce dependency only modestly. That's because of the two stumbling blocks that politicians love to ignore
when talking about work programs—the price tag and the
"dribble-out" phenomenon.

Cost estimates for GROW have left some welfare analysts in-
credulous. During the first year of the program, when 20 percent
of those eligible for GROW would be expected to participate,
roughly $40 million of the money would be for child care. Cali-
fornia alone expects to spend twice as much next year on child
care for a much smaller group of welfare mothers in its work program. Underestimating the cost of a job program is far more than
just a bean-counter's nightmare; as the experience with WIN
shows, inadequate funding can hinder efforts to reduce dependency. AFDC family heads, for example, have been "required" to
participate in WIN since 1967, but the requirement has largely
been meaningless. Underfunded from the start, WIN typically
registers hundreds of thousands of welfare mothers who end up
doing nothing, since there is no work or training available
through the program. Participation requirements make the pa-
per-shuffling routine worse, since lots of recipients can be served
only if the most job-ready mothers are helped. GROW provides

similarly perverse incentives for creaming by withholding matching funds for the direct costs of education or training—both of which chronic welfare recipients need to become employable.

Assume, though, for the sake of argument, that GROW's cost estimates are plausible and its incentives flawless. There remains the stumbling block of the dribble-out phenomenon: once job programs get rolling, some people drop out, and simultaneously the number that get exempted seems inevitably to grow. Historically, the most successful job programs have a placement rate of about 65 percent. That means one out of three participants doesn't get a job out of the "best" programs; the person gets sick, finds a job before the program is completed, gets married, or recycles through the program. Meanwhile, those who do see the program through typically fail to make enough money in their training slot or low-wage job to get off welfare. As David Ellwood reports, the most successful programs for poor mothers "boost earnings by perhaps a thousand dollars per year on average, surely not enough to insure self-support." Unlike many mothers of preschoolers, those on welfare typically cannot secure a decent-paying part-time job that will enable them also to care for their children.

These humble results might be dismissed as unrepresentative, part and parcel of the small, inefficient job programs of yesteryear, were it not for the loophole problem. GROW actually would grant far fewer exemptions than other work proposals, including the current proposal from the National Governors' Association. The NGA, for example, would not require mothers with children under three to participate in its work-education initiative—which lets almost 40 percent of all AFDC recipients off the hook before the program begins. By lowering the age of the youngest child to six months for exemption, GROW closes that loophole and purportedly covers 90 percent of the AFDC caseload.

Yet even in GROW the numbers would still add up: 10 percent of AFDC mothers with infants would be exempt; 40 percent of the people eligible for GROW would not be required to participate when the program was fully implemented. Some people would recycle back into the program after losing a job. Others would participate by getting their high school degree instead of working. The cumulative effect of the loopholes can be seen in the Administration's own projections. By 1992, when the program was fully implemented, 440,000 fewer families would be on welfare because of GROW, either because they had found jobs through the program or because they were deterred by GROW from ever going on AFDC. That's a 12 percent reduction—worthwhile, certainly, but far short of a "simple solution" to the welfare problem.

The modest record of employment initiatives has stirred renewed interest in more-radical solutions. Job-related reforms advocated in recent months have included abolishing AFDC and replacing it with a guaranteed government jobs program; and expanding the use of tax credits, to make it easier for mothers to work part-time without having to rely on AFDC. Recommendations for reforming cash benefits have included shutting off payments to a family after two years, and expanding child-support laws to provide single parents a guaranteed income. A far-reaching overhaul isn't likely in 1987, however, because the political consensus between Republicans and Democrats breaks down when more than philosophical support for job programs is at stake.

What's likely to emerge from the Republican-Democratic tug-of-war in Congress is some tinkering with the cash side of the welfare system, plus a compromise job program that includes more funding for jobs and training, with stiffer obligations for recipients. Should President Reagan win authorization for a series of demonstration projects at the local level, they undoubtedly would produce some useful ideas for curbing welfare dependency. Still, most of the experiments are expected to run for at least five years, so final results wouldn't be available until at least 1992, long after Reagan leaves office. In the meantime, the prospects for mothers to climb off the relief rolls the old-fashioned way—through earnings—remain dim, far dimmer than either Ronald Reagan or Ted Kennedy cares to admit.

A RETURN TO COMPASSION?[4]

They are the people the Reagan Revolution left behind. You can see their haunting faces peering out from the shadows in subway stations, you come across them in doorways or huddled on heating grates. Amid Reagan-era prosperity, they were merely an embarrassment. To the next President, these legions of the dispossessed will be something more: a poignant reminder that sooner or later the federal government will have to grapple with the social-policy failures of the Reagan years.

Reagan did not shred the social safety net, as some critics charge. Many entitlement programs for the elderly and other politically powerful constituencies escaped the knife. But his policies allowed more Americans than ever to fall through the gaps. Convinced that the Great Society was a colossal failure in social engineering, he all but killed federally subsidized housing construction, whacked away at job programs, and sharply restricted eligibility for a host of federal benefit programs. He pushed responsibility for many programs onto the states. When asked what would happen if some state governments failed to pick up the burden, he replied their poor residents could "vote with their feet."

Housing Crisis. Reagan intimates insist the President is a compassionate man who can easily be moved to tears by the plight of someone down on his luck. But his implacable hostility to the welfare state meant that he had little sympathy for the needs of the poor as a class of citizens. Reagan's policies have "created a set of social problems that simply were not there in 1980," says Marian Wright Edelman, president of the Children's Defense Fund. "We're going to be paying for them for a long time."

Ah, but how? The Reagan budget deficit has foreclosed expensive new initiatives. At the same time, demands for government services are rising. Poverty is growing, especially among the working poor and children. The ranks of full-time workers whose income falls below the poverty line swelled to 2 million in 1986, from 1.4 million in 1979. And the percentage of children living

[4]Reprint of an article by Susan B. Garland, *Business Week* staffwriter. Reprinted from the February 1, 1988 issue of *Business Week* by special permission. Copyright © 1988 by McGraw-Hill, Inc.

in poverty grew to 19.8% in 1986, from 16% at the start of the Administration.

A crisis in low-cost housing is driving many of the needy into the streets. Some 37 million Americans have no health insurance. As the U.S. population ages, the cost of care for the elderly will explode. And the AIDS epidemic could impose an enormous burden on the health care system. "The budget choices that will face the next President are really very grim," says Robert Greenstein, director of the Center on Budget & Policy Priorities, a liberal research group. "A lot of serious needs won't be met at all."

The Administration's conservative supporters have ready answers for these broadsides. They insist that the states and charitable organizations, rather than a cash-strapped federal government, should take the responsibility for meeting social needs. "Newer, bigger items face a new burden of proof," declares Education Secretary William J. Bennett.

What's more, Reaganites question the effectiveness of many poverty programs. "Twenty years after the Great Society, the underclass is more deeply entrenched than ever before," says Stuart Butler, director of domestic policy studies at the Heritage Foundation. Even Administration critics, who once looked reflexively to Washington for answers, concede that Reagan's relentless attacks on the merits of federal solutions to public problems have reshaped public thinking. "We have different expectations about the ability of programs to solve many of these problems," says John L. Palmer of the Urban Institute.

But the idea of a more compassionate government seems to be coming back in style. And politicians of all stripes are promising to do more for the disadvantaged. "There are some people in America, be they poor or handicapped, black or brown, veterans, farmers . . . who may be waiting for an invitation to participate," said one Presidential candidate. "I will be sensitive to the needs of the left-out and down-and-out in our society." Jesse Jackson? No, the speaker was Republican Senator Bob Dole of Kansas.

On the Fringe. Education could be one of the first areas to benefit from the new mood. Although Reagan gets credit for championing the "back-to-basics" movement, he pushed through large cuts in aid to education. Now an alliance of business, labor, and liberal groups is pushing hard for a greater commitment to both education and job training. An educational system that produces high school graduates who can barely read, they argue, not only dooms its students to a lifetime on the fringes of productive society but denies employers the skilled work force they need to meet the competitive challenges of the 1990s.

The post-Reagan budget deficits will force social-spending advocates to find creative ways to fund their agendas. One scheme: Tie each program to a specific new source of revenue. Such a system has already been proposed in legislation that would give the elderly new insurance protection against the costs of catastrophic illness. The benefits would be paid for by an increase in taxes and medicare premiums the elderly pay. A separate proposal for home health care for the disabled would be paid for by an increase in Social Security payroll taxes for workers earning over $45,000 a year.

Policymakers are likely to reach deeper into the pockets of business. Organized labor is teaming up with congressional Democrats to push legislation that would force employers to offer health insurance to all workers. Another measure would require employers to provide unpaid leaves so employees can care for newborns and ill relatives. This may only be the beginning. Says Urban Institute economist Isabel V. Sawhill: "If I were a businessman worried about the implications of the Reagan years, I'd look at mandated benefits."

Reagan's efforts to end government's social activism were a neat meshing of ideology and practical politics. His blistering attacks on "welfare queens" and government handouts skillfully exploited the politics of resentment. That inspired millions of working-class white males, many of them southerners, to vote Republican, a lot of them for the first time. "People fundamentally felt that something was out of whack when able-bodied young people were getting benefits from the federal government while the guy next door and his wife were working and making very little more," says Jack A. Meyer, president of New Directions for Policy, a research group.

"Unintended." Nothing symbolized the Administration's strategy better than its position on civil rights. For the first time, the Justice Dept. argued for whites in court that minority preferences in affirmative-action programs were unconstitutional. The Supreme Court repeatedly rejected the Administration's narrow view of the law, but the efforts drove a wedge between minorities and the White House. "The unintended result was to energize the civil-rights coalition," says Stuart E. Eizenstat, President Carter's domestic policy chief. Riding high after the defeat of Robert H. Bork, Reagan's nominee for the Supreme Court, civil-rights groups will be in shape to press their demands at the start of a new Administration.

But efforts to turn around some of the social policies of the Reagan years will run up against what may be his most enduring legacy. In seven years, Reagan has appointed more than half of all federal judges, almost all conservative and many of them young. The Reagan judiciary will restrain liberal bureaucrats well into the next century.

Reagan was far more successful in reshaping the courts than he was in bringing down the welfare state. Despite years of incessant budget cutting, the Administration never won a wholesale dismantling of programs. "It was a significant midcourse correction, but it was not a revolution," says Eizenstat.

Government benefits for the middle class were cut far less than programs for the poor. After being burned by an ill-conceived 1981 proposal to cut Social Security benefits, Reagan shrank from further assault on middle-class programs. But because these programs are a huge part of the federal budget, a future President may have to go where Reagan feared to tread. "Are we going to accept more and more transfer payments to the middle class in the 1990s?" asks Richard S. Williamson, Reagan's former assistant for intergovernmental affairs. "If so, the budget squeeze will continue."

One issue on which Reagan won a near-total victory could confront his successor with a crisis: a critical lack of low-income housing. Not only did the Administration virtually end funding for subsidized housing construction, Reagan pushed tax policies that made it increasingly unattractive for the private sector to build such units. Housing authorities are tearing down aging projects, and 500,000 privately owned low-income units could disappear soon, as their subsidized mortgages are paid off and owners pull the properties from the program. The crunch is especially severe for young families on the margin of poverty. "This is the group showing up on the streets," says William C. Apgar Jr., associate director of Harvard's Joint Center for Housing Studies.

Stepping Back. Reagan isn't leaving only problems behind. The Reagan Administration's determined efforts to reduce the government presence yielded some success. For example, the President leaves at least one class of government apparatus far stronger than the one he found—the role of the states. Early in his Administration the President consolidated and cut many of the 500 separate grant programs to state government, but gave the states more say over how the money should be spent. To the surprise of many, governors and state legislatures took up the challenge and became centers of innovation, pushing reforms in welfare, education, and job training. "The states have become what the framers of the Constitution intended them to be," says Democratic Governor Bill Clinton of Arkansas. "They are laboratories of democracy."

To a limited extent, therefore, Reagan succeeded in persuading skeptics that the federal government had to step back from its role as the answer to all of society's ills. But in the process, he demonstrated precisely the opposite: that a broad range of needs exists that only Washington can meet. Dealing with this challenge while living with a budget that provides very little in the way of resources will take all the skill and imagination a new President can muster.

EDITOR'S INTRODUCTION

The Reagan administration's policy of giving a greater share of welfare decisions to the states has resulted in innovative programs that have had a national effect. Many states—including California, Massachusetts, and New York—have experimented with workfare programs that have captured the imagination of social planners. Under these programs, those on welfare are expected to work to defray the costs of public assistance and to provide an incentive to gainful employment and independence. Workfare soon became a byword of welfare theorists, who have urged enactment of the policy on a federal level. Senator Daniel Patrick Moynihan introduced such legislation in Congress, and it has since been enacted into law. But this innovative approach remains controversial. Its critics argue that it is a punitive act targeted at single mothers and, more importantly, that it will produce no significant result. To its adversaries, workfare is merely another welfare reform mirage.

In the article from *Time* magazine that opens this section, Jacob V. Lamar, Jr. reports on the proliferation of workfare programs in twenty states; and in the second article, reprinted from *Progressive*, Laurie Udesky examines the much-heralded workfare program in California. Udesky is critical of the program in many respects. In another article, reprinted from *USA Today*, Michael Dukakis, governor of Massachusetts, claims extraordinary success for his Employment and Training Choices program, enacted in 1983 and known as ET. Unlike the California plan, the one in Massachusetts is voluntary, and provides more extensive training so that graduates can move into better paying jobs.

In a following article, reprinted from *Business Week*, Susan B. Garland comments on two new workfare proposals presented to Congress by Thomas Downey and Daniel Patrick Moynihan. She observes that both seem especially directed to long-term welfare mothers who collect more than half the benefits paid out. In an article from *Newsweek*, Mickey Kaus records the movement of the Moynihan bill, the Family Welfare Reform Act, through Congress. He points out that the House version of the bill restricts workfare programs because of pressure from unions, who fear cheap competition from workfarers; but the Senate passage of the bill adds an amendment mandating 16 hours a week of public-service work from two-parent families.

In a following article, Mimi Abramovitz in *The Nation* maintains that the workfare bill will hurt women and the poor. It will cheapen the costs of women's labor, placing them in low-paying jobs without providing them with Medicaid or day care. Finally, in his omnibus review in the *New York Review of Books*, Andrew Hacker raises questions of fairness in the new legislation. His article, "Getting Rough on the Poor," points out that a disproportionate burden will fall on women. Men, he claims, will get off easily; prospects of squeezing child support payments from absentee fathers are poor, since many are unemployed, in jail, or are drug addicts or homeless. The welfare mothers who will be put to work have no adequate provision for day care, and the experience of workfare programs in the states strongly suggests that after "training" they will find jobs paying hardly more than their welfare allotments—but with the difference that they will be deprived of Medicaid. The modestly budgeted act, Hacker suggests, is unlikely to have any meaningful result, while at the same time it will add to the burdens of poor women.

FROM WELFARE TO WORKFARE[1]

For five years Maria Unzueta's sole source of income was a monthly welfare check. Separated from her husband, the San Diego mother of four made do on benefits totaling $7,920 a year. But now Unzueta, 39, is part of a local job-training program for welfare recipients in which she works 40 hours a week as a hospital file clerk and makes roughly the same amount of money she was getting on the dole. Under the workfare program, she still receives child-care benefits worth about $130 a month, but she hopes to be completely self-sufficient soon. "For me it's important

[1]Reprint of an article by Jacob V. Lamar, Jr., *Time* staffwriter. Copyright 1986 Time Inc. Reprinted by permission from *Time* February 3, 1986.

to try and make it on my own," says Unzueta, "and provide an example for my children."

Requiring welfare recipients to work for their checks is not a new concept. Nor are the programs, which usually affect poor mothers with children to raise, as simple in practice as they are in theory. But workfare, which has slowly evolved from a somewhat cranky conservative notion to one with broad support, seems to be an idea whose time has come. Able-bodied welfare beneficiaries must accept occupational training and jobs in more than 20 states, and the number is growing.

In Washington, legislators are mired in trying to find ways to cut spending in accordance with the Gramm-Rudman deficit-reduction bill. Confronted with severe cutbacks in revenue sharing, states are searching for innovative ways to make their social programs more effective. Workfare could prove to be an important example for future experiments.

The idea has enjoyed an unusual bipartisan harmony: in state-houses around the country, Democrats and Republicans have joined forces to support legislation that combines the job programs traditionally favored by liberals with efforts to pare the welfare rolls advocated by conservatives. Jo Anne Ross, a Reagan appointee at the Social Security Administration, describes workfare as the "top priority of the Department of Health and Human Services." Says Joseph Califano, Secretary of the Department of Health, Education and Welfare during the Carter Administration: "If the kids are in school, then the mother can be working. Nearly everyone accepts that concept now."

Welfare has been a political battleground since federally financed public assistance was made law under the Social Security Act of 1935. Traditionally, conservatives have viewed welfare programs as handouts to the poor and an insult to the American work ethic. Liberals generally have considered it compassionate compensation for victims of economic and social circumstances beyond their control. But with the startling growth in the number of children being born to unwed mothers from the underclass, many of welfare's long-standing supporters have begun to question whether Aid to Families with Dependent Children programs may be exacerbating the problems they were designed to alleviate. Even some civil rights leaders and welfare recipients in the nation's inner cities are criticizing the system for helping perpetuate dependency from one disadvantaged generation to the next and for unintentionally encouraging the breakdown of the underclass's family structure.

California is embarking on the most sweeping statewide plan so far. Encouraged by the success of San Diego's local workfare system, the state legislature last September approved a program known as Greater Avenues for Independence, or GAIN. Approximately one-third of the state's 586,000 AFDC cases will be affected. As in most workfare plans, handicapped people and single parents with preschool children are exempt but may volunteer for the program. Welfare beneficiaries who do not register in GAIN stand to have their payments cut off.

After an evaluation of their skills, GAIN participants are given any necessary training, ranging from remedial math and language classes to high school equivalency courses. Once training is completed the welfare client has three months to find work in a job-search program. A trainee whose search is unsuccessful is enrolled in a one-year pre-employment preparation program to work off the welfare grant in an assigned job, with time off for job hunting. Typical jobs include clerical positions or maintenance work in a parks department, day-care centers or programs for the elderly; the pay is the California starting wage, currently $5.07 an hour. If after a year the client still has not found a job, he must begin the evaluation and training program again.

The GAIN bill won in the state senate by a vote of 32 to 2 and in the assembly by 60 to 9. Republicans were all for a mandatory work requirement, while Democrats liked the education, child-care and job-creation provisions that were written into the legislation. GAIN is enrolling members gradually and will be fully operational in 1988. Though the program is expected to cost $304 million a year, GAIN supporters estimate that it will have saved the state $115 million by 1992.

While California's program is being touted as a model for the future, other ambitious workfare operations are in place around the country. New York hopes eventually to enroll more than 200,000 of its 1.1 million AFDC recipients in a revamped workfare program that went into effect last November with the support of Democratic Governor Mario Cuomo. "We're not letting them sit at home and get into the welfare syndrome," says Cesar Perales, New York State's commissioner of social services. "Exposing them to the workplace has real value." A program in Massachusetts instituted in 1983 led to employment for 19,000 former welfare clients and saved the state an estimated $54 million over two years. Other notable programs are operating in Pennsylvania, West Virginia and Michigan.

Workfare first became government policy, at least in theory, more than a decade ago. Congress strengthened a Work Incentive (WIN) program in 1971 during the Nixon Administration. But WIN suffered from inadequate funding, mismanagement and weak enforcement. In 1981, with the advent of the Reagan Administration, Congress passed legislation granting states more flexibility in administering WIN. For the first time, AFDC recipients could work in public agencies rather than in private-sector jobs. States were also allowed to use part of a recipient's welfare grant as a wage subsidy to his or her private employer. Given these new liberties, state governments began cooking up fresh workfare programs.

"Obligation" is a word that workfare supporters use frequently, arguing that welfare recipients have not fulfilled their responsibilities as citizens. Lawrence Mead, professor of politics at New York University, makes such a case in his new book, *Beyond Entitlement: The Social Obligations of Citizenship* (Free Press; $19.95). His most controversial theme: the poor need to have standards of behavior set for them. "We have to say, 'You have a real obligation we're not going to let you get away from,'" says Mead. Workfare, he maintains, can give poor people the discipline he feels they lack. Mead advocates expanding workfare programs to include mothers with children above age three rather than simply those whose children are old enough to be in school.

Workfare's philosophical opponents see it as a sort of punishment for being poor. They contend that the vast majority of welfare recipients are young unwed mothers with few if any marketable skills, who are often forced to take demeaning, low-paying jobs under workfare. Critics question whether there is even enough work to go around for the programs' undereducated participants. Says California Democratic Assemblyman Tom Bates: "When Ronald Reagan says, 'Go to the want ads and look for jobs,' he doesn't point out that they're for electrical engineers and highly skilled people."

There are other well-reasoned objections to workfare: that it displaces people in the regular labor force; that by exempting single parents with preschool-age children, it excludes 60% of all adult AFDC recipients; that, as Ohio has experienced, welfare savings can be less than program costs; that workfare places too much emphasis on getting clients into the job market quickly rather than enrolling them in education courses that could help them gain entry to more useful and lucrative lines of work.

A report released last month by the House Government Operations Committee criticizes programs that do not provide adequate child care for participants. Said the study: "The lack of safe and affordable child care can foreclose the possibility of employment, training, education and even opportunity to job hunt." Moreover, say critics, workfare does not address America's most serious unemployment problem: the jobless rate among black teenagers is currently 41.6%, compared with 6.9% for the U.S. as a whole.

Nevertheless, growing numbers of officials think that work-for-welfare programs are at least worth trying. And many workfare participants seem to agree. In Des Moines, Ruth Breitzke, 34, has been working since September as a volunteer at the juvenile court in return for her welfare check. "I enjoy what I'm doing here even though I don't get paid for it," says she. "It gives you the feeling that you can get back into the working world. It gives you that boost."

WORKFARE[2]

Romelia Carrillo is a California success story. The mother of three children and a six-year welfare recipient, she landed a job as an on-call dietician's aid through the state's workfare program, GAIN—short for Greater Avenues for Independence. It requires all parents whose children are six or older and who receive Aid to Families with Dependent Children to find jobs or work for their welfare checks. As participants prepare to work, it promises, they will receive transportation, subsidized child care, and up to two years of training and education.

[2]Reprint of an article by Laurie Udesky, associate of the Center for Investigative Reporting in San Francisco. Reprinted by permission from *Progressive*, V. 51:7-8. Ag. '87. Copyright © 1987 by *Progressive*.

In October 1986, Carrillo was chosen "GAIN Employee of the Month." A brightly colored newsletter published by the social services department in Fresno featured her story. Carrillo, the article reports, "takes two buses to ride to work, but is glad to have a job to ride to. Carrillo . . . is very happy to have her job. She has been trained in many aspects of the hospital food service, including setting up trays, delivering them to tables, clean-up, washing the pots and pans, and putting the dishes away. She is looking forward to a long and steady association with the hospital."

But a talk with Carrillo paints a different picture. The young mother confirms her intense desire to work and be independent of welfare. Her hours are irregular, however, and at times her take-home pay dips to $400 a month. Her monthly expenses, she says, include $330 for rent, $137 for car payments, and $65 to $70 for gas and electricity. "But then," she says, the welfare department "cut off my food stamps, and me and my kids had to live on eggs and potatoes."

After three months on the job, Carrillo, like all GAIN participants, had her child-care subsidy cut off. She then had to squeeze an extra $67 a week for child care out of an already-strapped family budget.

"I'm struggling and I know I can't expect welfare to always pay my way," she says. "But it's been very hard."

Most disturbing is the fear that she'll lose the job overnight. "I like my job," she says, "but I've been late to work several times because one of my children is ill. When you're late to work, they count it as a sick day, and I've already used up all my sick time. If one of my children is sick again, I'm afraid I'll be fired."

Her voice drops in concern as she talks about her children. "The kids really miss me; I don't see them that much now."

The scarcity of available child care means she must depend on relatives and informal babysitters when she goes to work. Sometimes child-care arrangements fall through at the last minute.

"A couple of times, I've had to leave the kids alone. It's not good, to leave kids alone. One time my six-year old flooded the bathtub, and the water went all over the carpet in the hall and into the downstairs apartment."

GAIN is supposed to find work for thousands, mostly single mothers on the welfare rolls. Billed as a model program, it has caught the eye of lawmakers across the country. Many politicians, including some Presidential candidates, are looking to GAIN and other similar programs as solutions to the welfare problem. But as the case of Romelia Carrillo demonstrates, it is hardly a solution at all.

When Republican Governor George Deukmejian signed the workfare bill into law in 1985, he claimed it would "give welfare recipients the tools to break out of the endless trap of welfare dependency." Assemblyman Art Agnos, one of the liberal Democrats who joined conservatives in pushing GAIN, calls the program "the most advanced, progressive, state-of-the-art reform of the welfare system in the nation." The public is being wooed by slick advertisements produced by Louis and Saul, a Santa Monica firm that will be paid $1.5 million for selling GAIN over the next three years.

But the program is more hype than substance. Assemblyman Ernie Konnyu, the Republican who was the main author of the GAIN legislation, says the program will provide welfare recipients with "training and self-reliance so they can leave welfare and reduce taxpayer costs." California, however, has invested neither the planning nor the resources to make good on these promises. In what may be the best-kept secret of the campaign year, the state's Department of Social Services estimates that 97 per cent of all GAIN graduates will remain on welfare. And the kinds of jobs the workfare program offers can barely support one person, much less a family.

"They're training us to become clerks and busboys," says Kevin Aslanian of the California Coalition for Welfare Rights. "It's an assembly line, and you can't live on those wages. That's why we call this program PAIN—which stands for Painful Avenues to Nowhere."

The lack of well-paying jobs for GAIN graduates also worries John Ritter, GAIN manager for the welfare department in Solano County. "It's a real problem because a single parent with two kids needs at least $8 or $10 an hour just to survive," he says. "But the kinds of jobs we have here are service jobs running $5.05 an hour."

A study by Alameda County, cited by the *San Francisco Chronicle* backs up Ritter. Welfare recipients with one child would need to earn more than $6.44 an hour just to reach the same standard of living they had on welfare, the study points out. Single parents who work have much higher expenses than do those who stay at home; after starting a job, they may lose most or all of their subsidized food, housing, and medical benefits.

A single mother with two children who receives $716 monthly in welfare benefits, for example, would need to earn twice that to cover the added costs of child care, transportation, payroll taxes, and other new expenses. That amounts to a $9.25-an-hour job to reach the same subsistence standard of living she had on welfare—a wage far higher than that earned by most GAIN graduates. California's Department of Social Services reports that the median wage for GAIN employees is $5 an hour. In some counties, it drops as low as $4.

"You can't find a better job until you start with $5 an hour," says GAIN deputy director Carl Williams. "This program has everything conceivable to help people get work, but it's unlikely that unskilled, or modestly skilled, people can get $10 an hour at their first job."

GAIN's low wages reflect a Catch-22 problem with workfare nationwide:A recent Federal report on programs in thirty-eight states reveals that most participants were forced to take dismally low-paying jobs, with a median hourly wage of $4.14. Unsurprisingly, fewer than 50 per cent of participants were able to get off welfare after finding work.

This finding is not news to Dion Aroner, an aide to Assemblyman Tom Bates, a long-time critic of workfare programs. Bates opposes GAIN, says Aroner, because it is "not voluntary" and sets aside no money to develop jobs.

"Its creators didn't see it as a way to get families out of poverty," Aroner says. "They saw it as a way to get them off the welfare rolls."

Yet the program is not succeeding in doing even that. With workfare under way in sixteen counties, GAIN has found jobs for only 3,788 of its 27,800 participants. And although the state expects to spend more than $200 million a year on workfare, realistic welfare officials expect few GAIN participants to leave the welfare system. Asked how GAIN's single parents will be able to support a family on $5 an hour, deputy director Williams says, "Your question assumes people will be leaving welfare. We don't expect everyone to leave welfare." He explains that many workers will be eligible for reduced benefits. Pressed further, Williams estimates that only 3 per cent of GAIN graduates will be able to make it off the welfare rolls.

Holly Bailey of San Mateo is among this lucky 3 per cent. A thirty-five-year-old former welfare mother, Bailey was able to finish her nursing program through GAIN. "When I was getting welfare," she says, "it seemed like you were penalized for trying to go to school and do better in your life. But GAIN has been wonderfully supportive." The program paid for her child care, transportation, and two uniforms, she says. "It really made a difference to have that support."

Bailey now earns $1,800 a month as a registered nurse.

More typical, though, is the case of Linda Carevich, a mother in her thirties who enrolled in GAIN voluntarily in November 1986. With a high-school education and two children, she hoped to get a job as a laborer or some other position that pays well.

"We need to get the kinds of jobs men get and get paid what they get paid," she says. At her GAIN orientation, however, Carevich says she was told to apply for entry-level clerical jobs, bank-teller and child-care aide positions, and other low-paying jobs.

"I thought, 'They've got to be kidding!'" say Carevich. "I don't see how a woman like myself with two kids can get a $5-an hour job and still pay for child care and medical expenses. It's my children who would suffer. We'd be better off on welfare."

Licensed child-care facilities with openings are scarce or non-existent in many parts of the state, and that presents another problem for GAIN mothers, even though program administrators downplay it. Williams says he has heard "child-care shortages talked about *ad nauseam*, but I haven't heard of people who have had a problem."

One person who has is Marcelle Hall, a mother of three who fought to get into GAIN. She describes her search for child care as "frustrating and exhausting." The few day-care centers she found had long waiting lists, and Hall had grave reservations about the home-care providers she interviewed.

"Their places seemed run down and not set up well," she says. "I didn't trust them to take care of my kids. Because of this, my eight-year-old and eleven-year-old have been home alone all this time." While enrolled in classes, Hall got the call she had been dreading: "My kids had broken a glass door and were seriously injured. If they hadn't been able to reach me at school, they would have been home all alone, bleeding."

Heidi Strassburger of the Child Care Law Center in San Francisco thinks the GAIN legislation is seriously flawed for cutting off child-care money only three months after a parent finds work. Strassburger also worries that parents in GAIN may not know of their right to paid child care—or may be afraid to assert themselves. For these reasons, she says, GAIN "may actually create a larger pool of latch-key children" whose safety is jeopardized. The National Fire Protection Association, for example, reports that more than 20 per cent of all multiple-death fires involve unattended or unsupervised children.

The concern about latch-key children led one child-care agency in Kern County, California, to start up a children's hotline in 1984. Wendy Wayne, director of the Community Connection for Childcare, reports, "We have been receiving 600 calls a month from children who are terrified, lonely, or feel isolated."

Despite the dangers of leaving children unattended, welfare officials in Kern County have tried improperly to cut corners on funding child care for GAIN parents. The county initially refused to pay for child care for 89 per cent of its potential GAIN participants, stating in an internal document that the homes had "elder sibling(s) or a second parent" or friends to babysit "at no cost." GAIN requires, by law, that all child-care providers be paid.

Faltering start or not, GAIN supporters are quick to defend the program, citing the nonmonetary benefits.

"This program destroys the myth that people on welfare are lazy, shiftless, and don't want to work," asserts Assemblyman Agnos, who is now running for mayor of San Francisco. "The large number of people volunteering for the program has already ended that debate.

"We now have people who are trained, willing, and ready to work," says Agnos. "The question is, can the economy handle them?"

By transferring responsibility for GAIN to an amorphous "economy," Agnos sidesteps tough questions about the program itself. In addition to shuttling most participants into low-paying, dead-end jobs, GAIN is operating in a bureaucratic thicket. Social workers have as many as 200 GAIN clients each, far too many to serve effectively. In Fresno, angry eligibility workers went on strike for four days last March to protest intolerable working conditions in the GAIN program.

"Employees were so overloaded that they couldn't get their jobs done," says Sherill Perkins, an official of the Service Employees International Union, which represents the caseworkers. "A lot of GAIN participants are getting lost in the system."

Other headaches plague administrators as well. The politicians, in their rush to pass GAIN as an "emergency statute" in 1985, neglected to investigate what kind of training the state's welfare recipients would need to become self-sufficient. Welfare officials originally estimated that 15 per cent of those in GAIN would need remedial education. Now a state study shows the figure is actually 60 per cent—and counties are not prepared to foot the bill.

"The Department of Social Services had very little data on clients," says Bates aide Aroner. "No real surveys were done to see how many people would need remedial education. So now DSS has gotten caught with its pants down."

Many GAIN caseworkers say they're proud of clients who have passed a high-school-equivalency test for the first time. But GAIN doesn't allow participants more than two years of schooling or professional training, so it has met with skepticism even within its own ranks.

"Many people won't get the education they need to be independent," says Solano County's John Ritter. "The program can help people with two years of college finish their degrees—and that's great. But if you dropped out of school in the eighth grade, two years of schooling won't give you the skills you need to get a good-paying job."

Ritter and some other concerned officials have plans to try placing GAIN graduates in nontraditional jobs, including union apprenticeships. But far too often GAIN officials fall back on "job-skills" classes that stress a vague melange of positive thinking and grooming tips.

"We want to teach people that it isn't appropriate to wear fuzzy slippers and curlers to a job interview," says one welfare official. "We're also offering color-coordination classes. We may tell our clients, 'Sure, go out and become a bus-boy,' but we try to give them the motivation to hang in there and become a chef."

Some GAIN officials say they want welfare recipients to reach—but only as high as the welfare department thinks they should.

Mariana Talbot, a college senior and twenty-three-year-old single mother on AFDC, wants to go to graduate school in journalism and become a reporter. She has worked as news and features editor of her college newspaper, won several scholarships, and received many straight-A report cards. But when she asked a GAIN caseworker about graduate school, she was told to take her dreams elsewhere.

"I was told—and I've heard this so many times—'We're not out to subsidize your college education,'" Talbot says. "The caseworker told me, 'We have no sympathy for humanities students. If you want to go to nursing school, though, we'll pay for it.' Basically, they expect you to give up any right to choose your own career. It's such a paternalistic attitude, as if all women on welfare should be forced to do traditional women's jobs, whether they want to or not."

Talbot, whose child was born while she was still in high school, encountered similar roadblocks from the welfare department in getting her bachelor's degree.

"The system is definitely not set up to support women who have higher ambitions," she says. "Welfare officials don't respect you for pursuing a college education; they seem to resent it. I was never given any support. It's so ironic, because I'm doing everything in my power to educate myself and get a good-paying job so I can get off welfare forever." She adds that she intends to hire a lawyer, if necessary, to obtain the level of education she feels she needs to compete in a tight job market.

In one California county, a GAIN mother of three fought for—and won—the right to go to graduate school in psychology to become a therapist. Welfare officials, she says, "wanted me to get a job as a counselor with my B.A., but I couldn't feed my three kids on those wages."

The law does not limit the type of higher education a GAIN participant can aspire to, but GAIN officials apparently think that poor welfare recipients, unlike middle-class or wealthy students, do not deserve to enter a profession by earning a master's degree—in anything.

"No, GAIN will not pay for graduate school," says deputy director Williams. "This is an employment program. We're not going to pay for a graduate program in basket-weaving. There's no way the taxpayers would want to pay for it."

As things now stand, many women and men in GAIN must take the job that the welfare department thinks they should, even if it means earning less than their net income from welfare. If they refuse and lose their appeal in a lengthy "conciliation process," they can lose their aid.

Defending sanctions against GAIN parents who miss classes or refuse to take a job without "good cause," Assemblyman Agnos goes so far as to compare welfare mothers to school-aged children. Some women must be forced to participate in GAIN, he says, "just as we do with [children] in public education." A woman who balks "will lose her adult right to spend her [welfare] check as she chooses. The state will handle all her money." If, after three months, the woman is "still recalcitrant"—GAIN literature calls her a "second-time offender"—Agnos says, "she will lose the adult portion of her grant."

Such sanctions are under challenge by the Western Poverty Law Center, which has filed suit charging that a GAIN participant has the right to refuse a job if it means a net loss in income. It is illegal to force parents in GAIN "to take a job where the net income does not meet the basic needs of themselves and their children," concludes the complaint.

The GAIN program has been badly oversold, according to Casey McKeever of the Law Center. "For many people," he says, "GAIN will provide some useful services, such as education and job searches, and give them more self-confidence. But the program is incapable of helping the poor in general. It promotes jobs, but doesn't create them. It doesn't take into account the trend away from union jobs that have provided security to families for generations, and the trend toward service jobs with no security and often no benefits."

McKeever thinks GAIN may create a secondary work force easily exploitable by employers who could reduce wages, "knowing that women and men in GAIN must take the job even if it pays less than their welfare checks."

Whatever the good intentions, GAIN has little to distinguish it from unsuccessful workfare programs in other states. It's time that lawmakers in California and elsewhere create a voluntary jobs-training program and jobs to go with it. A voluntary program would also recognize a parent's right to stay home and take care of her children. The states should do more than pour millions of dollars into programs that "train" people for jobs that don't pay enough to support a family.

If, as Governor Deukmejian says, "workfare is a bridge, and all you have to do is cross it," we ought to make sure the bridge is leading somewhere.

THE GREATEST WELFARE REFORM: REAL JOBS[3]

It's not too late for the Congress and the Reagan Administration to agree on meaningful welfare reform. A quick look at the legislation passed by the House Ways and Means Committee, chaired by Rep. Dan Rostenkowski (D.-Ill.), and the welfare reform bill sponsored by Sen. Daniel Patrick Moynihan (D.-N.Y.) indicates that there is basic agreement on what's needed to help thousands of welfare families to become independent and self-sufficient. That, quite simply, is jobs. This long-awaited and painfully reached agreement could deteriorate, however, over relatively minor details. It would be wrong for our nation to miss this opportunity for true welfare reform.

Disagreements have developed over two questions: should families in which both parents are unemployed be allowed to receive welfare, and what age should a child be when the mother is required to look for work? Both are reasonable questions, but neither has a right or a wrong answer. More important, neither question should get in the way of providing opportunity to families on public assistance.

The states have led the way in designing programs that provide welfare clients with the opportunity to get the training and support they need to land real jobs with real wages. Congress now wants to help the states by providing for an increased Federal investment in "welfare-to-work" programs. Now, as never before, we must not lose sight of the fact that real jobs with adequate support services such as day care and health benefits are the key to reform. With such a policy, we can save billions of dollars and cut the Federal deficit at the same time.

[3]Reprint of an article by Michael S. Dukakis, Governor of Massachusetts. Reprinted from *USA Today* Magazine, March 1988. Copyright 1988 by the Society for the Advancement of Education.

Agreement on welfare reform didn't always exist. In my first term as Governor of Massachusetts (1975–78), I found my state confronting a strange paradox. As our unemployment rate dropped from nearly 12% to less than six percent in that four-year period, the number of families on welfare actually went *up*. Try as we might, we found this phenomenon impossible to understand or reverse. So, like most governors, I had my own fling at workfare—and it failed.

Retired involuntarily from the Governor's office in 1978, I watched a similar experiment by my successor fail as well. Why did workfare fail in Massachusetts, and why have similar programs across the country achieved so little success? Quite simply, it is because the overwhelming majority of families on welfare in this country are made up of single mothers with young children. Traditional workfare—a part-time "work assignment" in a dead-end job with no real wages, just a welfare grant as a paycheck—won't help these families to lift themselves out of poverty. Unless we want or expect those mothers to abandon their children for dead-end or make-work jobs, such programs are doomed to failure.

Support Services Are Essential

When I returned to the Governor's office in 1983, I put together a program with my Legislature that recognized the needs of welfare mothers and their children, one that acknowledged that most welfare recipients want to work. The Employment and Training Choices program—known as ET—says to mothers and their children: "We're prepared to be serious partners in your efforts to lift yourselves out of poverty. We're prepared to provide real training for real jobs; we'll provide day care for up to a year after you go to work and we'll continue medical benefits for up to a year as well, if your employer does not provide health insurance."

Contrary to popular myth, those on welfare are not all alike, not part of some permanent underclass, and not unwilling to work. Welfare mothers want to work and to provide a better life for their children, but they need different kinds of support to get there. Some require basic educational opportunities, like a chance to get a high school diploma or even to learn to read. Others need skills training so that they can compete for the wages necessary to support a family. Many must have help with day care if they are to be able to leave the house for training and eventually a job. Most also need to get jobs with health benefits if they are to be free of the welfare system.

The success of the ET approach is evidenced by the statistics: over 40,000 ET graduates have entered full- or part-time jobs since the program began in 1983; the average full-time job obtained through ET pays $13,000 per year; 86% of those who leave the welfare rolls are off welfare one year later; the average length of stay on welfare in Massachusetts has declined by 25% since ET began; and the number of families on welfare for five years or more has declined by nearly 30%.

The statistics are impresive, but they do not tell the whole story. Rather, it is the human factor of ET that so eloquently documents its success. Take 27-year-old Angela Wooten from Dorchester, for example. In August, 1987, she and 10 other ET graduates officially were certified as Emergency Medical Technicians (EMT's) by the Commonwealth of Massachusetts. Angela and her classmates had studied hard during the 18-week course offered through ET and Northeastern University. They had completed rigorous examinations and internships with Boston-area ambulance companies. Most already had been offered jobs.

Angela, who is a single mother, had been on welfare since 1984. She and her seven-year-old daughter had survived on less than $6,000 per year. "It was very hard. We never had anything. But I was surprised at how dependent on welfare I became. It was like being inside a nut. I was stuck in it," Angela explained.

In the spring of 1987, she heard about ET and began the EMT training program. In August, Angela spoke about her new outlook on life at her class graduation. "For the first time in a long time, I don't know what is happening on the afternoon soap operas—and I don't care," she said.

Today, Angela earns over $13,000 per year as an EMT at Boston's Brewster ambulance company, and she and her daughter have full health benefits. Angela believes that her work is both challenging and rewarding, and she says with a grin, "I won't ever go into a welfare office again."

Dawn Lawson, a Worcester mother, faced similar obstacles. She was on welfare from the time her nine-year-old son Brian was born. A teenage mother, she had managed to finish high school, but had no marketable skills. In 1983, she heard about the ET program and began a word-processing course, which included an internship at Norton Company, a Fortune 500 manufacturer with headquarters in Worcester.

"I was scared to death walking in there. I was so nervous, I could hardly talk," Dawn said. However, her newly acquired skills earned her a job offer that she accepted. Within a year, she was substituting for the secretary of Norton Company's president, and today she is in charge of managing the payroll and benefits of all of Norton's overseas employees.

Norton Company still offers internships to ET participants, and Dawn Lawson has seen her share of nervous young women who, like herself, lacked confidence and work experience. "I tell them I was just like they are. They can't believe it, but it's true."

Dawn now earns more than $17,000 per year, and the changes in her personal life have been dramatic since she graduated from ET and welfare dependency. She has purchased a car. She and her son have been able to move out of a crime-ridden public housing project. Brian has enjoyed karate lessons, summer camp, new clothes, and yearly vacations on Cape Cod.

Angela and Dawn are not unique. I have talked to dozens of ET graduates, and their employers, about their new-found feelings of self-worth and self-esteem and about the sense of independence that comes with earning a paycheck instead of a welfare check. "This is the most successful program I have ever been associated with," said Thomas J. Hourihan, vice president of corporate human resources for Norton Company. "The ET graduates I meet come to us with marketable skills and enormous motivation. These individuals want to work."

Lessons on Reform

ET has taught us some valuable lessons about the two questions that may be getting in the way of welfare reform.

Two-Parent Welfare Families. Currently, 26 states, including Massachusetts, allow families to receive welfare benefits when both parents are unemployed. In other states, the family is required to break up before they can receive public assistance. This is a ridiculous policy for a country which prides itself on being pro-family. It also is self-defeating. Why encourage family break-up if child-support enforcement is so difficult? I believe that a growing economy combined with a successful employment and training program can be the answer to the problem.

Since we began our ET program in October, 1983, the number of two-parent welfare families in Massachusetts has dropped nearly 60%, to just over 1,100. These families are the first to benefit from a decline in the unemployment rate and are least likely to remain on welfare for a long time.

When to Leave a Child So As to Take a Job. There is no answer for every family, and Congress should be careful about an across-the-board mandate below the current age of six. Currently 60% of welfare families in Massachusetts have children under age six. Existing Federal law exempts these families from having to participate in any welfare-to-work program. Yet, in Massachusetts, women with children under age six make up over 40% of ET participants. This is because the program offers extensive day-care services throughout the time a woman is in a training program and for up to one year after she obtains a job. At the end of one year, the cost of day care is on a sliding fee scale, according to the mother's income.

Massachusetts is not alone. In states as diverse as Florida, Illinois, Maryland, Michigan, Vermont, and California, state government has been opening the doors of opportunity to thousands of welfare families through education, job training and placement, and the full range of support services needed by single women raising families who are trying to break free of the welfare system. For the most part, these programs have depended on state funds. Now, it is time for the investment of Federal resources as well. In addition to the savings achieved when a family leaves welfare, we *all* get added benefits since the new worker becomes a new taxpayer. The states have understood the value of this effort, and we would welcome the addition of a Federal partner to this investment, one that is already paying dividends.

In Massachusetts, for example, after deducting all program costs, ET saved taxpayers over $100,000,000 in 1986 in reduced welfare benefits and increased revenue from Federal and state income and sales taxes. Two-thirds of these savings were reaped by the Federal government. Recently, the Massachusetts Taxpayer's Foundation—an independent organization that has monitored government expenditures in the state for over 50 years—released a special report on the ET program which concluded, " . . . the investment in ET has paid off for Massachusetts" and "the savings to the state far outruns the cost of the program."

If Massachusetts can save taxpayers over $100,000,000 a year, think how much we could save if the same kind of program was operating in all 50 states. That would be an added boost in our efforts to reduce the Federal deficit.

WELFARE REFORM MAY FINALLY BE IN THE WORKS[4]

In the winter of 1985, the cruel wind blowing in off Lake Michigan was a bitter reminder to Desiree Allen that she had hit rock bottom. A twice-divorced mother of two school-age children, she was living in her mother's home on Chicago's rough South Side, just scraping by on $500 a month in welfare and food stamps. Last year, though, Allen enrolled in Project Chance, a state program that provides education and job training for welfare recipients. Now she works with the disabled, supports her family on her $180-a-week salary, and may go back to school. "The program opened my eyes," she says. "It has given me a lot of self-motivation."

Allen's new paycheck, less than $10,000 per year, leaves her squarely in the ranks of America's poor. Still, her experience represents a glimmer of success in the battle against welfare dependency—and such glimmers highlight a fragile consensus emerging among liberals and conservatives. Both camps agree that transforming welfare into work opportunities can cut the roster of those on the dole and slash the costs of supporting the poor. "Welfare reform" has become the new call to arms, "workfare" its buzzword.

With optimism running high, Congress is considering what could be pathbreaking legislation to change the nature of Aid to Families with Dependent Children, the 52-year-old program known as welfare. "The current system is broken, and this is an attempt to fix it," declares Representative Thomas J. Downey (D-N.Y.), who is sponsoring a workfare proposal.

[4]Reprint of an article by Susan B. Garland, *Business Week* staffwriter. Reprinted from the November 2, 1987 issue of *Business Week* by special permission. Copyright © 1987 by McGraw-Hill, Inc.

Downey's bill, and one introduced by Senator Daniel P. Moynihan (D-N.Y.), would provide matching funds to state efforts to set up education, training, and job-placement programs for welfare mothers of children older than three. Because fewer than half of the nation's 8.8 million single mothers receive child support, Moynihan's proposal would also crack down on absent, noncontributing fathers by withholding their wages. A Republican alternative, offered by Colorado Representative Hank Brown, would require that all AFDC mothers whose children are older than six months join a work program.

Much remains to be worked out. Funding levels, particularly, will be subject to intense debate. A consensus bill will likely remain elusive for at least several months. Still, any agreement would be nothing less than remarkable, given the dissension that has long marked the welfare debate.

Welfare, reflects Tom Joe, director of Washington's Center for the Study of Social Policy, has come to symbolize this nation's internal schisms over the work ethic, marriage, charity, and parental responsibility. While opinion polls indicate support for health, food, and housing programs for the poor, they elicit scant sympathy for the able-bodied, overwhelmingly female, and disproportionately minority-group recipients of AFDC. "Welfare is the great American scapegoat," Joe says. "It brings out all of our religious and moral prejudices in a morally acceptable context."

Highly Visible

The federal budget for AFDC, adjusted for inflation, has been shrinking, while other poverty outlays have climbed. AFDC expenditures are dwarfed by the cost of social programs for the elderly: $194 billion for Social Security, $54 billion for public employee retirement, and $80 billion for medicare this year. Research by David T. Ellwood and Mary Jo Bane, poverty experts at Harvard University's John F. Kennedy School of Government, indicates that at least half of those on welfare leave the rolls within two years, and 85% leave within eight years—suggesting that most poor women use welfare as a source of temporary income while their children are young.

But the nation's attention is riveted on a highly visible, particularly troubled group of welfare mothers—the 15% who stay on AFDC for long periods and collect more than half of the benefits paid out. Mainly unmarried, 43% black and 12% Hispanic, these women are joining the rolls at younger ages than formerly, says Sheldon H. Danzinger, director of the Institute for Research on Poverty at the University of Wisconsin. He adds that the new recipients often are the daughters of welfare mothers.

For years the right and left have clashed over what to do about AFDC. Conservatives have insisted that welfare recipients have an obligation to give something back for what they get. That argument led to the original workfare approach in the early 1970s—state programs requiring some recipients to work off their welfare checks in government jobs at the minimum wage.

Charles Murray's influential 1984 book, *Losing Ground*, made the conservative case that the government's safety net is itself the problem. By providing an alternative to work and marriage, Murray argued, AFDC encourages out-of-wedlock childbearing and discourages private initiative in poor communities.

The liberal scholars of poverty, for their part, have ridiculed the notion that average monthly welfare benefits of $354—a 33% decline in purchasing power since 1970—create an incentive to stay on the dole. They argue that welfare does not foster single-parent families, noting that states with vastly differing welfare benefits show the same out-of-wedlock birth rates. Moreover, while the number of single mothers in the general population has risen sharply since 1970, the fraction of America's children on AFDC remained constant.

Liberals also criticized the early forms of workfare as punitive, calling it "slavefare." They said that workfare jobs did nothing to help the destitute attain self-sufficiency.

The Greater Good

In the past, attempts to tackle the problems of welfare's hard core have been both sporadic and feeble. The 1971 Work Incentive Program (WIN) required all AFDC recipients without preschool children to register with the state employment services and to participate in job training or job search—but in many cases, the massive registration efforts ate up most of the funding. Social policy for mothers of younger children was decided, in effect, by the failure of national child-care initiatives that would have enabled at least some welfare recipients to work. At that time, paying poor mothers to stay home with their children was deemed the greater social good.

In the 1980s, however, with 56% of mothers of preschool children in the work force, "requiring mothers to work is no longer considered unreasonable," says Harvard's Ellwood. Equally important, a growing body of experience suggests that welfare-to-work programs can be effective, though to varying degrees. In 1981, Congress gave the states leave to experiment along these lines using WIN funds. Most efforts consisted of simple job search assistance, helping short-term welfare recipients.

Still, New York-based Manpower Demonstration Research Corp., in a recent review of eight state workfare programs created since 1981, found modest improvements in earnings and employment rates compared with control groups. "We know the programs are a positive step, but these are incremental changes," says MDRC President Judith M. Gueron. "The key is to have realistic expectations."

While the Manpower study dispelled the myth that welfare recipients do not want to work, it also showed that workfare is no easy solution to years of debilitating poverty. Hard-core AFDC mothers need extensive remedial education, employment-skills training, job placement, and child care to prepare for jobs.

That is an expensive proposition. From 1975 to 1980, Manpower experimented with a program called "supported work." At 15 locations, welfare mothers and other hard-core unemployed were immersed in structured work situations for a year of job training and experience. They learned to get to work on time and to get along with the boss and fellow workers. The price tag, $6,000 for each participant, was high compared with several hundred dollars for simple job search assistance, but low when the alternative is years of welfare checks.

Faustian Bargain

High-profile programs in Massachusetts, California, and Illinois combine education and training with job placement, tailoring the assistance to participants' needs. Massachusetts' Employment & Training Choices, which offers "supported work" as one of its services, claims to have found jobs for 30,000 people in three years. Illinois' Project Chance says it has placed 77,000 people in two years.

However, follow-up is nonexistent. "We don't know how many stayed on the job for how long," says Elizabeth Solomon of the Illinois Commission on Intergovernmental Cooperation. Some skeptics suspect that many people counted as "placements" would have found jobs on their own.

The Downey, Moynihan, and Brown bills, to varying degrees, combine employment and training, which liberals like, with the conservatives' insistence on responsibility and work. By themselves, though, the bills can make no sharp dent in American poverty. Downey's plan, the most generous, earmarks $5.2 billion over five years. That is expected to remove from the welfare rolls only 50,000 of the 3.7 million welfare families. Experts say the Republicans' $1.4 billion alternative will spread too little money among too many people to have any real effect.

Finding a job, of course, is not in itself the whole solution. For unlike their married counterparts in the work force, workfare mothers will find themselves struggling with what Harvard's Ellwood terms the difficult "dual responsibility" of being sole breadwinner and nurturer. Jobs that get mothers off AFDC are likely to pay low wages and exclude health benefits: a Faustian bargain at best, since many of these women would find themselves in the growing ranks of the working poor, with incomes, below $11,203 per year for a family of four. By this standard, 32 million Americans are poor. Only one-third receive welfare.

Child care, which costs an average of $3,000 a year per child in the U.S., is another serious problem that will face workfare mothers. The Democrats' proposals would finance medicaid and child care for several months for those who start work—but then would terminate the benefits. "It's a catch-22," complains Helen S. Blank, child-care expert at the Children's Defense Fund. "Many may decide to go back to welfare."

To tip the balance, some policy analysts advocate expanding the earned-income tax credit and the child-care deduction for poor families. A separate bill now being worked up in Congress would provide low-income women with $2.5 billion for child care.

Even with the problems plaguing reform efforts, a low-wage job still is a first step, while welfare dependency leads nowhere. Also, demographic trends predicting regional labor shortages among young, entry-level, and service workers may make this the best opportunity in many years for undertaking work-based welfare reform.

Too Sanguine?

"In the past, welfare mothers were at the end of the hiring queue, and employers would have been out of their mind to take them," says Robert D. Reischauer, a senior fellow at the Brookings Institution. "Today, employers may be more willing."

That seems overly sanguine in the here and now. As yet, most states do not have the low unemployment that has enabled Massachusetts to place so many Employment & Training Choices graduates in jobs. Maryland is so concerned about job shortages that it is lending companies money to expand their operations and hire welfare recipients. The answer, says socialist thinker Michael Harrington—whose 1962 book, *The Other America,* helped ignite President John F. Kennedy's War on Poverty—is massive job creation, both public and private. However, it has long been a conservative article of faith to oppose expanded public-sector employment and the concept of guaranteed jobs.

Some experts argue that lawmakers should focus on combating the joblessness and substandard earnings that reduce the ability of young men in poor communities to support a family. Others believe that more attention and money should be directed toward prenatal care, preschool education, dropout programs, and teenage pregnancy prevention. What's really needed, they contend, is a broad approach that prepares children for the economic mainstream, so that they never need welfare at all.

IS IT HYPE OR TRUE REFORM?[5]

The *New York Times* says it is "the first major change in the welfare system in 50 years." It isn't. Democratic Sen. Daniel Moynihan, its principal architect, says it will "turn the welfare program upside down." It won't. *USA Today* says it "calls for a work program for recipients." It does—for about 6 percent of welfare families, in the distant year of 1997.

Maybe the Family Welfare Reform Act, passed with great fanfare last week, is just a lot of hype. But no, it's not that, either. Somehow, in the strangely productive political vacuum of the Reagan administration's final year, what was largely a make-believe reform got transformed into a law worthy of its name, if not its press clips.

In pushing his reform, Moynihan attempted to capitalize on the so-called "new consensus" on welfare. The consensus held, first, that America had a growing, unproductive "underclass," composed in large part of single mothers who (with their children) are dependent on welfare. Second, the way to break the "cycle of poverty" was to get these mothers into the work force. Crudely put, if conservatives would pay for the necessary training and day care, liberals would give up the idea that welfare mothers had a "right" not to work.

A key break came in 1981, when Reagan got Congress to let states require that welfare recipients work in exchange for their checks (*workfare*). This *was* the first major change in the welfare system in 50 years. Over half the states designed new programs. Hardly any of them command all recipients to work—they offer "work experience" as one of several options, including training or going to school. But many obligate recipients to do *something*. (Michael Dukakis's much-touted "ET" program is not one of these. It offers training but requires nothing.)

Moynihan's original bill used federal money to encourage these experiments. But states didn't have to do much of anything to get more recipients working. Meanwhile, the House passed a "reform" bill that only undermined the "new consensus." It actually restricted workfare programs, in part at the behest of unions fearing cheap competition from workfarers.

Republicans complicated the matter further. The Senate passed a GOP amendment to Moynihan's bill mandating 16 hours a week of public-service work (not just training) from two-parent families on welfare. This was largely symbolic—two-parent families are less than 7 percent of the 3.7 million welfare families. More important, the White House insisted that states be required to get a minimum percentage of their entire caseload (including single mothers) into some form of work, training or job preparation.

Some liberals balked, reasserting the old idea of welfare as a right and branding the 16-hour requirement "slave-fare." But ultimately the "new consensus" held. The 16-hour rule and the minimum "participation rate" were watered down and delayed—but by 1995, 20 percent of the recipients "required" to participate must actually do it.

That doesn't sound rigorous, and it's less rigorous than it sounds. Half of welfare families, including all mothers with kids under three, aren't in the "required" group. But any requirement is "better than nothing," a White House aide argues. The Congressional Budget Office thinks the new law will double (to well over 1 million) the number of recipients getting some kind of training. Significantly, the bill also allows states to require that young unwed mothers live at home, so going on welfare doesn't become a ticket to independence for teenagers. It beefs up child-support collection, setting uniform schedules and deducting support from paychecks. That may deter some potential fathers from making babies they can't feed.

"Hat Trick": Why did Democrats compromise instead of waiting for a possible Dukakis administration? A bit of congressional macho seems to have motivated one key negotiator, Rep. Dan Rostenkowski, who already brags about having achieved the "hat trick" of a trade bill, catastrophic health insurance and now welfare reform. Even if Dukakis wins, Democrats realize, the next Congress will be in a deficit-cutting crisis—no time to pass a $3.3 billion welfare bill. Democrats also won major concessions: welfare mothers who start work will be able to keep subsidized day care and Medicaid for up to a year.

Still, some House liberals talk openly of trying, in future years, to knock out even the compromise work requirements before they take effect. Meanwhile, conservatives hope to toughen the law. This year's "reform" didn't really answer the crucial question of whether welfare mothers must work—or even train. Most will still simply collect checks. Moynihan can be proud of his achievement, but it has hardly "redefined the whole question of dependency" (his words). It is, rather, the greatest reform of the welfare system . . . until the next reform of the welfare system.

WHY WELFARE REFORM IS A SHAM[6]

Congress is about to enact legislation that turns the controversial Aid to Families with Dependent Children program on its head. The changes made in this program, which was designed to help needy single mothers stay home with their children, represents a sharp break with the philosophy of the landmark Social Security Act of 1935, of which A.F.D.C. is a part. The new law transforms A.F.D.C. from an income-support program into a mandatory work and training program and shifts social welfare responsibility from the Federal government to families and the states. Billed as a way to strengthen family life, this "welfare reform" will in fact cheapen the costs of women's labor and weaken the basic principles on which the modern welfare state rests. This, in turn, is best understood as part of a broader conservative strategy, initiated more gingerly in the mid-1970s, to redistribute income upward and reduce the size of Federal government.

The new welfare program meshes well with current conservative thought. It claims to be forging a new social contract that spells out the reciprocal responsibilities between A.F.D.C. mothers and the state. In exchange for a parental agreement to become self-sufficient there will be a societal commitment to provide some of the means for self-support. Translated into practical terms: Women on welfare with children over age 3 (or 1 in some states) will be required to participate in work and training programs, and the state will more vigorously collect child-support payments from absent fathers. In return, the government will also help women on A.F.D.C. become employed by offering them social services—job placement, education and training programs, child care and Medicaid coverage. Women who refuse to participate in mandatory work programs face a reduction in (or loss of) benefits or work relief. But no sanctions are specified if the state welfare department fails to uphold its part of the contract.

Welfare reform has captured the support of many liberals because proponents initially promised a national minimum benefit,

[6]Reprint of an article by Mimi Abramovitz, associate professor of social policy at Hunter College School of Social Work in New York City. Reprinted by permission from *The Nation*, V. 247: Cover, 238–41. S. 26, '88. Copyright © 1988 by *The Nation*.

child care and Medicaid benefits, increases in services and an extension of A.F.D.C. to two-parent families in all states. In the end, however, the changes that emerged from the political process offered nothing more than very old wine in new and smaller bottles.

The national minimum benefit was the first to disappear from the legislative proposals. The loss of this long-advocated liberal reform leaves the states in charge of setting A.F.D.C. benefit levels. Not only has the amount of the welfare check varied widely from one state to another but from 1970 to 1985 the real value of the average A.F.D.C. grant plunged by 31 percent. In 1988 the maximum combined A.F.D.C. and food stamp benefits did not bring a family of three in any state up to the government's own poverty line. In thirty-nine states these benefits failed to reach 75 percent of this understated threshold. This not-so-benign neglect occurred even though the costs of A.F.D.C. leveled off in the mid-1970s and in 1987 accounted for only about 0.76 percent of the Federal budget. The final welfare reform bill provides few, if any, Federal incentives to the states to increase their welfare payments.

The original promise of enriched employment services for welfare mothers also was eroded. Instead of mandating the states to provide education, training and job placement programs as initially proposed, the Federal bill makes most services optional. The states will be required to provide only the least costly job search, basic education and "workfare" programs rather than the more expensive skill-building education and training services. Although most of the low-paying jobs open to welfare recipients lack child care and health insurance, Congress preferred to leave the provision of these benefits up to the states. The hard-won mandatory provisions finally enacted cover only nine months of child care and up to twelve months of Medicaid (the second six months subject to a premium). No one asks how women in low-paying jobs will pay for these services once the temporary benefits run out. Quality day care for poor children is also out of reach. Congress did lift the maximum reimbursement for child care payments from $160 a month to the prevailing market price, but the states still have considerable discretion in setting the rates.

The new welfare law makes the currently optional A.F.D.C.-UP program, which provides benefits to two-parent families in which the primary earner is unemployed, mandatory in all the states. But instead of making A.F.D.C. available to one- and two-parent families, a legislative compromise restricted the already limited A.F.D.C.-UP program in new ways. It permits the states to introduce a mandatory workfare component for the first time and to confine aid to six months in any twelve-month period.

The use of automatic child support deductions from the wages of absent fathers to enforce child support more effectively has been billed as necessary to increase parental responsibility and reduce welfare costs. It recognizes that nearly one in four children nationwide lives with only one parent and that 60 percent of their families are legally entitled to support, but that just over half have received even partial payments, and many have received no support at all. Garnishing wages to recoup program costs may force those absent fathers who can do so to support their children. But for poor men it may be more like squeezing blood from a stone. Past efforts at child support, like the current one, imply that fathers of children on A.F.D.C. are irresponsible parents who avoid supporting their children because the state is doing the job. To date this approach has produced only modest financial returns and has pushed many poor fathers away from even a minimal involvement with the home.

The new bill's shortcomings should be no surprise, given its conservative underpinnings. Proponents have used a variety of disingenuous and misleading arguments to sell as "reform" what is actually a regressive measure that hurts rather than helps the poor.

The advocates of spurious reform glibly invoke feminist ideas on the desirability of jobholding women to justify throwing welfare mothers off the rolls and into the labor market. To justify mandatory rather than voluntary work and training programs, welfare reform advocates point to the high labor force participation rate of women, ignoring the declining standard of living that has compelled more and more middle-class wives and mothers of very young children to enter the work force. They fail to mention that 43 percent of all A.F.D.C. children are under age 6, or that while two-thirds of all married mothers with young children are employed, less than one-third work full time, year-round. They also ignore the labor market's inhospitality to welfare mothers, who, like many other women, are very likely to fill part-time jobs and be paid less than the $7,000 annual minimum wage. Although some on welfare lack the necessary motivation, education or training for better jobs, many have been adversely affected by the decline of better-paying manufacturing jobs, the rapid expansion of part-time and temporary work, the unending segregation of jobs by race and sex, the persistently low minimum wage and other economic trends that from 1978 to 1985 increased the number of working poor by 50 percent.

The campaign for welfare reform also draws heavily on negative stereotypes of poor women. While the media celebrates professional women who give up their high-powered jobs for family life, welfare mothers who want to stay home with their children are viewed as unmotivated to work rather than unwilling to accept substandard wages and unlicensed child care, and as suffering from poor work habits rather than a poor education, limited job opportunities and abusive economic policies.

Similarly, the promise that welfare reform will break the "cycle of dependency" feeds on the negative vision of a female-dominated welfare culture that keeps families mired in poverty, dependent on public aid and in homes that, lacking a man at the helm, are by definition disorganized and incapable of properly socializing children. The widely held belief that public assistance causes family breakups, soaring illegitimacy rates and reliance on programs like A.F.D.C. from one generation to the next persists despite the failure of research since the mid-1970s to support these stereotypic assumptions. Public opinion has yet to accept what researchers now know: that poverty, not welfare, causes families to break up; that most daughters of welfare mothers do not end up on A.F.D.C.; and that most families leave welfare rolls within two years.

But these facts mean little to welfare reformers. Their real desire is to shrink the A.F.D.C. rolls and reduce the program's costs rather than meet the needs of poor women. Putting them to work would also help enlarge the cheap labor pool. During most of the postwar period, in keeping with the age-old rule that public aid must be less attractive than paid work, A.F.D.C.'s low benefits, restrictive residency rules and moralistic eligibility requirements (e.g., "suitable" homes and the "no man in the house" rule, threats of child removal and midnight raids) operated to keep poor white women and women of color off the rolls and in low-paying jobs. During the 1950s, a variety of complex social and economic factors caused unwed mothers and women of color to replace white widows as the predominant groups on welfare.

At this time many states increased their use of vaguely defined moral fitness standards rather than economic need to determine eligibility for aid, which effectively punished women for departing from traditional wife and mother roles and forced them to work. For black women such practices date back to slavery and continue white society's pattern of refusing to grant their families the same respect, recognition and protection accorded to the white middle class.

In the late 1960s, as the Supreme Court declared moral fitness and residency requirements unconstitutional, and as civil rights and welfare mothers' groups began to claim welfare as a right, Congress introduced more formal work requirements into A.F.D.C., notably the Work Incentive (WIN) program in 1967. By requiring women on A.F.D.C. to participate in work or training programs, WIN formally reversed A.F.D.C.'s policy of helping single mothers remain at home with their children. Unhappy with WIN's limitations, during the 1980s the Reagan Administration encouraged the states to experiment with the new welfare-for-work programs. Paving the way for the current welfare reform bill, the WIN demonstration projects provided incentives for the states to test a variety of new employment programs.

Today's welfare reform comes at a time when pressures from the private sector to increase the supply of low-cost labor have intensified. The Committee on Economic Development, the National Alliance for Business and the Labor Department all have expressed fears about the shortfall of young workers willing to fill an expanding number of entry-level positions, the skill level and analytic capacity of the emerging work force and the trend toward higher wages already evident in fast-food outlets, supermarkets, banks, hospitals and some offices.

By transforming A.F.D.C. from an income support to a mandatory work and training program, which increases the supply of women for the entry-level jobs historically reserved for them and thus lowers overall wage rates, welfare reform may help to ease industry's current labor-market problems. Indeed, most state welfare-for-work programs place A.F.D.C. mothers in low-paying jobs. The Massachusetts employment and training program participants average about $9,000 a year; in Santa Clara, California, they receive only $6.50 an hour, although state officials say that $11 is needed to stay off the welfare rolls. The New York–based Manpower Demonstration Research Corporation found that, on the average, welfare recipients in 1987 earned less than $4.14 an hour, or $4,000 below the poverty line for a family of four. A recent update, covering a longer period of time, reported that participants' earnings have increased only $300 to $500 a year.

"Welfare reform" meshes well with the Reagan Administration's ongoing effort to cheapen the cost of labor. Although it is not always seen in this way, A.F.D.C. is an economic way station for poor women who are temporarily without a paying job or a breadwinner. One source of the controversy surrounding the program may be that even its low benefits offer the potential of a financial cushion that enables women to avoid abusive marriages or insecure jobs. If properly funded at higher levels, A.F.D.C. might increase the economic independence of poor women and cause fewer of them to be available for the low-paying service jobs now on the rise.

The Reagan Administration is also committed to chipping away at the philosophical basis of the entire welfare system, including A.F.D.C. By replacing liberal tenets of entitlement, self-determination and Federal responsibility with more, conservative notions of contract, compulsion and states' rights, welfare reform erodes some of the fundamental principles that support the U.S. welfare state. In 1981, the Reagan Administration first declared that the idea of entitlement was wrong. Transforming A.F.D.C. into an employment program based on a contractual arrangement furthers this goal by implicitly undercutting the societal obligation to provide cash assistance. A contract between parties as unequal as a welfare mother and the state effectively weakens the protections against economic insecurity and loss of social rights that the welfare state, at least in theory, arose to provide.

The mandatory features of A.F.D.C.—forced work for recipients and automatic wage garnishments for absent parents—also undermine the democratic principles of self-determination and free choice. Coercive requirements substitute the market-based concept of exchange for the rights-based idea of entitlement. Preferring the stick over the carrot, the welfare reform denies poor women the right to decide for themselves whether staying home or going to work is best for their children, a choice still granted many women of the middle class. The implication that caring for one's children at home is not productive work (but caring for the children of others is) blatantly discounts the enormous contribution made by women's unpaid labor to their families and society at large. The system of coercion also blames the victim by suggesting that welfare mothers will not work outside the home and poor fathers will not support their children unless forced to do so by the government. This simply ignores the facts. The Manpower Demonstration Research Corporation found that 61 percent of the participants in San Diego's WIN demonstration found work, but so did 55 percent of the nonparticipants. Only 5 to 7 percent *more* of those who participated in a variety of WIN programs became employed than those who did not. While some poor men, like those of other social classes, are overtly negligent, many A.F.D.C. fathers simply lack the income needed to support their families.

Although it was dropped at the last minute, it's worth remembering that for months the welfare reform bill included a provision that would begin to carry out the Administration's continuing effort to defederalize A.F.D.C. Handing enormous discretion to the states, it would have allowed them to consolidate a variety of Federal social welfare programs, to use the funds to modify A.F.D.C. or create alternatives to it and to be exempt from various Federal requirements that safeguard clients' rights. Although it was defeated in committee, its near passage signals the difficulties confronting liberals who for years have sought to federalize A.F.D.C. in order to standardize its benefits and eligibility rules and make it less vulnerable to pressures of racism, sexism, antiunionism and opposition to social programs that often originate in the states.

The United States is one of the few Western industrialized countries without a national children's or family allowance that provides cash aid to all families regardless of their composition. The new welfare law has not changed this at all. True reform must include more participation by welfare mothers and must look past the current A.F.D.C. program to the entire social welfare system. This means a commitment to assuring economic security through income support programs for all families, with benefits at or above the poverty line and indexed to inflation. It means full-employment policies that provide jobs for all those ready and able to work but that also close the male/female and the white/nonwhite wage gaps, that enforce antidiscrimination and affirmative-action laws and that open white-male-held jobs to those now excluded from them. Caretaking roles must receive support regardless of who carries them out, and the gender division of labor that still leaves women exclusively responsible for children and the home must be revised. In brief, we must recognize equal rights and responsibilities within the family and in the workplace and assure that the needs of all people are satisfactorily met. Reform must ultimately go beyond questions of poverty to those of redistribution, full employment and genuine equality for all.

GETTING ROUGH ON THE POOR[7]

The Family Security Act of 1988 ("The Moynihan Bill") Report of the Committee on Finance, US Senate. US Government Printing Office, 190 pp., Free

Creating the Future: The Massachusetts Comeback and Its Promise for America by Michael S. Dukakis and Rosabeth Moss Kanter. Summit Books, 190 pp., $17.95

Poor Support: Poverty in the American Family by David T. Ellwood. Basic Books, 271 pp., $19.95

Challenge To Leadership: Economic and Social Issues for the Next Decade edited by Isabel V. Sawhill. Urban Institute Press, 326 pp., $22.95; $12.95 (paper)

Laboratories of Democracy by David Osborne. Harvard Business School Press, 380 pp., $24.95

The New Consensus on Family and Welfare edited by Michael Novak et al. American Enterprise Institute, 143 pp., $22.50; $9.75 (paper)

Remaking the Welfare State: Retrenchment and Social Policy in America and Europe edited by Michael K. Brown. Temple University Press, 312 pp., $34.95

Both political parties and most legislators now agree that Aid to Families with Dependent Children, the program commonly called "welfare," needs radical reform. The Democratic platform pledges to "help people move from welfare to work." The Republicans also say they will "reform welfare to encourage work as the

---

[7]Reprint of an article by Andrew Hacker, professor of political science at Queens College in New York City. Reprinted with permission from the *New York Review of Books*, October 13, 1988. Copyright © 1988 Nyrev, Inc.

ticket that guarantees full participation in American life." Indeed, the GOP now accepts that if single mothers are to become self-supporting, they will need subsidized child care. And Michael Dukakis, in a manifesto of his own published earlier this year, urges his Massachusetts employment-training program as a model for the nation.

Large changes in AFDC may be closer than most people realize. Both chambers of Congress have passed a stringent "workfare" bill—in the Senate the vote was ninety-three to three—which is likely to become law before the end of this year. The belief behind the Family Security Act of 1988, which was largely drafted by Senator Moynihan, is that welfare creates a dependent underclass. Hence the view underlying the act that the time for solicitude has passed; discipline must be imposed. In particular, the statute's sponsors seek to change the outlook and behavior of the 3.3 million women now on the assistance rolls. Under its provisions, even mothers with preschool children will be forced to find jobs and support themselves. Given the emphasis on compulsion, it is appropriate to ask how justified this policy is, and what are the changes it may bring about.

I.

Today most Americans feel that mothers of young children should not be deterred from working if that is what they want to do. Many wives choose not to work, and that too is viewed as a legitimate option. However, women who receive welfare tend to be judged by rather different standards. Under current AFDC rules, any single mother is allowed to apply for a stipend that will enable her to stay at home with her children. Even so, states vary in their readiness to make these grants and in the amounts they offer. But it hardly needs remarking that the program is barely tolerated. In opinion polls most Americans rate it a failure, if not a scandal and a shame. Its initial purpose was to give needy citizens a respite, while they got back on their feet. However, the public is persuaded that too many recipients have made dependency a career: among all US families with children still at home, almost one in eight is now on the welfare rolls, while as recently as 1960 only one household in thirty-three was receiving AFDC.

The aim of the new Family Security Act, according to one of its sponsors, is "to get these people off the welfare rolls and onto the payrolls." Most of "these people" are women, since it is mothers or in some cases grandmothers who head 90 percent of all AFDC households. (In the others, a disabled or unemployed father may be present.) Since at least 1965, when he wrote *The Negro Family*, Daniel Patrick Moynihan has been proposing policies designed to end the poverty and pathologies associated with life on welfare. Moynihan ensured that the committee report would carry a detailed discussion of the act's major tenets. The report contains much useful information, as do the recent studies by David Ellwood of Harvard's Kennedy School and Isabel Sawhill at the Urban Institute in Washington. While they share most of Moynihan's concerns, they are less sanguine about some of his solutions.

A typical welfare family tends to be imagined as having half a dozen children, with the mother on the rolls for at least a dozen years. But as Table A shows this is one of several widely believed myths. In fact, three quarters of the AFDC households have one or two children, while fewer than 10 percent have as many as four. Only about a fourth of the parents have been receiving assistance for five or more years; and fewer than 10 percent have been on AFDC for over a decade.

At the same time, the figures support the general view that most recipients are black or Hispanic, out of proportion to their share of the population. This is to be expected, since within those minorities more households are headed by women. While black and Hispanic women comprise 21 percent of all women aged fifteen to forty-four, they account for 45 percent of all women who head households, and 55 percent of those receiving AFDC. To look at the figures another way, altogether 57 percent of Hispanic single mothers are on welfare, as are 55 percent of the comparable black group, while among single white women with children the proportion is 34 percent. (Unless otherwise indicated, the phrase "single mothers" refers to women who are widowed, separated, divorced, or have never been married. Similarly, the only households and families considered here are ones with children under the age of eighteen.)

TABLE A

HOUSEHOLDS RECEIVING AID FOR
DEPENDENT CHILDREN (AFDC)—1986

Number of Children			Age of Youngest Child	
One	43.4%		Under 3	38.4%
Two	30.8%		3 to 5	22.7%
Three	16.0%		6 to 11	24.3%
Four or More	9.8%		Over 11	14.5%

Time on AFDC			Race	
Under 7 Months	17.2%		White	39.7%
7 to 12 Months	12.7%		Black	40.7%
One to Two Years	17.3%		Hispanic	14.5%
Two to Five Years	26.8%		Asian	2.3%
Over Five Years	25.9%		Other or Unknown	2.7%

Mother's Age			Mother's Education	
21 or Younger	15.8%		Under Grade 12	47.4%
22 to 29	41.3%		High School Graduate	42.9%
30 to 39	30.3%		Some College	8.5%
40 or Older	12.7%		College Graduate	1.2%

Fathers of the Children

	1986	1973
Not Married to Mother	52.6%	31.5%
Divorced or Separated	31.7%	46.5%
Unemployed or Disabled	9.0%	14.3%
Deceased	1.7%	5.0%
Other or Unknown	5.1%	2.7%

Source: Department of Health and Human Services

The figures also confirm popular concern that most of the mothers on AFDC have had their children out of wedlock. This itself is a significant shift from earlier years. Since 1973, the proportion of women receiving benefits because their husbands are unemployed, disabled, or deceased—generally seen as "legitimate" reasons—has declined by almost one half. And whereas the largest single category (46 percent) used to be women who were separated or divorced, it now consists of mothers who have never been married (52 percent; see Table A).

It is important to stress that most single mothers are not on welfare and in fact hold full-time jobs. Between 55 and 60 percent combine parenthood and employment, even when they have to settle for wages that barely support a household. Table B shows the incomes of the 6.3 million women who are single parents. That almost a quarter make more than $20,000 suggests how well they are coping, not only despite wage discrimination, but while caring for one or more youngsters, a burden borne by few fathers. That a further 27 percent earn between $10,000 and $20,000 tells us that they are not on welfare, since they have found they can make more on the job market. That so many single mothers have become self-supporting has bolstered the view that the rest should. (In addition to the 6.3 million single women who head households, there are another 1.8 million unmarried mothers who are not listed as heading households because they live with their own parents. Most of these younger mothers also receive benefits. Of the 3.3 million women family heads who are currently on AFDC, about 225,000 report that they are holding jobs, usually on a part-time basis.)

TABLE B
INCOMES OF WOMEN WHO HEAD HOUSEHOLDS
(1986)

$50,000 and Over	104,000	1.6%
$35,000 to $50,000	283,000	4.5%
$20,000 to $35,000	1,081,000	17.2%
$10,000 to $20,000	1,717,000	27.3%
Under $10,000	3,112,000	49.4%
	6,297,000	100.0%

Source: Bureau of the Census. Figures include women who are not currently married and have one or more children under the age of 18.

There is no way to live well on welfare. Even in the most generous states, stipends fall well below what the government defines as the poverty level. In 1986, annual cash allowances for a family with two children ranged from $1,380 in Alabama to $5,970 in Wisconsin, with the national average at $4,320. In 1986, it took an income of $8,740 for a family of three to escape the poverty category. Thus, as Table C shows, the typical AFDC stipend amounts to one seventh of the average American family income. Here, too, the states vary greatly, with the ratio of welfare to average US income ranging from 6 percent in Mississippi to 19 percent in Vermont. Even adding the value of food stamps, housing subsidies, and free routine medical treatment seldom raises a welfare family above the poverty line. (Apart from food stamps, the money value of various welfare benefits is difficult to estimate. For example: a recipient may have a public housing apartment that could command a market rent of $700. Or her child might undergo a series of operations that cost Medicaid more than $50,000.) Recent years have seen cutbacks in federal contributions, while states permit allowances to lag behind inflation. Whenever the government supports people on welfare, its manner of doing so ensures that they will be poor.

TABLE C

RATIO OF AVERAGE AFDC STIPEND TO MEDIAN FAMILY INCOME

Vermont	19.3%
Minnesota	19.0%
New York	18.3%
UNITED STATES	14.0%
Nevada	8.3%
Louisiana	7.6%
Mississippi	5.8%

In fact, there are millions of women who were once on the

welfare rolls and who are now self-supporting. Among them are
wives who were not employed when their marriages broke up,
and needed time to find a decent job. (Mothers can receive AFDC
assistance while going to college.) Follow-up studies of the welfare rolls have shown that more than half of all recipients leave
voluntarily before their third year. (See Greg Duncan, Martha
Hill, and Saul Hoffman, "Welfare Dependence Within and
Across Generations," *Science* (January 29, 1988), pp. 467–471.)

2.

The first part of Senator Moynihan's Family Security Act
deals with defaulting fathers. Moynihan likes to cite a remark by
the economist Stanley Lebergott: "Our national code of accepted
behavior includes the right of men to propagate children, and
then desert them." Lebergott calls this "men's liberation," which
he finds more pronounced than its women's counterpart. In 1950
only 6 percent of all households lacked a resident male parent.
Now the proportion is approaching 25 percent. When marriages
break up, the children almost always end up living with the mother. We seldom give this much thought, since people tend to assume that a woman will be a more natural parent. Few fathers ask
for even partial custody, since they take it as given that they cannot handle the job, a sentiment their wives usually share. (In the
rare cases where a mother asks the father to take the children,
she is seen as "walking out on the kids," an epithet we rarely hear
nowadays when a father packs his bags.) Except in the relatively
few cases of well-to-do fathers who pay adequate child support,
having the children remain with the mother means that either
she or the taxpayers end up paying most of the bills. And from
what we hear, the taxpaying public is not very happy about foot-
ing these costs.

A further consequence of "men's liberation" is that fathers
feel little obligation to support the children they have sired. Currently, 63 percent of single mothers receive no payments at all.
And while 37 percent do, by no means all receive the agreed-
upon sums. For those who do get checks, the yearly total averages

$2,215, which must often be spread among several children. A California study found that men earning $45,000 were as likely to ignore court orders as those making $15,000. For these reasons, the Family Security Act intends to make delinquent fathers pick up a greater share of costs now covered by AFDC. If they do, the reasoning runs, the role of government will diminish, since it will only have to provide supplemental funds when parental support is inadequate.

As matters now stand, when child support is computed, the needs of the mother and the youngsters seem of secondary concern. The first factor is how much the father is judged "able" to pay. Judges, lawyers, and lawmakers generally presume that a man will need to keep 80 percent of his earnings for himself once he is on his own. This is not surprising since most of those involved in these decisions are men. Almost all divorced men remarry, moreover, and many start another round of children. So securing support for their first set can be uphill work. This may be why Isabel Sawhill sounds grateful for a recent Wisconsin law mandating minimum payments of 17 percent of the father's earnings. However, the law also sets a ceiling of 34 percent, no matter how many children the man has produced.

Some strains might be eased if more single mothers married or remarried. In most cases, adding a man's income to her own would double the family budget. However, such statistics as we have show that after the age of thirty, women face dismaying odds in the remarriage market. In the thirty-five-to-thirty-nine age group, only four in ten divorced women can expect to remarry. Former husbands face no similar hurdles, and usually choose younger women as their second mates.

However, the fastest growing group of AFDC families consists of women who were not married when their babies were born and have not married anyone since. As Table A noted, in recent years these mothers and their children have risen from under a third of the welfare rolls to more than half. In most of these cases, the mothers conceived children with no expectation that a male parent would be taking up residence. In most such cases, moreover, those participating in making the baby tend to be young and poor. So far as the young men are concerned, David Ellwood writes in *Poor Support*, "fathering a child out of marriage is often seen as a badge of manhood, rather than a troubling set of new responsibilities." Thus fewer than 12 percent of out-of-wedlock fathers provide even token support payments. At the same time, girls choose to have and keep their babies; in their case, becoming a mother is often a badge of womanhood.

The legislators who drafted the Family Security bill apparently feel that if government gets tougher about making fathers pay, then many men may try to deny paternity. So the law will allow states to require "blood tests and genetic typing" for suspected fathers. That done, a federal bureau will then grade each state on its "paternity establishment percentage," listing how many fathers have been found for out-of-wedlock children. The states will also make fathers supply their Social Security numbers when a baby is born, to be used by agencies charged with finding delinquent dads. If some fathers protest that they are unable to help, since they are unemployed or poorly paid, states may order them to take part in training programs, so they may augment their earning power.

This is an ambitious, if not intrusive, program, based on the premise that creating a human life carries long-term obligations. Unfortunately, many nonpaying fathers simply lack the cash. A considerable number are among the 850,000 men now in our state and federal prisons or local jails. Others are drug addicts or homeless, or are youths who have yet to hold a steady job. While every dollar they pay will help, their prospects as providers are not very promising.

For this reason most of the provisions of the Family Security Act concern women. As has been noted, the aim is to get them off welfare and onto payrolls. First, mothers under twenty-two who have not graduated from high school will be obliged to complete a high school education. (They may do so, in some states, through special courses leading to a high school "equivalency" diploma.)

After that the act provides for "mandatory participation" in job-training programs for all women with children over the age of three. The 40 percent of current AFDC mothers with children under three would not have to take part, although many of them would still be required to leave the house and return to school. However, the bill also allows a state to limit its exemptions to women with children under the age of one; in that case, almost 90 percent of the women would have to attend school or training sessions. During this period, the bill says, AFDC allowances and medical benefits would continue, and some form—just what is not clear—of child care must be made available.

Upon completing a training program, a mother is presumed ready to go to work, and would be require to accept any "bona fide" offer of employment. The presumption is that such a job will pay wages that equal or exceed her welfare stipend, plus the value of food stamps and other services. The legislation also assumes that she will be able to make suitable arrangements for the care of her children. If a mother refuses to enter a training program or accept a "bona fide" job, she will be removed from the AFDC rolls. To ensure that her children will not suffer, "protective payments" for them may be made to a "third party," bypassing the mother. Just who is meant by a "third party" and just how it will use the payments to care for a child, the act does not specify.

If all AFDC mothers with children over three will have to attend school or job-training sessions, and will have to take full-time jobs sooner or later, then 1.5 million new places for child care will have to be added to those now being used by working mothers. As it happens, the funding portion of the bill does not provide for new child-care services. Indeed it assumes that states will allow women on welfare to make much the same arrangements as currently employed mothers. The most recent census survey found that 31 percent of women who are now working leave their children at home, and 37 percent drop them off at someone else's house. Thus only 24 percent have them in child-care centers, nursery school, or kindergarten, and 8 percent take them along to work. (Nor do these figures include after-school arrangements for children in the elementary grades.)

But mothers on AFDC may be more likely to need organized child care. This raises questions of quantity, quality, and cost. For one thing, we hear that children from lower-income families need special attention to compensate for the limitations at home, and experts insist that child-care centers should have professional staffs, with one college-trained adult for every three or four children. Yet, curiously, the report on the bill assumes that $120 a month—$6 a working day—will provide suitable care for youngsters of preschool age. The centers that Harvard University runs for its clerical employees charge upward of $825 a month and the much-cited Swedish system has similar costs. What kind of child care will the Family Security Act be able to provide with only a small fraction of those budgets? And what kind of job training will the women get?

3.

Neither David Ellwood nor Isabel Sawhill expresses much confidence in the job-training programs currently available. Ellwood entitles his discussion "Big Promises, Modest Payoffs." As he sees it, "No carefully evaluated work-welfare programs have done more than put a tiny dent in the welfare caseloads." One project he cites spent close to $10,000 per participant; yet a follow-up study found that its graduates were averaging only $10 a week in wages more than a group that had not had any training. Sawhill reaches a similar conclusion about a five-state project. There, "employment rates for participants in the job-training programs were three to six percentage points higher than for other welfare recipients." Applying those figures to the whole AFDC population, she estimates that the proportion of households receiving assistance would drop by only five percentage points. As it turns out, much of the training has less to do with specific jobs than with basic literacy, and with such matters as dress and deportment, with knowing how to fill out forms or use an alarm clock. Those who are placed in jobs usually start out doing unskilled work. Nor is this surprising. According to Senator Moynihan, half of New York City's welfare mothers have never held any kind of job.

At the same time, there have been success stories. The most notable has been Massachusetts' education and training program ("ET"), which has had the strong support and attention of Governor Michael Dukakis. He and Rosabeth Kanter write of its record in *Creating the Future*:

Since the program began in October 1983, more than 43,000 welfare recipients have found full-time or part-time employment through ET. Average full-time wages have provided families with income that doubled the average welfare grant; and of those who left welfare through the program, 86 percent were still off welfare one year later.

Dukakis and Kanter introduce us to Ruby, Dawn, Kathy, and Julie, whose case histories show how "self-motivated client participation" reduced the average stay on welfare in Massachusetts from forty months to twenty-eight months. Those on the rolls "for five years or more fell by more than 25 percent in three years."

Is this simply campaign-season hyperbole? The analysis of the Massachusetts program by David Osborne, a Boston political writer, adds a few qualifications to the statistical claims of Dukakis and Kanter. Some two thirds of ET's graduates have found full-time employment, defined as working thirty hours a week. In all, about 60 percent hold jobs that pay enough to get them completely off welfare. Of these, some would have found work without counseling or training, not least because in Massachusetts' prospering economy employers are looking for workers. The state gains a further edge from the fact that 64 percent of its welfare mothers have completed high school, compared with 53 percent throughout the nation. And 51 percent of them are white, against 40 percent throughout the country; this means fewer face discrimination or come from segregated neighborhoods.

Osborne emphasizes, moreover, that the Massachusetts program is not compulsory: no one is forced to participate. By confining itself to volunteers, ET avoids any appearance of being Draconian, but it is open to the criticism, as Osborne says, that it is "placing those who are the most job-ready and ignoring the rest." It may not be able to help the women who need help the most, and its methods may not be applicable under a compulsory plan such as the one Moynihan recommends. Osborne makes a convincing case, however, that ET has been imaginatively managed. Along with encouraging women who want to work, the state welfare officials have found ways to recruit employers and to minimize their risks. Thus, according to Osborne, one Massachusetts program can assure a company that it will have "reliable employees, because those who cannot perform—almost a third of those who begin the process—wash out *before* the company is asked to hire them." He is particularly impressed with the record of the Bay State Skills Corporation, an umbrella agency overseeing several training plans. It keeps in constant touch with employers across the state—such as General Electric and Digital Equipment, and medical centers and cable television services—to ascertain their work-force needs. As one BSSC staff member put it, "We do not train for jobs which do not exist."

The Dukakis approach has tended to bypass the deeper problems of many welfare recipients. By choosing to concentrate on those most likely to turn in good performances, the program has built a record of success which can be displayed to the public. Still, you have to start somewhere. An experiment that begins with selective candidates usually comes up with tips and techniques that can be extended to people in more difficult situations. Certainly, a central lesson from Massachusetts is that welfare reform needs strong political support, something other pilot programs have lacked.

4.

The central issue posed in the controversy surrounding AFDC and the Moynihan bill is whether welfare should cease being an option for most single mothers. Under the Family Security bill, after a series of training sessions, women now on AFDC will be expected to become self-supporting, when presented with "bona fide" offers, however much they may object to those jobs. David Ellwood calls this "imposed work," and he condemns it on moral and practical grounds. He makes the point that only 27 percent of married mothers work throughout the year at full-time jobs. Moreover, he notes that as many as one in seven women on welfare have physical or mental disabilities that are not dissimilar to those afflicting men in similar surroundings.

So at this point several questions need sorting out. For most of us, work is not a matter of choice, since we must take some kind of job if we don't want to live in poverty. Nor do we always end up in positions we would have preferred or chosen. Even so, we do not call our employment involuntary or imposed. Why, then, should the withdrawal of AFDC benefits be seen as forcing people to work? After all, welfare allowances are unlike unemployment benefits and Social Security pensions in that they have never been viewed as entitlements. Welfare dependency is not a right but a dispensation bounded by rules. In response, Ellwood asks why we worry so much about the presumed indolence of unmarried mothers. He presents a different view:

Single mothers ought to have the flexibility of wives. Some wives choose full-time work, some choose part-time work, and some do no market work at all. Many argue that single mothers should be able to make the same decisions.

If we provide sufficient welfare support to give single mothers a full choice, we have to recognize that some single mothers will choose not to work at all, just as many wives do.

Ellwood proposes raising AFDC payments above the poverty line, so that single mothers who choose to stay at home will have a measure of comfort and self-respect. But might not this attract even more young unmarried women to the welfare rolls? It is not that teen-agers have babies in order to receive welfare funds. In fact, many actually want to become mothers, and the availability of AFDC allows them to act out that desire. Others are deterred because they know that welfare will keep them in poverty. Ellwood wishes to raise the stipends, for obvious humane reasons. A concern he does not address is that more generous allowances might encourage an even greater number of fifteen-year-olds to embark on motherhood.

The ideological convictions many people have about the family and welfare are both intense and often contradictory. There is, for example, the conservative position that a good mother will want to stay at home with her children. And as they grow older, she will be there when they return from school. Once the children are on their own, making a home for her husband is an honorable occupation. Nor are these wives and mothers considered "dependent" in any invidious sense: what they do is deemed to be full-time, productive work. Many husbands are willing, even eager, to support this arrangement. (George Gilder and Phyllis Schlafly have long espoused this view, and they speak for a not inconsiderable number of women who have no desire to work and husbands who want their wives at home. Nor is this entirely a right-wing position. See Deborah Fallows, *A Mother's Work* [Houghton Mifflin, 1986], which I reviewed here in the issue of August 14, 1986).

Why, then, are conservatives so adamant about wanting to get single mothers out of their homes and onto full-time payrolls? The reasons become evident in *The New Consensus on Family and Welfare*, a report by the conservative think tank American Enterprise Institute in Washington. It opens with the axiom that "no able adult should be allowed voluntarily to take from the common good without also contributing to it." Married women who stay at home are not seen as a social cost, since they are supported by their husbands' earnings. But it is only if she has such support that a woman can be said to contribute to "the common good" by attending to her children.

So the American Enterprise Institute's position is that women who do not happen to have resident husbands should not ask to be subsidized by society. This stricture is most plainly applied to those who have children out of wedlock; women who engage in irresponsible reproduction should not ask for a free ride. Giving them money will only increase the tendency to reproduce. Nor is much more magnanimity shown for women who have gone through a divorce. If the wife initiated the break-up, she should have foreseen the consequences, not least of which is that husbands give very little to their former families. But an even larger number of women, many of them older and with teen-aged children, are left by their husbands. Interestingly, the American Enterprise Institute feels that they, too, should join the labor force. The implication seems to be that had she worked harder at being a good wife, she probably could have kept her husband.

The AEI report also suggests that mothers who rely on AFDC are bad models for their children. If they will not get or stay married, then they should redeem themselves by work. Thus becoming married to a wage earner is itself seen as redemptive. This reasoning is reflected in the federal law, which makes special provision for one group of single mothers—younger widows with school-age children, whose deceased husbands had held steady jobs and contributed to retirement accounts. Women in this position do not have to apply for welfare, nor are they expected to become self-supporting. Since they cannot be faulted for losing their husbands, the Social Security Act entitled them to survivor's benefits. Currently some 300,000 widows are supported under this statute. They may receive as much as $20,000 a year, almost five times the average AFDC award. If they choose to work, as many do, they still receive separate payments to assist with their children.

The position of many feminists is ambiguous in different ways. Their strongest support has gone to women who want or need to work. Hence the stress in feminist programs on equal employment opportunities, on the right to have child care, and to be paid by the standard of comparable worth. (One common argument for abortion is that it allows women to continue with their careers.) True, some feminists have said that staying at home is a legitimate choice, yet the prevailing sentiment remains that both housewives and mothers on welfare should be making more of their lives. While it is never stated in so many words, the feminist ideal is a woman who combines a career and motherhood.

These and related issues are considered in *Remaking the Welfare State*, a collection of essays examining the campaigns against welfare by the Reagan and Thatcher governments. I particularly recommend the one by Wendy Sarvasy, who shows how both feminists and conservatives have used goals of the women's movement "to justify forced paid employment for poor mothers." If one accepts the view that households should be self-supporting, then those headed by women fall under this rubric. Current demands for equal treatment make it difficult to request special dispensations for family heads of a particular gender. Nor is Sarvasy pleased with measures that exact payments from defaulting fathers. In so doing, she argues, the state ensures that a "woman is still dependent on the father of her child for a private income supplement." It would, she argues, be better to have an expanded system of public benefits than to sustain a moribund relationship.

What Sarvasy wants, very simply, is to have society acknowledge that "nurturing or caretaking is work," whether it involves the "care of children, sick parents, or perhaps a friend with AIDS." She wants taxpayers to be willing to pay for that work. She asks that a single standard of respect, if not payment, apply to middle-class housewives, widows receiving pensions, and single women striving to make it on their own. All are "citizen nurturers and should be treated as important members of society." The word "nurturer" here seems to apply to practically any altruistic person, including many men. She also joins Ellwood's plea for a guaranteed income well above the poverty level, to be available for many kinds of households. Where she goes further is in proposing salary checks for unpaid tasks we now deem to be labors of love or domestic duty. At no point does Sarvasy concern herself with the costs of her proposal. Quite clearly, it would require a drastic change in the way we define and distribute income, especially if public agencies were to set the salaries of "nurturers" and "carers." Still, her essay raises important questions about what it means to contribute one's efforts to the society one lives in, indeed what one chooses to consider "work."

I have reserved for last what is perhaps the most troubling issue in the AFDC debate. Most of the mothers receiving welfare are Hispanic or black, whereas most of those who want to replace welfare with work are white. The motives of the welfare reformers are difficult to disentangle here. Thus there is the view that too many blacks and Hispanics are on a self-destructive course; and since liberal subventions have not worked, it is time for discipline. Hence some believe that if women are made to take productive jobs, it will improve their characters and deter them from having more babies. Single mothers who already work are held up as examples, as are many aliens and immigrants, particularly Asians, whose families, which often include grandparents and relatives, tend to stick together and stay off welfare. Moreover, as Table D shows, some states have shown that women will find work if admission to welfare is kept sufficiently stringent. It seems evident that many of the women who are now receiving AFDC in Wisconsin, Ohio, and Illinois would have managed to find jobs for themselves had they been living in Texas, New Hampshire, or Idaho. One problem with welfare is that it tends to cast its recipients as helpless people, who would languish without public assistance. The sterner states take the position that the great majority of single mothers are resourceful human beings, who can and will support themselves if that is made their only choice.

TABLE D

PERCENTAGE OF SINGLE MOTHERS RECEIVING AFDC

Wisconsin	78.7%
Ohio	75.3%
Illinois	68.2%
UNITED STATES	52.4%
Texas	33.9%
Idaho	28.6%
New Hampshire	21.6%

Sources: Department of Health and Human Services and Bureau of the Census

Or models showing poor women at work are found in the past, when there was nothing like today's public assistance. In 1940, for example, some 2.4 million women—most of them black—supported themselves and their families by working as domestic servants in other people's houses. The equivalent figure in today's labor force would be 5.2 million. However, the Bureau of Labor Statistics estimates that only 900,000 women now have "household employment." Many are aliens; and the real figure may be higher because of unreported hiring and off-the-books wages. While seldom explicitly stated, the implication is often drawn that welfare mothers could do that kind of work.

Over half of the Hispanic and black mothers on AFDC had their babies out of wedlock and have not subsequently married. (For black mothers, the proportion exceeds 75 percent.) Not only conservatives regard this reproduction as irresponsible; liberals and others see it as unfair, above all, to the children and as posing the sad prospect of millions of children growing up without adequate care. Thus much of the debate over work derives from the fear that growing numbers of black and brown Americans are no longer under the kinds of controls that once restrained the poor, and are producing children who may be a burden to society. Here welfare dependency is seen as part of a wider malaise, involving not only drugs and crime, but a more generalized tendency to give up and drop out. The solutions proposed range from better kindergartens and counseling to sterilization and incarceration. But since rules and laws haven't had much effect on men, it should not come as a surprise that policies, programs, and directives are increasingly being aimed at women.

At this point it is unrealistic to try to estimate the costs and gains of universal enforced work. Regarding Dukakis's ET program, the Massachusetts Taxpayers Foundation, a business research group, concluded that "the savings to the state far outrun the cost of the program." People who were once burdens under AFDC are now taxpaying workers. However, the report also notes that ET's outlays will rise if it moves beyond volunteers to less promising candidates. But here successes will bring offsetting savings, since long-term welfare recipients tend to incur more expenses. The Family Security Act asks for an annual appropriation of about $2.8 billion, to assist states in providing child care and other services. According to its sponsors, the bill will be "budget neutral," which means it will pay for itself and "not worsen the budget deficit." In addition to trimming the welfare rolls and creating more taxpayers, it predicts new revenues by securing greater payments from fathers. And it can be argued that as more families become self-supporting, the tenor of society will improve, so we will not have to pay so much for things like remedial education and prison cells.

Still, Ellwood's phrase "imposed work" lingers. The original aims to Aid to Families with Dependent Children were enlightened and humane. Women who found themselves on their own—most of them widowed or divorced—would be supported for a time while they created new lives. In addition, social workers would aid in this transition by advising on budget planning and other preparations. In fact, millions of single mothers still use welfare in this way, and they are not considered a problem. The difficulty is that too many others linger on the rolls for prolonged periods. Also, social work professionals have generally given up on this group. Hence the impulse to call AFDC a failure, and to remove it from the statute books.

Nor are the reasons mainly financial. The truth is that most Americans find the presence of a welfare class unseemly: it conflicts with the way are supposed to organize ourselves. Since milder measures have not moved long-term recipients, they must be treated like those once castigated as slackers or work-shy. And therein lie the reasons for misgivings with the Family Security Act's insistence on employment. By returning to the harsh rules of an earlier era, it spells the abandoning of yet another of the dreams that were going to make this century different.

III. CHILD WELFARE

EDITOR'S INTRODUCTION

Section Three addresses the special problem of children in a welfare system. Often these children of poverty belong to broken homes, or are so badly mistreated or abused that they require placement, if it can be found, in foster homes. In other cases, they exist as members of homeless families who live in shelters or in welfare hotels, where their well being is endangered. As the "culture of poverty" worsens, so does the problem of poor and neglected children. In fact, child abuse cases have been soaring in recent years; teenagers in urban areas have been dropping out of school in disturbing numbers, and teenage pregnancies—even pregnancies among girls as young as ten or eleven—have been increasing. Critics argue that too many children are now slipping through the safety net of the welfare system or are provided for so inadequately that when they reach adulthood they will become a social burden.

In the first of the articles in this section, Michael Robin in *The Nation* focuses upon the high incidence of black infant mortality. The same subject is taken up by Marian Wright Edelman, in the magazine *USA Today*, and is linked to federal budget cuts targeted at poor children and families. Edelman also deplores cuts of programs that would provide poor children with immunization shots, and the federal emasculation of low-income housing that has resulted in child homelessness.

In a following article, reprinted from *New York* magazine, Dinitia Smith reports on New York City's foster care crisis. As she notes, the city's Office of Special Services for Children is understaffed and overburdened with babies to place, often on a night-to-night basis, in foster homes. The problem of placement is made more difficult by the fact that most of these babies are unwanted even by foster parents who are paid to take them in. In a disturbing article from *New York Times Magazine*, Andrew Stein, President of the City Council of New York, reveals how critical the condition of poor and displaced children in the city has now become. An estimated 3,000 babies, he points out, are born addicted to drugs every year; 10,000 children live in shelters and hotels for the homeless; and 12,000 are so abused in a single year that they have to be put in foster care. Finally, David Whitman, writing in *U. S. News & World Report*, reveals that although candidates in the 1988 presidential election talked of helping children, very little is being done to improve their lives. Because of restrictions imposed by the federal deficit, only the most modest efforts to aid children seem likely in the future.

A RIGHT TO THE TREE OF LIFE[1]

In the 1920s demonstrators protesting the lack of decent health care for poor mothers and their infants marched on the Capitol in Washington with banners that proclaimed, "A Baby Saved Is a Citizen Gained." That cry badly needs to be resurrected today.

While the status of fetuses holds center stage in American politics, the right to life has not yet been extended to thousands of black infants who die needlessly every year. Today, a black infant is twice as likely as a white infant to die before his or her first birthday. The most recent national infant mortality data broken down by race show that in 1981, 20 black babies per 1,000 died in their first year, as opposed to 10.5 white babies per 1,000. Had the black rate in 1981 been the same as the white, 5,584 of the 11,756 black infants who died that year would have lived.

As the overall U.S. infant mortality rate continues to decline—it was 11.2 per 1,000 in 1982—the rate for blacks in some areas of the nation is rising, exceeding that of many Third World countries. In 1981 the infant mortality rate in black neighborhoods of Chicago was as high as 55 per 1,000; in central Harlem it was 28 per 1,000; and in parts of Baltimore, 59.5 per 1,000. In addition to numerous communities, thirteen states reported that the rate for blacks had increased in 1982. Most of those states are in the South, where infant death rates have been about 20 percent higher than in the rest of the country.

[1]Reprint of an article by Michael Robin, public-health social worker and freelance writer. Reprinted by permission from *The Nation*, V. 238:698–700. Je. 9, '84. Copyright © 1988 by *The Nation*.

Why are black babies so much more vulnerable than white babies? According to public health officials, the main reason is that the percentage of black newborns designated as low-birth-weight babies (under 5.5 pounds) is twice that of whites. As Myron Winick, professor of nutrition and pediatrics at Columbia University put it, "Pound for pound, the poor baby does as well as the rich baby; black babies do as well as white babies. The difference in mortality can be explained entirely by the fact that babies from these disadvantaged groups weigh on the average half a pound less at birth than middle-class babies."

Many underweight babies are born to mothers who haven't had access to good prenatal care. Most public-health officials acknowledge that an expectant mother who receives no care is three times as likely to have a low-birth-weight baby as one who sees a doctor regularly. A recent study by the Children's Defense Fund reported that about 10 percent of all pregnant black women in the United States don't get prenatal care. In 1979, 386 Detroit women, or 1 percent of those who gave birth in the city that year, did not see a doctor until the day of delivery. Among their babies the death rate in the first year was a shocking 88 per 1,000. And in Washington, D.C., the city with the highest infant mortality rate in the country—20.3 per 1,000 in 1982—21 percent of nonwhite women receive inadequate medical attention while they are pregnant.

Despite its profamily rhetoric and its stated concern for the unborn and newly born, the Reagan Administration has severely cut many of the programs that specifically benefit pregnant women and infants. Federal budget cuts in Title V maternal and child health programs have meant that hundreds of poor women and their children have been turned away from prenatal and maternity services. About 90 percent of the Maternal and Infant Care clinics in ten states surveyed by the Children's Defense Fund had resources either cut or frozen in 1982. In Lexington County, Kentucky, the number of women receiving no prenatal care rose from 32 per 1,000 in 1980 to 55 per 1,000 in 1982, partly because the clinics had to refuse hundreds of needy women.

In addition, the Administration has frozen funds for the Special Supplemental Food Program for Women, Infants and Children, better known as WIC. Although 9 million people are eligible for the program nationwide, the budget allows enough money for only about 2.5 million. According to a number of studies, WIC has been extraordinarily successful in reducing the incidence of low-birth-weight babies and has saved taxpayers' money. A Harvard University study shows that every $1 spent on nutritional supplements saves $3 in medical costs later for the care of a low-birth-weight baby.

Federal programs to improve maternal and child health have also been hampered because they are administered by the states, where eligibility standards vary widely; as a result, many poor mothers and children have been excluded. In 1984, to be eligible to receive Aid to Families with Dependent Children (A.F.D.C.), a family of four in Oregon could have an annual income of up to $7,362; a similar family in Texas could earn no more than $3,618. Overall, the Southern states have the lowest eligibility ceilings and the lowest benefits. They also have the greatest number of poor mothers and children—and, not coincidentally, the highest infant mortality rates.

Moreover, with Federal cuts reducing their budgets in the last few years, most states have tightened welfare eligibility requirements or have not raised income standards to keep pace with inflation, leaving thousands of poor women of childbearing age with no health insurance: in twenty states, women who do not qualify for A.F.D.C. automatically lose benefits under Medicaid as well. In 1982 the Reagan Administration further limited access to prenatal care by effecting regulations that disallow Federal A.F.D.C. reimbursements to state programs for women who are pregnant for the first time. Previously thirty states provided welfare benefits for first-time pregnancies; now only six provide assistance throughout a first pregnancy, and thirteen only after the sixth month.

Any initiatives to expand health services to poor women and their children would almost certainly bring cries of "budget busting" from the Reagan Administration, but the simple truth is that universal access to services would be more equitable—and cost-effective. While it costs a total of about $1,500 to $2,000 to provide prenatal and delivery services to a pregnant woman, it costs more than $1,000 a day to provide intensive-care services for a premature or low-birth-weight baby. Fewer low-birth-weight babies would also mean fewer children who are retarded or are delayed in their development, which would also save millions of dollars in special care.

It is time progressives took up the right-to-life banner, but for a different purpose. We should make sure that the Medicaid maternal and child health reform bill—a modest effort to extend coverage to poor women and children not eligible for Medicaid—gets adequate funding from the House-Senate conference committee that will soon be considering it. And we should press this year's Democratic Presidential candidate to put maternal and infant health high on the nation's political agenda. Unlike many issues that get far splashier press, this is a matter of life and death.

WHO WILL PROTECT THE CHILDREN?[2]

Baby C was born prematurely with lung disease. His parents lived in a car. His mother received no prenatal care and inadequate nutrition. The family lived on handouts from neighbors and hospital staff. By the time Baby C died at seven months of age in a Michigan hospital, the mother was pregnant again with Baby D. Baby D was delivered stillborn in the car five days after Baby C's death. The state of Michigan paid for a double funeral.

These two American children should not have died. Nor should American infants in some inner-city neighborhoods who suffer infant mortality rates comparable to infants in Honduras—poorest country in Latin America.

We are living in a nation and world that have lost their moral bearings. Nearly 40,000 children die *each day* from malnutrition and infection while the nations of the world spend one trillion dollars each year, $2,700,000,000 each day, on weapons of death of no use to the hungry and sick children of the world.

An escalating arms race and nuclear proliferation hold hostage not only the future we hold in trust for our children, but also steal the present from millions of the world's children whose principal daily enemy is relentless poverty and the hunger and disease it breeds.

[2]Reprint of an article by Marian Wright Edelman, president of the Children's Defense Fund, Washington, D.C. Reprinted from *USA Today* magazine, March 1986. Copyright 1986 by the Society for the Advancement of Education.

In today's affluent America, poverty is the greatest child killer. More American children die each year from poverty than from traffic fatalities and suicide combined. Twice the amount of children die from poverty than from cancer and heart disease combined.

Yet, for the fifth consecutive year, in the face of the highest child poverty rate in 18 years, our national leaders have targeted poor children and families for billions of dollars in new budget cuts. Under the Fiscal Year 1986 Administration budget, children would lose $5,200,000,000. This is on top of $10,000,000,000 a year in cuts already made in survival programs for poor children and families since 1980.

At the same time, the Administration proposed a $32,000,000,000 increase in defense spending in Fiscal Year 1986, on top of $178,300,000,000 in defense increases since 1980 to make American children more "secure" from external enemies. Even if the no increase beyond cost of living stance of the Senate prevails, the defense budget will go up another $10,000,000,000 next fiscal year. By 1990, if current Administration budget priorities succeed, every American will be spending 19% less on poor children and families and 86% more on the military.

Defending Our Children

American children need defense against the enemies within. Over a five-year period, more American children die from poverty than the total number of American battle deaths during the Vietnam War. Yet, our national leaders dream about a multibillion-dollar "Star Wars" system to make our defenses impenetrable against enemy missiles. Why can't they dream of a smaller achievable war against child poverty—a war that saves and enhances, rather than takes and threatens, human life? Every poor American child could be lifted out of poverty in 1986 for less than half of the Administration's proposed defense spending increase for that year alone.

American babies need defense against preventable infant mortality and birth defects. For two consecutive years, the decline in our national infant mortality rates—already a sad 15th in the world—has stalled. The national death rate for black infants between one month and one year of age actually increased by six percent between 1983 and 1984. By 1990, 22,000 American babies will die primarily because of low birthweight. We can prevent at least one in eight of these infant deaths and thousands of handicapping conditions simply by providing their mothers with prenatal care at an average cost of $600 each. For less than three days of current Defense Department spending or about one-fifth of the DoD cost of living increase next fiscal year, every poor mother and baby could be provided Medicaid, and thus prenatal care, coverage. Instead, the Senate proposes to cut Medicaid again by another $1,300,000,000. How many four-pound babies will it take to balance the Federal budget?

Tens of thousands of American preschool children need defense against preventable disease. While our nation plans to build 17,000 new nuclear weapons over this decade at an estimated cost of $71,000,000,000, the Administration budget only allows for a single month's stockpile of vaccination serum. Unless Congress adds to this request, 2,000,000 fewer children will be immunized against DPT at a time when half of all black pre-school children are not fully immunized against DPT and polio.

American children need to be protected against increasing child abuse. Every American supports a strong defense and well-defined national security goals. I certainly do. Still, don't children have a similar right to security against sexual and other abuse in day care centers and at home? An estimated 1,500,000 children were reported abused and neglected in 1983, an increase of 200,000 children over the previous year. Why, then, are we cutting funding for programs designed to prevent and treat child abuse? One hour of our current military expenditure rate would pay for all Federal child abuse prevention programs.

American children need defense against growing homelessness. A 1984 Department of Housing and Urban Development study indicated that 22% of the homeless in shelters, not including runaway shelters, are children under 18. Over 66,000 children are currently living without adequate, permanent shelter. Rather than seeking to provide decent housing and minimal income supports to help families weather unemployment and loss of shelter, our national leaders are emasculating low-income housing programs and cutting millions more from the tattered survival net of Aid to Families with Dependent Children. AFDC recipients, 66% of whom are children with an average daily benefit of $3.67, have been cut $1,700,000,000 since 1980.

American children need protection against too early parenting, which locks new generations of children and women into poverty. Recently released data from the Alan Guttmacher Institute show that the U.S. leads nearly all other developed nations of the world in rates of teenage pregnancy, abortion, and childbearing. The rates for white teenagers alone are twice as high as those of Canada, France, and England, even though we have similar rates of sexual activity. The maximum difference in birth rates occurs among girls under 15, the most vulnerable teenagers.

The costs of adolescent parenthood are enormous—for the teenage parents, for their children, and for society; 72% of all white female-headed families and 85% of such black families with mothers 25 and under are poor.

In 1983, 525,000 babies were born to teenage mothers, 10,000 to girls 14 and under. Over 300,000 of these girls had not completed high school and 36,000 had not completed eighth grade. About 31% of these births are paid for by Medicaid at an annual cost of $200,000,000, and 60% of all AFDC mothers had their first child as a teenager. Yet, we are being told by some that we can not afford $50,000,000 this year to establish more comprehensive school-based clinics, which have demonstrated their effectiveness in reducing teenage pregnancy rates. That's equivalent to one MX missile. Surely, one less missile would not cripple our national security, but teenage parenthood will surely cripple the lives of thousands of children and their children.

Five "Weasels"

Sojourner Truth, an illiterate slave woman, feminist, and anti-slavery fighter, had a knack for stating big truths simply. She said once: "I hear talking about the Constitution and the rights of man. I comes up and I takes hold of this Constitution. It looks mighty big, and I feels for my rights, but there aren't any there. Then I say, 'God, what ails this Constitution?' He says to me, 'Sojourner, there is a little weasel in it.'"

Well, there are some big weasels gnawing away at the constitutional and moral underpinnings of our democratic society that we must identify and fight. The first one is the *greedy military weasel* that can never seem to get enough. It currently spends $800,000,000 a day; $33,000,000 an hour; $555,000 a minute.

Just a minute's worth of the military weasel meal would pay for 14,000 monthly food packages to feed pregnant women and infants that the Administration cut this year.

Between now and 1990, this weasel will spend another one and one-half trillion dollars. If I had spent $1,000,000 a day every day since Christ was born. I would have spent less than our national leaders want us to believe the Pentagon can spend efficiently over the next five years. We must all curb this weasel before, in Pres. Eisenhower's words, it "threatens to destroy from within what we are seeking to protect from without."

The second big weasel that threatens our democratic equilibrium is the *unfairness weasel*. Not only have the poor been sent to the front lines of a Federal budget deficit reduction war almost nobody else is fighting, they have seen their Federal taxes skyrocket while rich individuals and corporations got the biggest tax break in the nation's history in 1981.

The amount of Federal tax paid by those with incomes below the Federal poverty line increased 58% from 1980 to 1982 alone. In 1984, a working single mother with three children and a below-poverty income of $10,500 paid $1,186 in taxes—more than Boeing, General Electric, Dupont, Texaco, Mobil, and AT&T together paid in 1983, although these huge corporations earned $13,700,000,000 in profits!

The President has touted the Grace Commission's recommendations for deficit reduction through social welfare program cuts. He has been silent about the fact that the W. R. Grace Company earned $684,000,000 profits from 1981 to 1983, paid no net Federal income taxes, and received $12,500,000 from the government in negative income taxes through rebates or sales of "excess" tax benefits. If we just raised the Grace Company tax rate to *zero*, we could pay for 9,000,000 of the free school lunches Pres. Reagan and the Congress cut from children.

In May, 1985, the Senate of the United States cut child nutrition again. Nobody is seriously pushing to enact a minimum corporate tax. I don't know any standard of fairness that can justify this outcome in a democratic society.

The third weasel is the *ignorance weasel*, which has created an enormous accuracy gap in public policy decision-making. Citizens have to dig hard to stay informed and hold their leaders accountable. With great skill and sloganistic simplicity, the President has seized on a few kernels of truth about waste and abuse which infects some social programs, just as it infects some defense contractors, and tainted a whole harvest of progress that lifted millions of children and elderly citizens out of poverty in the 1960's and 1970's. Head Start works. It keeps children in school, at grade level, and out of costly special education. In the decade after Medicaid, black infant mortality rated decreased 50%.

Each American must confront and let his or her Senators and representatives know what choices they want him or her to make for our nation this year and every year. Their decisions on military, tax, and social program spending will dictate the nation's choices—indeed, shape the national character—for decades to come. They are far too important to leave to the politicians or the experts.

The fourth weasel eating away at our democratic foundation is the *bystander weasel*. Without exercise, democracy atrophies. It is not a spectator sport. I worry about those who opt out of often discouraging political, bureaucratic, and community processes or who refuse to vote or to write letters to their representatives or take a position on one needed step because of the complexity and controversy surrounding often critical life and death issues.

Each of us must reflect hard within ourselves, our families, and our communities about the national ideals we want to see America reflect and then try "little by little," in Dorothy Day's words, to live them and be moved to act in two arenas—in the personal arena through greater service to those around us who are more needy and in the political arena to ensure a more just society. One without the other is not enough to transform America.

The fifth weasel is the *ineffectiveness weasel*. I'm always surprised by the unrealistic notions that too many of us hold about the steps required to overcome problems and bring about changes. Often, we presume something a failure before we have even begun to try to consider it. Change is possible, but it's very hard work.

Bringing About Change

The first step in changing anything is to try to see a problem whole and then to break it down into manageable pieces for action. One must then go step by systematic step to change the pieces until the whole is affected. It is so easy to be overwhelmed and discouraged by all that needs to be done, or to tell yourself it's okay to bow out because you can't make a difference anyway, or that it's too big for one individual or a few people or groups to tackle.

Pick a problem you care about or a piece of the problem that you can help solve while trying to see how your piece fits into the broader social change puzzle. Tailor your remedies to the specific needs identified and that you can do something about, and build from there over time.

Many of us are puzzled about how to translate our instincts for decency into positive action. Societies have traditionally acted out their compassionate instincts within the extended family or local community. The structures of modern life require us to act out our decency at the state, national, and international level as well, a difficult psychological and social transition. The transition has been made more difficult because the government is so complex, people do not understand how its resources are divided, and because they have been told—falsely in many instances—that what they tried to do did not and could not work.

Step two is recognizing that getting change is no guarantee of keeping change. It will take never-ending citizen monitoring to protect our children against poverty and nuclear disaster. Individuals and groups who care about the poor must fight constantly to translate laws and rights and policies into the daily lives of children, families, the poor, elderly, and homeless. It's like keeping your own house clean. The national house gets dirty all the time unless someone cleans it up regularly.

The third step is understanding that there are no short cuts to curing most of our social and economic problems. Thorough homework—good facts coupled with good analysis—is essential if good remedies are to follow and if an effective case is to be made for a particular cause. Too many good intentions and causes are wrecked and victims are left unhelped by fiery rhetoric, political grandstanding, and simplistic remedies that sometimes create more problems than they solve.

Step four in the change process is follow-up. Most institutions, public or private, are seldom self-policing. Competing interest groups seeking their ear, coupled with natural inertia, almost assure that any one-shot effort to correct a problem will be agreeably ignored. Being a change agent for poor children or for responsible arms control, or for anything, means being a good pest and wearing down those you want to do something. You always have a better chance of getting something done if you are specific, address one problem at a time, outline what the person responsible can and should do, have thought through why it is in their self-interest to do it, don't mind doing the work for them, and make sure they can take credit for getting it done.

The last twin weasels I want to single out are the *lack of confidence and low aim weasels*. Do not ever cease to believe that you as individuals can make a critical difference if you simply care enough, and bring to that caring skill, targeted action, and persistence.

Our nation *can* eliminate child poverty and curb the teenage pregnancy epidemic. Our individual and collective wills can achieve these goals. Our nation must stop turning our national plowshares into swords and bringing good news to the rich at the expense of the poor. You and I are the voices, hands, and minds that must redirect its priorities. Our nation's creaking institutions can work better, but it is you and I who must make them work for our children's sake.

Benjamin E. Mays, the former president of Morehouse College—a role model for me and for thousands of other black men and women, including Martin Luther King, Jr.—summed up our mission when he said:

It must be borne in mind that the tragedy of life doesn't lie in not reaching your goal. The tragedy lies in having no goal to reach. It isn't a calamity to die with dreams unfulfilled, but it is a calamity not to dream. It is not a disaster to be unable to capture your ideal, but it is a disaster to have no ideal to capture. It is not a disgrace not to reach the stars, but it is a disgrace to have no stars to reach for. Not failure, but low aim, is sin.

CHILDREN OF THE NIGHT[3]

On the twelfth floor of 80 Lafayette, a big, grim municipal building near City Hall, an attractive 45-year-old woman is dashing frantically from phone to phone, engaged in a strange sort of

[3]Reprint of an article by Dinitia Smith, freelance writer. Copyright © 1986 News America Publishing, Inc. All rights reserved. Reprinted with the permission of *New York* Magazine, December 1, 1986.

brokering. "We've got a *lovely* sibling group here," Betsy Mayberry says seductively into the receiver. "They're really good kids."

To someone else she says, "I've got six babies, five of them under a year old, and three siblings, six, five, and four."

And to another, "They have to be *white*? I don't have any white!"

Later, in a moment free of the phones, she confides, "It's like the stock market." But Mayberry isn't trading stocks; she's finding beds for foster children.

Betsy Mayberry works for the Office of Special Services for Children, the beleaguered agency that runs the city's foster-care system. Lately, finding beds for abused and neglected children has become a constant, frenzied search. For each child placed, workers have to make as many as 30 calls. Tonight, about twenty children are already waiting throughout the city in precinct houses and Special Services field offices. More will arrive as the evening wears on. Four floors above Mayberry, eleven babies and toddlers are crammed into a makeshift nursery in a conference room. (It has since been improved.)

In part because of the crack epidemic, the number of children being placed has jumped by as much as 70 percent over certain months of last year.

Some of the children waiting for placement will wait all day and far into the night. Then they may be driven in Big Apple cars to foster homes in distant boroughs or even in upstate New York. If beds can't be found, the children may end up going to Emergency Children's Services at 241 Church Street. Although officials deny it, for a time last spring, some children were even sleeping in the Special Services field offices.

The children have been removed from their parents for a variety of reasons—a school has noticed that they're covered with bruises, they're showing signs of sexual abuse, a neighbor has discovered they've been left alone for days, for example. Mayberry and her staff try to put each child in a foster home that could, if necessary, take the child for a long period. But often, only temporary beds are available. In the morning, some of the children return to city offices, and the process begins again.

"We have newborns who've been in six different foster homes in a week," says Mayberry. In Brooklyn, a fifteen-year-old boy spent December through May in the field office at 345 Adams Street, sleeping in a different foster home every night because a permanent bed couldn't be found. A twelve-year-old girl who'd been raped by a relative had to stay in the hospital for fourteen days because no home was available. "My supervisor told me if [the girl] were light-skinned, we could find a place in Long Island," says her caseworker. "Now, what am I supposed to do?"

The chaos in the placement process is just one symptom of a foster-care system that's diseased to its core. The children are the victims. Once caught up in the system, many spend their youth in foster care without going back to their families or being adopted. Some move regularly from foster home to foster home, losing all sense of permanency. Many are introduced to a life of crime or vagrancy. Some of the foster homes have themselves been accused of abuse.

Assessing blame for this situation is almost impossible. Outside critics fault the private foster-care agencies that dominate the system. The private agencies say they're getting by with limited resources, and they blame the city for dumping sick and seriously troubled children on them. City officials say they're doing all they can.

Meanwhile, the city bureaucracy that runs foster care is a shambles. Overburdened workers have threatened to file abuse and neglect petitions against the city itself. Lawsuits have dogged the system. One—a suit that accuses the private foster-care agencies of racial and religious discrimination against black children—has become a real-life version of Dickens's interminable *Jarndyce* v. *Jarndyce*. After thirteen years of litigation, a tentative settlement has been reached, but it may take years to go into effect.

The current crisis has arisen despite a widely praised reform effort, which has gone sadly awry. The Child Welfare Reform Act of 1979 changed the emphasis from foster care to the delivery of concrete *preventive* measures designed to keep families together. In part because of the act, the number of available beds has declined. Meanwhile, though, critics say, the city has provided few of the services that were supposed to reduce the need for beds.

"Children are a vulnerable constituency," says Barry Ensminger, a lawyer who worked on foster-care reform while on the staff of City Council president Carol Bellamy. "They don't vote. They don't speak out. Children have never been a priority with Mayor Koch, and Special Services for Children has historically been left to flounder."

The story of the current foster-care crisis is a case history of failure at virtually every level. After all the reforms, dollars, lawsuits, and efforts by well-meaning citizens, the system has come to this: overburdened workers calling around the city, trying to find beds for the night for dozens of hapless children.

"I'm desperate," Betsy Mayberry says into the phone.

In a windowless former conference room on the sixteenth floor of 80 Lafayette Street, five-week-old Lisa (The names of all children have been changed.) spends her day sleeping in a small crib. Lisa has fine black hair and skin the color and texture of ivory, and her features are precisely formed. She is wearing a pink-and-violet stretchy—the clothes she arrived in. Lisa's mother and father are both addicts. When Lisa was born, there were traces of cocaine in her bloodstream. For a while, she was in the custody of her grandmother. But her grandmother works, and she says she can't care for a young infant. She finally gave Lisa up for foster care.

This is Lisa's second day in a row here. Yesterday, at 8:35 p.m., the New York Foundling Hospital said it had a spare bed in its crisis nursery, a unit for children whose parents are frantic and are afraid they may become violent. But the bed was available for only a night. So this morning, Lisa has come back to 80 Lafayette. At eleven o'clock, her grandmother comes to visit her and stands over Lisa's crib with tears streaming down her face.

By mid-afternoon, Betsy Mayberry and her co-workers have made about 30 fruitless calls in an effort to find Lisa a place to go tonight.

All around Lisa, babies are crying, toddlers are playing on the floor. There are toys, stuffed animals, a dollhouse, a table and chairs for older children. Pictures of Martin Luther King Jr. and Jesse Jackson have been torn from magazines and pasted on the yellow-gray walls. Homemakers, some in blue smocks, play with the children and try to keep the place clean.

Lisa has a touch of pinkeye and could infect other children. Her parents provided no medical records.

At 8:15, a foster home is finally found for Lisa in Brooklyn, and a transportation worker arrives to pick her up. "Come on Sugar," says the worker. "They've been giving this baby such a hard time!" The worker collects Lisa's bottle and bundles her up in a pink blanket. For Lisa, it's another bed for the night.

The Current Foster-Care system has its roots in the seventeenth century. In those days, orphaned and abandoned children were farmed out as indentured servants or given shelter in alms-houses alongside the homeless, the mad, and the mentally retard-ed. The public reacted against this treatment of children, and in 1806, the Ladies Society for the Relief of Poor Urchins and Small Children established the first orphanage in New York City. In 1853, a group of prominent New Yorkers helped found the Chil-dren's Aid Society for "the training and the general improvement of the conditions of the homeless and friendless children roaming the streets of New York." Children's Aid sent the children out to farms in the Midwest, which were thought to be healthier set-tings. Some became indentured servants, and others were adopt-ed.

Eventually, Children's Aid evolved into one of the more en-lightened childcare agencies. Meanwhile, Roman Catholic and Jewish groups established agencies to care for immigrant chil-dren. Traditionally, these and other voluntary agencies have giv-en preference to children of their own religion, and it remains state policy to place children with foster parents of the same race and religion whenever possible.

As blacks began to migrate north and as Puerto Ricans ar-rived during the 1950s, the population of foster children changed. Today, 60 percent are black, 22 percent are Hispanic, and 12 percent are white. Getting a precise total is hard, because children are in and out of foster care all the time, but officials say there are about 17,000 children in foster care—an increase of 6 percent over a year ago.

New York City, which this year will spend $233 million on foster care, has one of the most unusual systems—and one of the most Byzantine. In virtually every other major city, foster care is run by the municipality itself. In New York, the system is con-trolled largely by private, voluntary children's agencies—organizations such as the Children's Aid Society, the Jewish Board of Family and Children's Services, and the New York Foundling Hospital.

The private agencies recruit foster parents (most of whom are black) and run group homes for the children. Despite being paid with city and state money, the agencies have traditionally had a great deal of independence. Foster parents, for example, some-times specify the age, sex, race, and even the skin tone of children they will take. Homes that house groups of children can turn away any child they consider "unacceptable" under their contract to the city, and they control about 90 percent of the available beds.

When a child needs foster care, Special Services for Children usually contacts a private agency. Assuming a bed can be found, the younger children are sent to private homes (there are about 6,620 in the city, some of which can furnish several beds) and the older children to group homes (about 5,050 beds are under contract to the city).

The city pays the agencies directly, and the agencies then pay the foster parents and administer the group homes. Foster parents are paid according to the age of the child. They get $267 a month for an infant, plus a $40-a-month clothing or diaper allowance. The fee increases as the children get older or if they are handicapped. Group homes get about $65 a day per child, but that money has to pay for food, shelter, clothing, staff, social workers, medical expenses, court costs—everything.

The city's past efforts to run group homes have sometimes been disastrous. The names Jennings Hall, Callagy Hall, and the Children's Center—homes that were established because many private agencies didn't want to take black children—linger in memory as symbols of the world's cruelty to children, and all were closed down by 1976. The few residences for older children that the city still runs are judged by foster-care experts to be inferior to the facilities run by most of the private agencies.

Elizabeth Morgan, as we'll call her, is in many ways a typical foster mother. She is black, she is middle-aged, and she has two grown children who are now out of the house. She lives in a well-kept home in a working-class section of Long Island with her husband (who works in the shipping and receiving department of a local store), a sixteen-year-old adopted son, an eight-year-old grandson whom she's raised since birth, and four foster children. "Foster children need more love and more attention than your own," says Mrs. Morgan.

Mrs. Morgan has been taking in children for nineteen years, and she's a success story, having won an award for her skill from the Human Resources Administration. Alan, who was one of her first foster children, came when he was ten months old; the Morgans adopted him when he was three.

Of the foster children now living with the Morgans, Johnny, twelve, a handsome, caramel-skinned boy, arrived last March through the auspices of the Jewish Child Care Association. Johnny's mother had died, and

*the man Johnny thinks is his father had neglected him. When Johnny first
arrived, he boasted, "I can wash my own clothes, I can clean." Mrs. Morgan surmised that Johnny had been doing these things for himself for some
time. "I can cook franks and eggs," he told her.*

*"But you can't use the stove in this house," Mrs. Morgan said. It's one
of her policies. "I give them very few chores," she says. "They're learning.
They can't be expected to do what an adult can."*

*The twins, Jeannie and Patty, thirteen, arrived at the Morgan house
last June through the Emergency Foster Boarding Home Network, of
which Mrs. Morgan is a member. The twins' mother was an addict, and
they'd been left to fend for themselves.*

*The twins are big, bouncing, apparently happy girls. Soon after they
arrived, they began calling Mrs. Morgan "Mommy," and Mr. Morgan
"Daddy." "It's fun here," says Jeannie, her hair braided in corn rows. "If
you want something, they get it for you," says Patty, who wears her hair
swept back straight. Family disputes are settled by a "congress." "Daddy's
the president, Mommy's the vice-president," says Jeannie.*

*Finally there is Charlie, fifteen, who came last August. Charlie, who
is slightly retarded, is another neglected child. (Retarded children are often the targets of abuse and neglect.) He's thin and friendly, with slightly
distorted features.*

*"Show how you play the drums, Charlie," says Mrs. Morgan, as visi-
tors brace for an assault on their ears. Charlie goes down to the basement,
where his instruments are set up, and proceeds to drum up a storm. The
routines and riffs are complex, the beat precise.*

It's impossible to understand New York City's present foster-
care crisis without taking into account *Wilder* v. *Bernstein,* a remarkable lawsuit that has haunted the system for thirteen years
now. The suit was filed in federal court by the New York Civil
Liberties Union on behalf of Shirley Wilder, a thirteen-year-old
black girl, and other black foster children. Wilder is now 26, and
the case is still going on.

Wilder's father had petitioned the courts to have his daughter
declared a "PINS"—a person in need of supervision—and he
gave her up for foster care. None of the private agencies would
take her, the suit contends, because she was a black Protestant.
The courts were forced to put her in a state-run home for juvenile delinquents, although she wasn't a delinquent. Even while
the suit was pending, she was discharged and began living in the
streets, soon giving birth to a child, which she gave up for adoption.

The suit, which was brought against the city, the state, and the private agencies, charged that race had always been a guiding force in foster-care placement and that black children are almost inevitably put in inferior facilities. Over the years, some of the evidence in the case has been startling. A nun from New York Foundling Hospital, a Catholic agency, testified in a sworn statement that, until 1976, children from the hospital were regularly sent to the Museum of Natural History to have their race determined by anthropologists. (Gerald E. Bodell, the lawyer for New York Foundling Hospital, says this never happened.) And a city worker swore she had been sent to hospitals to peek under children's diapers at their genitals to determine the children's "true" color.

The suit argued that the city's contracts with the voluntary agencies were an unhealthy mix of church and state. To this day, for instance, many children in Catholic agencies are routinely denied birth-control education—despite federal, state, and local laws saying that foster children of childbearing age must have it.

The Civil Liberties Union lawyer who brought the suit and stayed with it all these years is Marcia Robinson Lowry. She argues that at its heart is the fact that "the city has no control over the agencies. The agencies can turn away children they don't want. They don't even have to tell the city what beds they have on a daily basis. And because the system is filled with black and Hispanic children, the Catholic and Jewish agencies have lost their incentive to provide good services." All this, Lowry contends, has contributed to the present crisis.

The private agencies have vigorously denied wrongdoing. "The Wilder case should never have been brought," says Richard E. Nolan, a lawyer with Davis Polk & Wardwell who represents many of the Catholic agencies. "Many of our agencies have a majority of black children, and they provide excellent care. We are able to do the job cheaper and better than the priests who devote their lives to child care, and because the voluntary agencies supplement city funds with their own endowments." (Early on, the nonsectarian and Protestant agencies were dropped as defendants, leaving only Jewish and Catholic groups.)

In 1983, the city and the Civil Liberties Union drew up a settlement, over the strong objections of most of the voluntary agencies. Judge Robert J. Ward, the third judge to handle the case, finally approved the agreement on October 8. The three-year delay, according to the judge's clerk, was due to the complexity of the case and the large number of defendants.

Lowry says the settlement provides guidelines that would make it harder for voluntary agencies to discriminate against black children. In particular, the agencies would have to take children on a first-come, first-served basis, except in the rarest of instances. "This is a system that is very resistant to change, but now we finally have the tools," says Lowry.

The Jewish and Catholic agencies didn't sign the settlement, however, and it's not clear whether they will appeal—thereby prolonging the case.

Robert McMahon, executive director of the St. Christopher –Ottilie home in Seacliff, Long Island, says he particularly objects to provisions in the settlement that would force agencies to accept any child. Given all the children who need beds, "I don't think I should have a vacancy," McMahon says. "On the other hand, if they want to bring a fire-starter or a heavy drug user when I have two kids just experimenting with drugs, the place would blow up."

Molly is eighteen, with long brown hair and powdery pale skin. She still recalls the day in the Bronx when she was three and she was taken away from her parents. Molly's mother and father were drinkers. There were given up for adoption. "They tried to do it as pleasantly as possible because we were little," says Molly, describing the day the police and the social worker came. "My mother was kinda out of it. They brought us stuffed animals while they talked with my mother. Then my mother started to cry, and they said, 'You have to come with us.' My brother, who was four and a half, held my hand, and we just left. I started to cry, 'Don't take me away from my mommy!' The first foster home was very nice. I cried at night for my mom, and my brother would comfort me.

"They said they would never take us away from each other, and when they did, it hurt even more. They took my brother away because he was goofing off; he was a little older and smarter and was understanding more than I."

Finally, when she was sixteen, a potential adoptive parent was found for Molly in upstate New York. Molly's prospective mother was single, a teacher and an actress. "A lot of times, she wasn't home. I would throw tantrums and lock her out of the house and do evil stuff like that. It was so hard to deal with a one-to-one relationship with a human being, a mother-daughter relationship. I'd never had that with my mother." Finally, the woman called the police and told them to take Molly away.

But Molly kept running back, hitchhiking upstate. "Finally, in 1984, when I ran away to her at Christmas and she called the cops, I realized if she doesn't let me stay for Christmas, she must really be serious."

Molly ended up at a group home in Westchester run by the Cardinal McCloskey agency. Sometimes group homes, where responsibilities are shared, are thought to be easier on adolescents like Molly, who have never formed a relationship with a parent. Molly is doing well now, living with a couple, their three natural children, and two adolescent foster children. She's attending high school and working as a recreation therapist in a mental hospital. One day, she hopes to have a job working with children. "It was a struggle," says Molly, "but I finally made it!"

While *Wilder* v. *Bernstein* plodded on through the seventies, the foster-care system came under regular attack. Agencies were accused of warehousing foster children to collect money from the city. An audit by City Comptroller Harrison Goldin's office found that one third of the children in foster care were being held years longer than necessary. In many cases, the children were living in terrible conditions.

"Supervision was poor, monitoring was poor. Tranquilizers were being used on some of the children. There was sexual activity between counselors and the kids," says Clara Barksdale, the former executive director of the Council on Adoptable Children.

The criticism culminated in 1979 in passage of the Child Welfare Reform Act, which ordered every county in the state to cut back on foster care and to work instead to keep troubled families together. The act was considered a model piece of legislation. Money would be spent on so-called preventive services—on providing counseling, day care, and homemakers for overwhelmed parents. The approach seemed enlightened and the budget figures made sense—preventive services are cheaper than foster care.

The number of certified foster beds declined from 21,954 in June 1984 to 20,389 last June, a drop of 7 percent. A new state payment policy discouraged agencies from recruiting foster parents.

Reducing the *need* for beds, however, has proved far more difficult than reducing the number of beds. The severe housing shortage for poor people continues to send families out into the streets. Pregnancies among teenagers—whose children are prime candidates for abuse and neglect—remain enormously high. And, most recently, the crack epidemic has torn apart countless families.

At the same time, the city has never provided the concrete services required by the new law. One 1983 state study of families who were investigated for possible abuse or neglect of their children found that 40 percent of the services recommended by caseworkers had not been provided. A private 1985 study of parents in crisis found that 49 percent of the services suggested by preventive-service social workers had not been provided. Existing services weren't exactly monumental offers of help. David Tobis of Welfare Research, Inc., the group that did the private study, says that "most of the services being provided consisted of counseling to help people adjust to poverty."

Eight-year-old Michael, who has been selling himself to the "sex hawks" in Times Square, is sitting in the room at 80 Lafayette where they send the "bad boys"—the older children, some of whom are seasoned veterans of foster care. (Since this story was reported, the authorities say they have created a "teen lounge" for the older kids.) Michael has been at 80 Lafayette since 11:15 in the morning, when police from the Times Square Truancy Squad spotted him washing windshields. It's 4 p.m. now. Michael is plump, and he has light brown hair worn in an Afro.

Michael's mother doesn't have a home. Sometimes she picks him up from school and takes him to sleep with her in a park. This morning, when the police found Michael, he said he was just trying to get some money to help out his mother.

"I had two hamsters," he tells a counselor. "One was very sick and died right in front of my face." Suddenly, he starts to cry. "I'm gettin' worried," he says, wiping away his tears with his fist. "I'm supposed to know if I'm goin' back to my mom or to a foster home. My mom doesn't know where I am. My mom should be worried about me. She said if anything ever happened to me, she'd do herself in."

While the foster-care system was trying to adjust to the new law, the Office of Special Services for Children was going through its own crisis. In 1984, Irwin Levin, a supervisor in the Brooklyn field office, charged that Special Services had failed to investigate properly a series of child-abuse cases that resulted in the deaths of nine children. Levin was demoted and fined. The case came to the attention of the press, and after an official investigation supported Levin's claims, Mayor Koch gave him his job back and refunded his fine.

Soon afterward, the city was accused of failing to investigate abuse cases at the Praca Day Care Center in the Bronx. James Krauskopf, commissioner of the Human Resources Administration (HRA)—the parent agency of Special Services—and Gail Kong, the head of Special Services, resigned. In the aftermath, the city got more aggressive about finding children in need—further increasing the numbers in foster care.

In February 1985, Eric Brettschneider was hired to run Special Services for Children. Then 38 and the father of two young children, Brettschneider was the fifth administrator of the agency in ten years. At the time he was hired, he was executive assistant to Queens borough president Donald Manes (who was known as a friend of foster-care reform). Earlier, Brettschneider had been executive director of the Queensborough Society for the Prevention of Cruelty to Children and an official with the State Department of Social Services. Even the system's severest critics say he genuinely seems to care about children.

Brettschneider himself, while hardly downplaying the problems he faces, cites several accomplishments in his 22 months. "We've seen dramatic improvement in our ability to respond to reports of child-abuse cases within 24 hours," he says. He has also opened a new field office in Brooklyn and made plans to hire new workers. He's trying to reduce caseloads and paperwork.

But Brettschneider has been unable to avert the crisis in foster-care placement.

Three-and-a-half-year-old Tommy sits by himself in the conference-room nursery. He has golden-brown skin and is neatly dressed in a white shirt and beige pants with orange-and-brown suspenders. One day, when Tommy's mother took him to the doctor, the pediatrician found a ball bearing in his ear. As the doctor was about to remove it, Tommy's mother had a psychotic breakdown. He was put in foster care four months ago, but on this morning, Tommy's foster mother had brought him to 80 Lafayette, saying she has had a death in her family and can't take care of him anymore. Tommy is very quiet. Though he follows people with his eyes, he usually talks only to television sets or machines. In her report, Tommy's caseworker raises the question of autism. Right now, he's playing with furniture from a dollhouse, making an imaginary scene. There's the little dining table, the four chairs surrounding it—everything is neat and perfect.

At 7:45 p.m., Little Flower Children's Services in Brooklyn calls to say it has a bed for Tommy and another child. At 8:35, though, Tommy is still on the sixteenth floor, waiting for a transportation worker to come and get him. He sits on the couch outside the nursery eating a dinner of meatballs. All around him, the offices are dim and quiet. Suddenly, there's a sound in the darkness. "What's that?" Tommy whispers. He's not autistic after all.

Critics charge that the city should have recognized the need for more beds as early as the summer of 1984. When Brett-schneider came on, one of his first moves was to halt admissions to the worst foster-care agencies. His intent was to stamp out abuses, though one effect was to reduce the already dwindling number of beds.

Last spring, an unusually large number of abused and abandoned babies began entering the system. Brettschneider and others blame much of the increase on crack. "These are babies born to crack-using parents," he says. "Many crack addicts use other drugs, and foster parents are reluctant to take the babies because of their medical problems and the fear of AIDS."

The city couldn't cope with the influx. Children waiting for placement were held in dingy city offices without toys or medical attention. They weren't sent to school, and they never went out to play.

On April 23, Special Services exploded. More than 60 workers stormed into Brettschneider's office demanding more beds for the kids, protection from angry adolescents, and reduced caseloads. The average caseload is 30, but some people carry 50 cases. The turnover rate for workers is about 55 percent annually. "It's inhuman," says Betty Greene, a caseworker in Manhattan. "It hurts us badly to see these children come in here defenseless, some of them at the point of death—and to recycle them this way."

Brettschneider listened to the workers' complaints for more than an hour. In the end, he could only agree that they were laboring under difficult conditions.

That evening, administrators dragged the furniture out of the sixteenth-floor conference room and began setting up a nursery. Security was tightened. More emergency funds were made available so workers could buy food and clothing for the children. Still, the underlying problem remained: Children continued to be recycled, night after night.

On May 20, the Legal Aid Society filed suit in federal court in Manhattan demanding what seemed like basic rights for children awaiting placement: That children taken from their parents before 5 p.m. have a bed by seven; that they be guaranteed three meals, clean clothes, and some time to play outside every day; and that older children be allowed to attend school. "My experience is that to get results from the city, you file a lawsuit," said Rose Firestein of Legal Aid.

On May 27, a decision was reached in another lawsuit. This one charged that the city had never provided the children and their families with the services required by the Child Welfare Reform Act. "It's idiotic and unbelievably cruel not to take every step possible to keep children out of foster care," said Robert Hayes, director of the Coalition for the Homeless, one of the groups that brought the suit. After listening to arguments, Civil Court judge Edward H. Lehner ordered the city to get busy and help families *before* their children were abused.

Throughout the summer, Special Services scrambled to find beds. City-run, short-term facilities were opened for children in a Queens nursing residence, a former East Harlem school, and a Brooklyn day-care center. HRA wouldn't let *New York* tour these shelters, but Firestein described the Queens residence in particular as "appalling." "I've worked as an attorney for prisoners in southern jails, and this was worse than some of the conditions I saw there," she said last July.

"It's better than keeping children in offices overnight," explained Brettschneider. Within months of their opening, the state ordered the short-term facilities closed because they lacked state approval. The Queens residence was closed in August, but the other two centers remain open while the city negotiates with the state.

At the end of July, a partial settlement in the Legal Aid suit over the plight of the children awaiting placement seemed to promise relief: The city agreed to a timetable for coming up with a plan to provide food and other services in the field offices.

Yet this fall, children were still being placed in different homes every night, and Legal Aid was seeking a new injunction. The conditions in the city offices had markedly improved, however. Doctors, nurses, nutritionists, teachers, and toys were provided to the children, though the recreation program was still inadequate.

Overall, since last spring, Special Services has added 112 new beds in foster homes—many of them recruited through an extensive media campaign. Another 104 beds have been added in group care, including a new shelter for children under two, run by the New York Foundling Hospital. More shelters are planned, but meanwhile, babies are being placed in group facilities with older children, a solution of grave concern to Legal Aid lawyers. The alternative—putting babies in their own group homes, where, if the past is any guide, they won't get adequate attention—seems equally grim.

In the middle of the crisis—on June 12—HRA commissioner George Gross resigned to become head of the state's Financial Control Board. He was the third HRA commissioner to resign in the last five years. It took Mayor Koch four months to find someone who could—and would—do the job, but on October 22, he announced that William J. Grinker, a management consultant and former Ford Foundation official, would take over.

Grinker faces a continuing crisis. During October, 140 babies, many of them the sons and daughters of parents on crack, were waiting in the city's hospitals for foster homes—a fivefold increase over the previous year.

Even Brettschneider thinks there's worse to come. "Every holiday season, there is an increase in the abuse and neglect of children," he says. Those interested in becoming foster parents can call 266-CARE.

At 8:30 p.m. at 80 Lafayette, Betsy Mayberry (who's been working since 9 a.m.) is sipping Pepsi-Free and chewing gum for dinner. Just as she thinks her workday may be ending, she puts in a call to Emergency Children's Services, which opens at 4 p.m. and stays open through the night.

"Whaddaya got?" she asks a social worker. "How're you doin' there? . . . *Twins!* . . . What ethnicity are they? . . . Black like you?" She lowers her voice. "*Sweet* like you?" The social worker says that the twins, a boy and a girl, are four and a half. Their six-year-old brother had been coming to school with bruises. Today, the three children were removed from their parents, and they are now sitting in the Brooklyn field office waiting for a home. Mayberry starts calling.

One worker is talking to the Angel Guardian Home in Brooklyn. "We really need the beds," the worker says. "You're our last hope." But Angel Guardian is full tonight.

Suddenly, the room is quiet. The twins and their brother walk in, holding hands. For a moment, the workers pause to watch them as they move across the room, barely visible above the desktops.

The older boy has a big bruise on his cheek. His mother's boyfriend has been beating him up. The twins are dressed in identical gray-and-white jackets. The girl's hair is done in braids. She wears a T-shirt with STARLET written across it. "They say she has marks on her back, too," says the worker who brought them in. The younger boy is rubbing his eyes and seems dazed. He has a cold and possibly a fever.

The girl heads straight for a pile of toys in the holding area. "I'm having a good time, I'm having a good time," she cries into a little plastic phone.

"They're a handful!" says the worker. They don't seem to get tired."

The older boy pushes a toy car across the floor while caseworkers make phone calls. The girl looks up anxiously. "Where's my brother?" she asks.

Someone offers the three of them bologna sandwiches, which they eat off paper towels. Mayberry doesn't want to split the children up because the older boy is a kind of a parent to his younger siblings—often the case with abused and neglected children. But it's 11:45 now, and the only beds Mayberry can find are in two homes in Queens. The children will have to be separated. It will probably be weeks before a home can be found for all of them, Mayberry says.

"You're going to *Queens!*" a worker tells the children. They smile excitedly. She helps them on with their coats. "Wave bye-bye," she says. The children wave.

Outside, a sleek black Big Apple car waits, its motor running. The time is 11:50. The street is dark and deserted. The children climb into the back of the cab, leaning forward onto the front seat and looking out eagerly. It's as if they're going to the zoo.

Now Mayberry no longer stays late to make placements. A night manager is on the job until the early-morning hours. Mayberry or one of her colleagues calls in at 2 a.m. to get a report. As for the twins and their older brother, four months passed before they were finally reunited in a long-term foster home.

CHILDREN OF POVERTY[4]

Imagine the mayor of New York calling an urgent news conference to announce that the crisis of the city's poor children had reached such proportions that he was mobilizing the city's talents for a massive rescue effort not unlike the one that saved us from bankruptcy 10 years ago. I believe some such drastic action is warranted, even essential, because our city is threatened by the spreading blight of a poverty even crueler in some ways than that of the Great Depression half a century ago. Almost 40 percent of our children—700,000 boys and girls—now live in families with incomes below the poverty line. Senator Daniel Patrick Moynihan has estimated that half of the babies born in the city in 1980 can be expected to be on our welfare rolls before they reach the age of 18.

Social critics, including Mr. Moynihan, have been telling a tale of two cities to describe the kind of community New York has become: while the city enjoys prosperity, the "new" poverty goes unchecked. The richest Congressional district in the nation shares a boundary with one of the poorest. And it was precisely during the last two banner years of economic growth and enhanced city budgets that the child poverty rate accelerated dramatically.

Today's children of poverty are suffering in ways that would have dumbfounded those who knew the Great Depression: an estimated 3,000 babies born addicted to drugs every year, 10,000 children living in shelters and hotels for the homeless, 12,000 children who were abused or neglected so severely last year that they had to be removed from their homes and placed in foster care.

All too many poor children in New York are denied dignity even in death, according to a recent report by the Coalition for the Homeless. The report revealed that almost half of the infants under the age of 1 who died in the city between 1981 and 1984 were buried in potter's field in unmarked graves that their families thus could not visit.

[4]Reprint of an article by Andrew Stein, president of the City Council of New York and formerly Borough President of Manhattan. Copyright © 1986 by The New York Times Company. Reprinted by permission from the *New York Times Magazine*, June 8, 1986.

All this poses a practical as well as a moral issue for the city, for the way we deal with the problem will determine the quality of life for all of us in the future. There is no question that the problem is enormously difficult, but it is not yet hopeless. Many sensible steps can be taken to attack the situation, including the appointment of one person—a "czar" if you will—to oversee all agencies that serve children, efforts to engage the private sector, revamping of the workloads of caseworkers and the increasing involvement of the school system. There are others as well.

This is not to say that the solutions will be easy. The problem is exacerbated by the rate of family breakdown, and the cruel choices this presents for the city can be illustrated with the story of 3-year-old Giovanny Maria of the Bronx, recorded in the Surrogate's Court this spring. His fate came to be decided by a judge because, shortly after his third birthday, his mother decided that being a parent had become too much of a burden.

Giovanny's mother was planning a trip to the Dominican Republic and did not know when, if ever, she might return. The boy's father was unknown, so she left Giovanny with a friend.

The friend was a 20-year-old single woman with a ninth-grade education, unemployed and living on public assistance and food stamps. Last November, she and Giovanny began living in a single room in a three-story rooming house, where they shared a kitchen and two bathrooms with 20 other people.

Under the circumstances, these living arrangements were felt to be the best possible by a caseworker for the New York City Office of Special Services for Children, whose function is to intervene to protect the welfare of children like Giovanny: The caseworker was sent to Surrogate's Court to support a petition to have the mother's friend declared his legal guardian.

Giovanny's prospective new mother failed to appear for the guardianship hearing, leading the lawyer for the city to wonder whether she was fit to care for the child. Still, the caseworker told the court that, under the circumstances, the boy should remain where he was. She recounted her investigation of Giovanny's life in the rooming house.

"He didn't have any marks on him and he looks well cared for," she testified, although she conceded that because the child spoke little English and she spoke no Spanish, she had reached her conclusion without ever communicating directly with the boy. As for his living conditions, she said they seemed adequate:

the communal bathrooms were "moderately clean" and the room the child was sharing with his prospective guardian was "spacious, well heated and clean." But it seems clear that the only valid argument for continuing the arrangement was that the alternatives were far worse—either a homeless shelter for the woman and child or a foster home for the child.

Judge Bertram R. Gelfand, Bronx County Surrogate, ordered the city to remove Giovanny from the "deplorable" conditions of the rooming house and to "place this child in a more appropriate environment which will more likely protect his health, safety, welfare . . . [and] give him the opportunities in life to which he, and every child in our society, is entitled."

The judge, in a rebuke to the city for the inadequate resources it devotes to its child protective services, urged the city to staff the agency with more professionally qualified social workers, at higher salaries. (Giovanny's worker had a degree in communications and was earning $19,000 a year.) The judge also reflected on the city's budget priorities: "This court is sensitive to the constrictions of budget limitations. However, in a budget-making process that is necessarily based upon fixing priorities, the cost of assuring the development of children into useful citizens is minuscule against the costs of endlessly continuing to expand the criminal justice system . . . create new expanded drug and alcohol abuse programs and swell the ranks of those who cannot provide for themselves, all because, in early childhood, people were denied the fundamental education and upbringing necessary to meet the challenges of life."

Citing the confidentiality provisions of the state's social-service law, a spokesman for the Special Services agency said it could not reveal what happened to Giovanny after the judge's decision. Nevertheless, we can reasonably speculate that foster care would not have been a desirable solution. Unlike adoption, foster care is not a permanent arrangement, and many foster "parents" participate simply because they get extra income. They may take a child in for a day, a week, a month or longer, then send the child back. Too many foster-care children ultimately end up in shelters for the homeless.

Despite the problems with the system, it is being strained beyond its limits by the magnitude and pervasiveness of poverty and family breakdown. Children are being abused and mistreated at record levels, abandoned like excess luggage, and we are simply running out of places to put them.

The Special Services agency projects that it will have to cope with reports of abuse and neglect involving 69,000 children in the coming fiscal year. The number of cases has been increasing at a rate of about 10 percent a year. David Tobis, a senior associate at Welfare Research Inc., a respected policy studies group, has concluded that in some neighborhoods "as many as 20 percent of the children have been reported to be abused or neglected during the past five years."

The total foster-care population in the city is now about 17,000, one of the largest in the country. But while the demand for foster care has risen, the availability of beds has contracted.

This spring, hundreds of children, from infants to adolescents, were piling up in agency offices and sleeping on benches, while overburdened and harrassed caseworkers labored through the night trying to arrange temporary foster-care placements for them. On any given day this spring, up to 30 healthy infants were lingering in hospitals, at a cost of several hundred dollars a day for each infant, because there were no foster beds.

Reports of child abuse are coming in so fast that workers in some agency regional offices are assigned 10 or 11 new cases a month, despite the fact that New York State's Department of Social Services has established a guideline of 4 to 5 new cases a month as the number that a trained caseworker can manage with any degree of professional competence.

According to Mr. Tobis, this was a crisis waiting to erupt. In fact, in a 1985 speech to the Conference on Setting Municipal Priorities, he warned that the foster-care system was being overwhelmed by the rising number of abused children needing placement.

"Recent events show again that the city's priorities are all wrong," Mr. Tobis said. "We spend half a billion dollars on child welfare services but most of it is used to remove and confine children after they have been damaged by poverty and neglect. We have no early warning system to identify children's problems before they overwhelm families and the city's budgets."

The courts now seem to agree. In a recent ruling, Civil Court Judge Edward H. Lehner in Manhattan ordered the city to come up with a "service plan" for intervention in families that face removal of children for placement in foster homes.

The city has now taken heed of some of the criticism of the Special Services agency. In an otherwise "lean" budget dictated by Federal cutbacks and decreased revenues, Mayor Koch this spring singled out the crisis in Special Services for Children, and requested funds to hire 323 new caseworkers and support staff.

Surely that is good news for the overburdened and unappreciated caseworkers. Yet even if the city retains the new personnel it intends to hire, we are still speaking about emergency treatment, not cures. The gridlock in the city's principal agency serving abused children is merely a symptom of a more fundamental and complex social disease.

To understand what is happening in the city we must return to poverty and its related disorders—family disintegration and teen-age pregnancy. The likelihood of a child's growing up poor is four times as great if he is born into a household headed by a woman rather than a traditional two-parent home. And it is even more likely if the mother is a teen-ager.

New York City has been massively afflicted by this "feminization of poverty." Though the city's population declined 11 percent between 1970 and 1980, the number of people living in female-headed families rose by almost 30 percent. The city's welfare rolls now consist mainly of minority-group women and children. Demographic projections suggest that this most vulnerable group will continue to grow as a percentage of the population at least through the next decade.

The most potentially destructive of these trends is the epidemic of teen-age pregnancy. Although the total number of teen pregnancies in the city has decreased in the last decade (as a result of a decline in the teen-age population) pregnancies among 15- to 19-year-old females went up from 12.3 percent to 13.1 percent between 1975 and 1984. The city's Adolescent Pregnancy Interagency Council has projected that if the present rates remain constant, 1 out of 4 girls 14 years old today will be pregnant at least once before her 18th birthday; 1 out of 8 will have had at least 1 abortion before reaching 18; and nearly 1 out of 11 will be a mother before she is 18.

The 13,000 babies born to teen-agers in 1984 represent a staggering social and economic cost. Seventy percent of those new babies and their mothers can be expected to end up on public assistance within 18 months, according to the Interagency Council.

Pregnant teen-agers are far less likely than other expectant mothers to receive prenatal care, thus increasing their risk of bearing low-birthweight babies requiring extensive medical care at public expense. Teen-age pregnancy is the single most important factor causing girls to drop out of school, and contributes substantially to the city's huge high-school dropout rates: 40 percent overall, 70 percent among minority groups.

Earlier this year, the Washington-based Center for Population Options released a study estimating that the cost of teen-age pregnancy (taking into account only direct Federal and state expenditures for Aid to Families With Dependent Children, Medicaid and food stamps) was $16.5 billion in 1985.

What we are experiencing throughout the country, but most particularly in major urban areas such as New York, is the result of an unprecedented reversal of fortunes among our age groups. Historically, poverty had always struck hardest at the elderly, because they were most likely to be infirm, without work or without income. That held true until the mid-1970's. Then a disproportionate number of children began to be poor, a phenomenon exclusive to the United States among the industrialized nations. In the last two decades, the poverty-rate curves for children and the elderly crossed each other. For children, the rate rose steadily, from 12 percent in 1965 to close to 25 percent in 1985. For the elderly, poverty declined just as steadily, from a high of 35.2 percent in 1959 to 12 percent in 1985. The Federal Government last year defined the poverty line as $10,990 for a family of four.

The White House task force on families concluded in 1984 that most of the poverty among children would disappear with economic growth were it not "that the rates of divorce and formation of single-parent households remain high."

Almost everyone agrees that the American family is in trouble, but there is wide disagreement as to the causes. Why is it that of all the industrialized democracies, the United States has the highest rates of divorce and teen-age pregnancy, along with resulting child abuse, teen-age suicide, drug addiction and alcoholism?

Neoconservative writers on poverty, who have the ear of the Reagan Administration, have argued forcefully that the federally sponsored social programs and the "explosion" of welfare payments of the 1960's and 70's created a "culture of dependency" in the urban black ghettos. Starting with the War on Poverty, Washington began sending the wrong message to the poor, these commentators argue—that they weren't responsible for any-

thing, that their condition was the product of racism and other
defects in society, and that it was all right for young men to stay
out of the labor force and for teen-agers to have children, because the government would take care of them.

New York City's government has been depicted by such critics as particularly profligate in its social spending. They believe
that the city consequently gets (and deserves) its exceptionally
high rates of social pathology, such as teen-age pregnancy and
family disintegration.

Yet the empirical evidence doesn't always fit the theory. New
York City certainly has a very serious problem of births to teen-
age girls, for example, but in 1980 it was only 26th among the 30
largest American cities.

The Washington-based Children's Defense Fund, a private
advocacy group, published a survey recently comparing states'
rates of teen-age births with 1983 payment levels of Aid for Dependent Children. The results are startling; practically every
state whose payments were more than 50 percent of the Federal
poverty level also had teen-age birth rates below the national average. On the other hand, almost every state with low payments
had teen-age birth rates higher than the national average. Thus
a substantial correlation was found to exist between lower welfare
payment levels and higher indexes of social pathology. This is exactly the opposite of the outcome predicted by neoconservative
theory.

The Reagan Administration is not likely to be convinced by
any evidence that higher payments might be socially beneficial,
but neither is it about to end all welfare benefits to working-age
adults, as some conservative writers urge.

Instead, we can expect more of the same—payment levels
that continue to lag behind inflation, and further cuts in Federal
programs that provide essential social services to the poor. At the
present time, for example, the entire Federal budget for preventive services for children (in the form of grants to the states and
demonstration projects) is $207 million. That is about $130 million less than the Federal Government's public relations budget
and about half the amount the city of New York allots to Special
Services for Children.

Liberals and conservatives will no doubt continue debating
the causes of family disintegration and poverty. But while the debate rages, millions of American children become poorer. In

New York City alone, over half a million remain on the welfare rolls. The tale of two cities is no mere metaphor. It describes a process of decay that is already unraveling our social fabric and damaging our most precious democratic institutions, particularly our public schools.

One-third of the pupils now in New York City public schools are on public assistance. At the same time, the middle class continues to desert the schools.

Clearly, New York must do better if it is to survive as a community into the 21st century. The middle-class can remove its children from the public schools, but it cannot escape the consequences of child poverty on this scale. Ultimately, the children of the middle class and the children of the underclass will be sharing the same streets.

I believe that the situation is not altogether hopeless. Despite Federal cutbacks, the city's $21.5 billion budget, when added to the immense resources of our private sector, could supoort a massive rescue effort. What is needed is not necessarily more public spending, but inspired leadership.

Imagine if the Mayor, in announcing a massive rescue operation as I suggested earlier, appointed a czar to lead the city's effort—a person of national stature, a leader and advocate for children and someone with proven administrative skills. Imagine that this czar would have the Mayor's full backing to coordinate and oversee the performance of all city agencies that serve children.

Suppose the czar began a concerted effort to enlist the private sector, the universities and the foundations, to work together with the city to develop innovative programs for children in distress.

We might also imagine some common-sense proposals that the czar would immediately put into action.

For example, the head of the city's Human Resources Administration could begin a television crusade, appealing to the public to open its hearts and homes to the increasing numbers of foster-care children. The agency would create an early-warning system to identify families at risk and provide them with necessary social services before a crisis arose and the children had to be removed.

The city, as noted, has already started an effort to improve the situation of the Special Services for Children agency, but much remains to be done to reduce paperwork to give workers more time for personal contact with the children and families they are supposed to serve and to improve morale, which is at an all-time low. Staff attrition at the agency is more than 50 percent a year, up to 70 percent in some of the more swamped offices. Caseworkers resign so fast that administrators have a hard time filling the agency's allocated positions.

Under our imagined czar, paperwork for caseworkers doing protective services for children would be drastically reduced, so that the workers could devote more attention to the children.

Other actions could be undertaken as well. The city now houses 3,400 families with children in decrepit privately owned hotels, at rates of up to $3,000 a month. To end this scandal, the city could immediately lease these hotels and contract with private, nonprofit agencies to provide better services and management.

As for schools, the Board of Education, in conjunction with community school boards, could be pressed to implement immediately its family life/sex-education curriculum for all schoolchildren and to expand the teen-pregnancy-prevention networks in coordination with outside social-service agencies.

Alternative high schools, small and caring institutions, are among the most effective means for saving at-risk students from dropping out. The city's 80 private and public colleges could be asked to volunteer to be host to at least one alternative school on their campuses and provide other educational resources to enrich the high school programs.

Summer programs in the city's schools could be increased. Major corporations would be asked to provide instruction and training in computers and other technical subjects.

The Board of Education and the Human Resources Administration, the two mammoth agencies that together have contact with almost all the city's poor children, and whose combined budgets surpass $10 billion, would be mandated to coordinate their efforts on behalf of at-risk children.

The list could go on. There is no shortage of ideas that deserve to be tried and excellent programs just waiting to be set in motion.

None of this is utopian. I have seen the programs work. At Middle College High School, on the campus of La Guardia Community College in Queens, I talked to youngsters who had already dropped out of the system and were saved because of the special, intimate nature of that school and because of its dedicated teachers and principal. I heard Robert Scott, a student at High School Redirection in Brooklyn, say that at the age of 18 he had won a Golden Gloves championship but couldn't read or write—until that alternative school changed his life. And I saw him put his arm around two of his teachers and say, "Thank God for these two."

The city could double the number of alternative high schools within two years (there are now 14). Given the political will, all the proposals on the above list can be accomplished—and more.

Alone, the city can't eliminate poverty among children; it can't put back together families that fall apart, or are never formed, because of that poverty. But if we move the problems of poor children to the top of our agenda, we can find the means to intervene and save many from utterly shattered lives. In saving them, we would be saving ourselves.

THE HOLLOW PROMISE[5]

Can the government save a troubled child? George Bush and Michael Dukakis insist that it can. Yet while the candidates tout their plans to invest in kids, the truth is that federal programs for troubled and impoverished children have generally fallen short of their well-intentioned goals. Even Marian Wright Edelman, who heads the Children's Defense Fund and favors major expansions in federal programs, is starting to question the prochild rhetoric in the 1988 campaign and the Congress. "This is the year," she sighs, "when politicians are talking more about children than ever and accomplishing next to nothing on their behalf."

The point is not, as some conservatives suggest, that all efforts to help children are doomed. There are dozens of model programs that provide good educations for inner-city ghetto kids, furnish hot meals to hungry youngsters and teach abusive parents

[5]Reprint of an article by David Whitman, senior editor, *U. S. News & World Report*. Reprinted by permission from *U. S. News & World Report*, V. 105: 41-4. N. 7. '88. Copyright © 1988 by *U. S. News & World Report*.

not to beat their children. But the individual success stories are often misleading. In fact, even the best large-scale programs for at-risk children, sponsored by Republican and Democratic Presidents, have produced modest results. To help America's troubled kids, the next President will have to surmount these antichildren barriers:

1. The Deserted "Gucci Gulch"

The simplest explanation for why programs for children get whittled down lies in "Gucci Gulch," the hallway outside the powerful Senate Finance Committee hearing room. When the subject is tax reform, the gulch is packed with natty tax lobbyists. But when the panel discusses foster care or hungry children, the expense-account crowd stays home. "When we talk about children up here," grumbles Senator Daniel Moynihan (D-N.Y.), "you can shoot deer in the hallways."

Children have no natural lobbyists, nor do they vote. True, *parents* vote, and when their self-interest is at stake, as in the battle over child care, congressional hearings are well attended. Still, children's advocates do not have a thimbleful of the power that, say, the elderly wield on Capitol Hill. The Children's Defense Fund, the country's most influential child-advocacy group, has two persons in its government-affairs section. KidsPac, a modestly funded lobbying group, is the sole federal PAC for children. Recently, the group hired its first salaried employee. "You flatter us," laughs founder Bill Harris, "by calling us an organization."

2. The Partisan Asphyxiation

George Bush wants to "be a leader for children." What politician doesn't? Being prochild is a little like favoring world peace. The slogan works only so long as the particulars are ignored. Democrats claim that a higher minimum wage, more public housing and extra day-care subsidies are prochild. Republicans contend that abortion restrictions, tax credits for families with children and school courses promoting chastity are prochild. This philosophical dispute routinely asphyxiates efforts to help children.

Last month, the Senate had the opportunity to vote on two important pieces of legislation affecting children: The child-care bill, which expanded and regulated day-care programs, and a modest bill allowing parents 10 weeks of unpaid leave from their jobs when a child is born, adopted or seriously ill. With the backing of business lobbyists, Senate Republicans were able to stall votes on both bills by claiming they were antifamily and too costly. The legislation's chief sponsor, Senator Christopher Dodd (D-Conn.), observed in disgust afterward: "Never in the history of American politics has there been a constituency so popular but with so little political clout as the American family."

3. The Don't-Help-Mom Fixation

No obstacle to helping children is quite as intractable as the parent. As Douglas Besharov, a social-policy expert at the American Enterprise Institute, says, "You can't put food on the table for the child without putting food on the table for the mother." Helping moms, conservatives argue, makes them and their children more, rather than less, dependent.

Even liberals disagree on what assistance Mom should receive. Some believe welfare benefits must be expanded; others think getting families off welfare takes priority. Last September, CDF's Edelman wrote every senator asking each to *oppose* the welfare-reform bill because, among other things, it did not sufficiently help two-parent families. But Democratic vice-presidential candidate Lloyd Bentsen championed the bill for providing more work and training for welfare moms and dads, saying it would "help millions of poor children and their families break out of the cycle of poverty." Inevitably, children will suffer while politicians battle over how best to help their parents.

4. The Power Vacuum

George Bush wants to be known as the "education President." So does Michael Dukakis. Yet neither candidate can make major reforms in the public schools since 94 percent of public-school funds come from state and local governments. The states also make most divorce and child-support laws and set the guidelines used to license day-care centers and to treat abused and neglected children.

The President nudges, rather than controls, programs for children. The spread of youth gangs is a prime illustration.

George Bush thinks that the nation's "No. 1 crime problem is street gangs," and he has pledged to form a federal antigang unit and expand federal powers to prosecute juveniles. Yet there is little evidence that such law-enforcement crackdowns accomplish much.

In Los Angeles, the police have special antigang units and have arrested gang members repeatedly in neighborhood sweeps. Yet over the last decade, the number of gang members in Los Angeles quadrupled from 15,000 in 1977 to 60,000 last year, mostly due to the lure of fast drug money. A pilot program that tried to rehabilitate youths within their own neighborhoods in the nearby San Fernando Valley had limited success. But locking up gang members in large prisons typically seems to make them even more hardened criminals. Barry Krisberg of the National Council on Crime and Delinquency says that "the prospect of three-piece-suited FBI agents chasing 15-year-olds around urban neighborhoods is ridiculous."

5. The Over-5 Problem

In the struggle to help kids, the most perplexing issue is what to do for poor children who have passed their fifth birthday. Just about everyone, including George Bush and Michael Dukakis, now agrees that programs like Head Start, prenatal care and childhood immunization should be reinforced because they promote healthier children and reduce the number of kids who will repeat grades at school. Yet what will the candidates do about the 9 million poor youngsters who have already entered school? Michael Dukakis has vaguely pledged to "invest in our urban neighborhoods." George Bush will ask affluent suburban teens to go into the inner city to reshape the ghetto.

It's unlikely that these, or any, federal policies will stop impoverished teenagers from drinking, taking drugs or having babies prematurely. Most programs that help teens tend to provide too few services in too little time and with minimal community commitment. For instance, strategies for teen-pregnancy prevention, from sex education to school-based health clinics, have generally yielded disappointing results.

"Just Say No" programs, which teach unwed teens to be chaste and are a conservative favorite, are a good example. The "Sex Respect" course, now taught in about 500 schools, seems to cause short-term changes in students' *attitudes* toward premarital sex, but there is little evidence it changes their *behavior*. Sabrina White, 16, of Atlanta became pregnant about a year after she took a course on postponing sex. She had unprotected sex with her boyfriend because, even though "the teacher taught us we could get pregnant from just one time, I was listening to my friend. She didn't get pregnant." In an age of casual sex and widespread student drug use, four or five classes on the dangers of drugs or sex just aren't likely to have much long-term impact on peer-conscious teens.

One program that has fared slightly better is Michael Dukakis's Alliance Against Drugs in Massachusetts, which has the schools work closely with police and community groups. Older, trained students, and athletes from the revered Boston Celtics, are enlisted to teach elementary and middle-school kids about how to avoid drugs. Six new residential-treatment programs for youths have been opened in Massachusetts during the last five years alone under the program, in part because of local input. Since the alliance was started in 1984, drug use among students has fallen faster in Massachusetts than in most other states. Still, a third of high-school seniors in the state use marijuana, cocaine or some other drug besides alcohol at least once a month.

6. The Impotent Matchmaker

In part, the limited success of the alliance highlights the reality that no government reform will have much lasting impact on poor children so long as the number of unwed mothers continues to soar. George Bush described the problem last month by drawing an odd analogy with the space-shuttle tragedy. He said that "families, too, explode, and so do communities, but like machines they can be put back together again." In fact, broken families often can't be put back together, at least not by government fiat.

While Democrats and Republicans have deplored antifamily welfare and tax policies in recent years, more-casual attitudes toward marriage are largely responsible for the growing number of single moms. In a new study, two liberal welfare analysts, Mary Jo Bane and Paul Jargowsky of Harvard University's Center for Health and Human Resources Policy, review the effect that government policies on taxes, birth control, divorce, abortion, welfare, teen-pregnancy prevention and short-term fiscal initiatives have had on the decline of marriage. Their unadorned conclusion: "No government policy will reverse the increase in the proportion of children in female-headed families. . . . The most important causes of changes in family structure lie outside the realm of policy." Put more simply, no federal bureaucrat can replace a father.

7. *The Success Shortfall*

When conservatives and liberals talk about prochild initiatives, they rarely discuss the fact that even the *best* national programs only modestly reduce the chances that children will fail in school or wind up in unemployment lines and hospitals. Participants in the oft praised Job Corps, for instance, earn about $10 more per week on average than similarly situated teens who did not go through the program. These modest gains are worthwhile, since youths who fail in school or end up in jail or hospitals, cost a lot of taxpayer money. Yet the enduring frustration of most policymakers is that they can rarely ensure that poor children will end up with opportunities similar to those of middle-class kids.

One such example is the widely touted Women, Infants, and Children program, which provides prenatal and postnatal nutritional guidance and food vouchers to mothers of disadvantaged children. Even well-regarded WIC providers face long odds in places like Chicago's West Garfield neighborhood. About 27 out of every 1,000 babies in that low-income black community die before their first birthday, a rate more than twice that of the state average. One reason is that almost all mothers in the neighborhood rely on infant formula instead of more-nutritious breastfeeding.

One nationally renowned nonprofit organization, Bethel New Life, Inc., has tried to help. Gilda Ivy, the able nutritionist in Bethel's WIC program, has for years encouraged clients to breast-feed, sponsoring breast-feeding fairs, luncheons, speakers and even breast-feeding support groups. Yet the local myth that bottle-feeding is more sophisticated seems unshakable. At Bethel, only 13 of the 954 infants on Ivy's case load are breast-fed. Ryusann Brooks's reservations about breast-feeding are typical. She tried it with her baby boy twice, then quit. "I knew it was a healthy thing," Ryusann said, "but part of me was thinking my sisters didn't do it, so it must not be so important." Parents, it seems, will cling to prevailing cultural mores, sometimes in spite of the best government advice and aid.

8. The Copycat Shortage

The ingredients of successful programs for disadvantaged children are no secret. Typically, they provide a wide range of services, have dedicated staffs that work intensively with clients, involve parents and community groups and aim, where possible, to help preschoolers. For instance, the Homebuilders program in Tacoma, Wash., has dramatically reduced foster-care placements of abused and neglected children by providing a kind of "family intensive care." On some occasions, a caseworker virtually moves in with a troubled family.

Yet the very reasons that model programs like Homebuilders are successful also make them hard to replicate. Charismatic leaders, committed parents, dedicated staff and extensive, comprehensive services are hard to bottle. For instance, model inner-city schools cited by conservatives like former Education Secretary William Bennett typically have inspirational principals, a phenomenon that Yale Prof. Edward Zigler dubs the "Jesus Christ effect." "The problem," says Zigler, "is that there just aren't that many magnificent people in the world."

9. The Cost Squeeze

While the candidates talk optimistically about helping children, the federal government is running a $152 billion deficit. Several underfunded children's programs (like Head Start and WIC) deserve more money, but so do other neglected programs. A 1988 poll by the Public Agenda Foundation shows that 1 out of 2 taxpayers is willing to pay about $25 extra a year to expand a few well-regarded programs such as Head Start—but not much more. The voters, in short, consider children a worthy investment so long as they remain an inexpensive one.

In the end, the hurdles facing the children's crusade should prompt skepticism but not despair. While the federal government's attempts to help children have a mixed record, the proliferation of innovative state and local initiatives is encouraging. So, too, are the thousands of community-development corporations and businesses that have started to pitch in to help disadvantaged children. It's worth remembering, moreover, that poor kids in earlier generations had a rugged lot.

Thirty years ago, poverty, malnutrition and infant mortality were far more widespread than today. Fifty years ago, policymakers were fighting to abolish child labor. That is a reminder of one important lesson: The lives of America's children improve slowly. But that fact also cuts two ways. If, in 1992, Michael Dukakis or George Bush asks the nation's children, "Are you better off today than four years ago?" the answer is likely to be "No."

IV. HOMELESSNESS

EDITOR'S INTRODUCTION

One of the most widely publicized aspects of the "culture of poverty" is homelessness. The bag ladies and indigent men who sleep in Penn Station have become familiar to millions of Americans through the press and television; and the army of the homeless poor have been the subject quite recently of Jonathan Kozol's controversial and widely discussed book *Rachel and Her Children: Homeless Families in America*. The number of the homeless poor has risen dramatically in the 1980s, but social planners hold differing views about them. In the opening article of Section Four, Marjorie Hope and James Young, writing in *Commonweal*, survey the causes of homelessness. They emphasize that withdrawal of government subsidies has made low-income housing unprofitable at the same time that housing rents have soared. Thousands of people have been left without shelter as a result. They note, too, that the government's policy of deinstitutionalizing the mentally ill, without effective treatment at community-based systems, has left the mentally disabled to fend for themselves. In none of the European countries, the writers argue, has there been such neglect of the poorest and most disadvantaged members of society.

In a following article, reprinted from *New Leader*, Richard J. Margolis calls attention to the elderly homeless. They are, Margolis remarks, at the bottom of the homeless hierarchy, not always easy to detect, easy prey to predators and disease, and more vulnerable than all other groups to death from hypothermia. Startlingly, in the northeastern states, elderly people make up about 30 percent of the unhoused. Then, Ellen L. Bassuk, writing in *Scientific American*, turns to another significant group of the homeless, the mentally ill. As she observes, shelters do no more than provide overnight lodging, and thus do not begin to meet the needs of the mentally handicapped. In the article from the *Yale Review* that follows, Jonathan Kozol takes issue with Bassuk and other social commentators, whom he feels have overstressed the mental illness aspect of homelessness. The fundamental problem, it seems to him, is the chronic shortage of low-income housing.

Kozol's book on homelessness, in turn, is the occasion of an article in *Commentary* by Thomas J. Main. Main argues, first, that Kozol grossly exaggerates the number of homeless in America; his estimated 2–3 million is not confirmed by any of the many surveys that have been undertaken, which arrive at a figure closer to 400,000. Secondly, he asserts that mental illness cannot be dismissed as a major factor in the homelessness problem. Even if more housing were made available, it would not solve the problems of the mentally ill. In a final article, reprinted from *America*, Mickey Leland, a Democratic congressman from Texas, explains that he has introduced the Homeless Persons' Survival Act in the House, which would provide for the multiple needs of the homeless. It would provide mental health assistance, nutrition, and access to federal benefit programs. It is important to note, however, that his bill to alleviate the suffering of the homeless was killed in committee before reaching the floor of the House.

SINKING INTO HOMELESSNESS[1]

Hunger and homelessness are haunting the president these days. The public doesn't seem to buy the findings of his hunger task force, namely that it was unable to "substantiate allegations of rampant hunger." And on January 31 he referred to the "people who are sleeping on the grates" as "the homeless who are homeless, you might say, by choice." Yet two months later, he personally intervened to postpone the closing of a large shelter in a federally-owned building in Washington—a shelter that hundreds of people seem to have chosen as preferable to the grates. It is possible, of course, that the president was uncomfortable with *his* choice, since the Community for Creative Nonviolence, which operated the emergency refuge, had planned a protest march that would have brought the issue up to the White House gates.

[1]Reprint of an article by Marjorie Hope and James Young, who teach sociology at Wilmington College in Ohio. Reprinted by permission from *Commonweal*, V. 111: 368–71. Je. 15, '84.

Homelessness has become an election-year issue. Clearly, the fact that some two million Americans are roofless represents only the tip of the iceberg; it is less a problem in itself than a symptom of deeper, ongoing problems. Although Mr. Reagan would hardly agree, it is a symptom of the bankruptcy of our militarized economic system.

Homelessness baffles the public. If official unemployment (i.e., all civilian workers) is down to 8,772,000, a "mere" 7.8 percent (a figure which excludes the involuntarily underemployed and those who have given up looking for work), why does this phenomenon persist? Whay are there so many more undomiciled people in 1984 than in 1975, when the recession of the 1970s hit its worst point?

Let's compare the two years in terms of the four major causes of homelessness: unemployment, displacement from housing, deinstitutionalization of the mentally ill, and inadequacy of social benefits.

In 1975 official unemployment was higher: 8.5 percent. On the other hand, according to the Center on Budget and Policy Priorities, in that year 78 percent of the jobless enjoyed unemployment compensation; in March 1984 only 37 percent of the unemployed received it. (During the 1975 recession, unemployed workers were eligible for up to 65 weeks in benefits.) Today some 5,544,630 "officially" jobless and some 1,457,000 "discouraged" jobless, or a total of 7,001,630 Americans, are without work *and* without unemployment compensation. Never since the inception of the program have so many unemployed been left without benefits.

Back in 1975 black unemployment was 13.9 percent. Today it's 16.6. Black teenagers (whose unemployment rate is currently 46.7 percent) and blacks in their twenties are disproportionately represented among the chronically homeless. In nine years the economy has moved steadily in the direction of high technology, leaving behind those who are limited in education, work training, and job experience. The majority of the chronically homeless—however able-bodied they may be—are simply unemployable in today's economy.

Displacement from low-income housing is one of the most widespread factors in homelessness. According to the Legal Services Anti-Displacement Project, displacement afflicts some 2.5 million Americans each year; moreover, some half million lower-rent units are lost each year through conversion, abandonment, inflation, arson, and demolition.

Let us focus on one example. Condo conversion has been accelerating since 1975. Research shows that 86,000 units were converted between 1970 and 1975, and 280,000 more in the following four years. Most existing tenants cannot afford the converted units because monthly costs often double; HUD has estimated that about two-thirds of the occupants move out. Many such condos were single-room occupancy hotels (SROs), traditional havens for single persons on welfare. In New York City alone, SROs have declined from about 50,000 units in 1975 to less than 14,000 in 1982. On the Upper West Side of New York, where many of these SROs have succumbed to conversion, rents for one-bedroom apartments now bring $700 or more. Moreover, this process has been aided by tax abatements of up to 100 percent. This pattern is being repeated in all large metropolitan cities.

As homelessness was growing in the past decade, so, too, was the proportion of income that the poor pay for shelter. The 1977 *Annual Housing Survey* reveals that in 1976 more than 5.8 million households paid over half of their incomes for shelter, including utilities. In 1980 (the latest year for which figures are available) more than 7 million households were paying over fifty percent of their incomes for shelter.

Space limitations preclude exploring the complexities of housing problems. The point is that displacement is a symptom of the overall shortage of low-income housing. The basic reason for the shortage is that housing for people with low and moderate incomes is no longer "profitable" on its own, without government subsidy. In the past decade, but especially during the first three years of the Reagan administration, the role of the federal government in the housing field has been shrinking. Even Congress' recent approval of 100,000 newly subsidized units (a victory for housing advocates over President Reagan's initial opposition) represents only a third of what it provided annually in the 1970s.

In virtually every city across the country, Americans have become alternatively repelled, mystified, and intrigued by the spectacle of men and women living in cardboard boxes, or washing their laundry in public restrooms, or getting on their knees in buses and screaming.

The mentally ill constitute about a third of the homeless population. Most have been discharged from institutions to community-based "systems." Yet according to Dr. John Talbott, president-elect of the American Psychiatric Association, fewer than 25 percent of the patients discharged from the state mental hospitals remain in any mental health program. Many are not even referred to such a program. Others are merely given a bus token and directions to a welfare office.

Despite mounting public criticism, the release movement, which began in the mid-1950s, has continued. In 1975 there were 193,721 persons in state mental hospitals; by 1982 they numbered only 125,200.

Community-based treatment and special housing facilities have not grown commensurately. In 1963 mental health professionals set 2000 community-based centers as a national goal; only 717 have been created. In the years 1977–82 New York State spent $3.1 billion on mental hospitals and only $540 million on services in the community. The picture is similar in other states. Furthermore, growing numbers of the mentally disabled on the streets are young "chronics" who have *never* been in an institution.

For the mentally ill, sheer survival is even more important than treatment. Ten years ago thousands of them lived in SROs; now these hotels are disappearing. Three years ago many more were receiving social security disability or Supplemental Security Income (assistance for the indigent aged, blind, or disabled). During the first two years of the Reagan administration, more than 350,000 recipients—nearly a third of them psychiatrically impaired—were dropped from disability rolls. They included hallucinating ex-patients who had not worked for years, paranoid persons who had been fired from their jobs, and at least one incontinent man who wore seven pairs of pants at one time.

Under the Reagan administration, many recipients of assistance have been dropped from the rolls. Hundreds of thousands of "working poor" families receiving supplemental Aid to Families with Dependent Children (AFDC) have had their supplement (an incentive to work) cut down or cut out—despite the administration's avowed espousal of the work ethic. Supplementary Security Income has disqualified thousands of recipients. Daycare (which made it possible for poor mothers to work), Medicaid, and school feeding programs have been cut. True, overall outlays for food programs have increased, but only because of the increase in food prices and in the number applying. Over one million people have lost their eligibility for food stamps since 1981, and average food stamp benefits have been cut by 14 percent. Today the average stipend amounts to 47 cents per person per meal.

State governments were supposed to sew up any holes in the safety net. Instead, pressed by recession and cuts in federal aid, they *lowered* case welfare benefits by 17 percent between 1979 and 1983. In the largest state-federal public assistance program, AFDC, the average monthly stipend per person was $72.40 in 1975 (adjusted to 1967 figures, $44.89). In 1982 it was $102.80 (in 1967 values $35.67). Industry average weekly gross earnings, by comparison, rose from $190.79 in 1975 to $330.65 in 1982—nearly keeping up with inflation. Clearly, the poor have been the real victims. The National Low Income Housing Coalition points out that if we adjust for inflation, since 1980, for each dollar cut from low-income programs (housing and other programs) $4.15 has been added to the military budget and $2.26 to interest on the public debt.

Statistics are telling, but they don't tell the whole story. Bureaucrats in their office towers tend to assume that human needs are neatly segregated. Hence, if we have a food stamp program and some people are able to get along on that, then anyone who is hungry must be a poor manager, or a glutton, or a cheat. Or, in presidential confidant Edwin Meese's view, a lazylegs who finds standing in a line for food "easier than paying for it."

Real life isn't like that. Unemployment, lack of low-income, housing, eroding welfare benefits, and lack of resources for the mentally disabled often converge to produce homelessness. And in real life, hunger and homelessness are two dimensions of the same problem. Let's look at a real case—in Washington, the president's own backyard.

Bill (a few details of Bill's life have been altered to conceal his identity; the figures and circumstances are nevertheless real) is twenty-five, unemployed, black, and mentally ill although he has never been hospitalized. He has an engaging smile and a playful manner; he likes to play hopscotch with imaginary companions.

For nearly a year Bill received General Public Assistance, $189 a month. To qualify for this he had to be judged temporarily disabled by District of Columbia doctors. (Doctors for the Supplemental Security Income program, which would have paid him up to $304 a month, turned him down as not sufficiently disabled.) For a run-down hotel room Bill paid $50 a week, leaving him with less than nothing to pay for all other expenses except those covered by food stamps and a medical card—i.e., clothing, transportation, non-prescription medications, tobacco, repairs, telephone calls, laundry, soap, toilet paper, and the like. How was he to survive? Bill had little choice. Sometimes he hustled; other men on the street persuaded him to be a runner in the numbers game. Sometimes he sold his food stamps—at about half their net worth. Since this left him quite hungry, he spent the last half of each month standing in line—often for one or two hours, sometimes in rain or snow—for a bowl of soup or spaghetti, dry bread, coffee, or Kool-Aid, and perhaps an apple. Some weeks he could not afford to pay the rent; then he was homeless and hungry.

Recently the D.C. doctors determined that because Bill had failed to fill out recertification papers that had come to him in the mail—papers that mystified and frightened him—he was no longer qualified as disabled. In D.C. an unemployed but "able-bodied" person is eligible for food stamps and some medical aid, but no cash assistance whatsoever. Today Bill lives on zero income—hustling when he can, eating where he can, alternating between sleeping on park benches and bedding down in barn-like public shelters. He has not taken his psychotropic medications in months, for no one is supervising them. He has lost weight, and developed a chronic cough and ulcerated legs.

As hunger and homelessness take on stronger dimensions in this election year, there is growing talk of solutions—short-term ones. The food stamp program can be expanded. City and state governments, as well as the Federal Emergency Management Administration and the Department of Housing and Urban Development, can provide more assistance for emergency shelters. Churches can make more pleas for funds, material, and volunteers.

Some advocates and workers in the field, notably those who belong to the National Coalition for the Homeless, are pushing for a three-tiered approach: basic emergency shelter; transitional accommodations where clients would receive intensive help in obtaining social and health services; and permanent housing (which can include, for the chronically mentally disabled, supportive residences where services are built into structures of everyday life).

In all three tiers of housing, religious groups have had the most humane—and most economical—approach. As one worker put it: "The church brings a compassionate, caring dimension that you don't find in big bureaucratic city-run shelters." The churches have also pioneered with new efforts. For example, Saint Francis Residence in New York offers its mentally disabled residents a variety of social services, comparative privacy, and opportunities to work out long-range individualized plans. Yet even Saint Francis cannot exist without considerable government support.

Almost no politicians are talking about preventive measures. Yet the homeless promise to be a long-term problem.

While those of the "new poor" whose jobs have not disappeared forever may be reabsorbed into the economy, the chronically homeless form a new class, or underclass. They are here to stay, unless Americans change their basic social philosophy from making it up by their bootstraps to one based on fair shares.

We should hardly be surprised by the number who have been sinking into homelessness during the last decade. It was predictable. In the past five years growing numbers of critics have pointed out that decarcerating mental patients into an uncoordinated, ill-funded community-based "system" was not working. For years we have talked anxiously about technological unemployment, yet never has government provided meaningful training or jobs programs, as many European nations have done. As for housing, clearly only the federal government can finance low-income housing on the scale needed. Yet the National Low Income Housing Coalition points out that only 19 percent of the renter households with incomes below $3,000 lived in subsidized units in 1980. Less than one American household in sixteen is living in such units. This is the lowest proportion among the so-called civilized countries.

Although most European countries have been struggling with high inflation and high unemployment, they do provide social supports. For example, in 1982 unemployment reached nearly 14 percent in Britain, yet few families were known to have been turned out of their homes or to have had to sell their possessions. (The government owns 60 percent of the rental housing stock, which makes eviction more unlikely, and also assures a more manageable waiting list.) In the same year, jobless Americans who did receive compensation got only an average of 63 percent of previous earnings; in West European countries the average was 85 percent. Family allowances have never been adopted here. The United States has the distinction of being the only industrialized country in the world without such allowances; sixty-one others, including many that are poor, find this an effective way to help keep families together and off welfare rolls. Because all European countries have some form of national health care, unemployed persons have not had to choose between food, shelter, and medical treatment, as thousands have had to do here. Moreover, deinstitutionalization has been carried at a slower, more controlled pace. It is no coincidence that in European countries, where real safety nets persist even in hard times, homelessness is a comparatively rare phenomenon.

Emergency shelters and breadlines are not the answer to homelessness in the richest and most powerful country in the world. We do have three major choices. We can decide that the homeless are redundant, non-productive casualties of today's society, and simply write them off or hope against hope that somehow the overburdened churches will fill the gap. We can, if we consider them to be nonproductive, provide supportive services and some sort of guaranteed annual income. Or, if we still believe in liberty and justice for all, government, churches, and individuals can make concerted efforts to *prevent* homelessness.

"IS THE NEXT STEP PENN STATION?"[2]

One rainy morning Dorothy Lykes, not knowing where else to turn, telephoned the Gray Panther office in New York City. Roger Sanjek tells the story in his report on "Federal Housing Programs and Their Impact on Homelessness" (1982):

"Mrs. Lykes was 78, terminally ill with cancer and weighed 70 pounds. Her husband was in the hospital, also terminally ill. Most of their Social Security was going for his hospital bills. The city had taken possession of their Bronx home, which they bought in

[2]Reprint of an article by Richard J. Margolis, freelance writer. Reprinted with permission of *The New Leader*, February 10, 1986. Copyright © 1986 by the American Labor Conference on International Affairs, Inc.

the 1950s, because they could not pay the property taxes. Nor could they pay the $300 a month rent the city was asking from them for living in their own home. Mrs. Lykes asked: 'Is the next step for me to move to Penn Station?'"

It was not so idle a fear. Increasingly now, our older citizens are being forced to move out of their single rooms, their rented apartments, even their own homes—places and neighborhoods they have lived in for generations. And in more cases than is generally recognized these refugees have no place to go. To the pain of relinquishment is thus added the nightmare of homelessness.

Nor was Mrs. Lykes' reference to Penn Station at all farfetched, as the notebooks of Ellen Baxter and Kim Hopper make clear (*Private Lives, Public Spaces*, 1981): "Penn Station: . . . an elderly black woman carrying three bags was sobbing and wincing each time she took a step on her extremely swollen leg. . . . For the past nine years she had worked for a couple as a live-in domestic on the East Side. The lady of the house recently became ill and was placed in a nursing home. . . . They no longer can afford to pay her because of hospital costs."

People on Social Security or Supplemental Security Income (SSI) can find themselves left out in the cold, too—eloquent testimony to the weakness of our old-age pension system. Here are Baxter and Hopper again: "Subway entrance: An impeccably dressed, small-framed woman in her late 60s stood quietly in the entranceway at 2 A.M. . . . She had 'no place to go nights.' She said that . . . with rents so high she couldn't afford both a place to stay and food to eat. She picks up a Social Security check at the bank every month but it is barely enough to get by on."

The exact total of homeless Americans remains in dispute. A 1984 Housing and Urban Development (HUD) study placed it at 350,000, but few believed so low a figure. "I think we should just dismiss the HUD report and go on," snapped Congresswoman Rose Oakar (D-Ohio), "because it is so absurd, why even relate to it?" The Community for Creative Non-Violence (CCNV), a Washington-based organization that has spearheaded the drive for more shelters nationwide, claims the total is closer to 3 million, and growing every year.

Whatever their number, a surprising proportion belongs to the ranks of the aged. The New York Coalition for the Homeless reports that in the Northeast states it has studied, elderly people make up about 30 per cent of the unhoused. Mary Ellen Hombs and Mitch Snyder note in their CCNV analysis that those who "populate our city streets" are mainly "the old, the sick, the mentally ill, the unemployed, the disabled, the displaced and the disenfranchised. . . . " Sometimes a single individual will embody all seven characteristics.

Like the rest of our society, street people have developed a hierarchy of sorts, and the elderly are always on the bottom. They are easy prey to predators and pestilences. To cite a single instance, doctors at the Los Angeles County Medical Center see as many as 125 hypothermia cases each year, and most of the afflicted are aged and homeless. "Hypothermia" means reduced core-body temperature, which is caused by undue exposure to the cold. It can be fatal. Among the most vulnerable elderly, states Dr. William Clem of Los Angeles, an authority on the subject, "exposure to temperatures of even 50 degrees Fahrenheit, particularly . . . in combination with . . . dampness, can result in hypothermia."

Nor can the municipal and charitable shelters any longer shield their elderly supplicants. A 1984 Gray Panthers' survey, called "Crowded Out," observes: "As the epidemic of homelessness sweeps younger and stronger men and women into the city's shelter system, the elderly homeless . . . are being driven out by sheer fright. Massive human warehouses cannot protect the frail. . . . "

Often it is difficult to distinguish the homeless from everyone else. Baxter and Hopper found that "Their presence during late night hours when commuters have gone home and stores have closed . . . is the only telling sign. After midnight is a prime time for research."

Hombs and Snyder have placed special emphasis on the invisibility of the elderly, which makes them all the easier to discount: "Thus, the older woman next to you on the bus may be going nowhere in particular, riding only to keep warm or dry or seated. . . . In the world of the streets, invisibility equals access, and those who can pass unnoticed into public places . . . suffer less abuse and harassment. . . . Consequently, one can find homeless people who sleep sitting up to prevent their clothing from being wrinkled. . . . "

The anxiety to escape public notice has its ironic parallel in the attitude of Federal officials. HUD's absurdly low estimate of the total number of street people, and Ronald Reagan's widely quoted opinion that most of them are "homeless by choice," both seem calculated to persuade the rest of us that we live in the best of all possible worlds, where there are no victims to be found other than self-chosen ones.

The aged homeless, in particular, have been generously doused with vanishing cream. Carol Bauer, a HUD functionary, assured a Congressional committee, for example, that "our current programs are adequate to provide a coordinated package of housing choices designed to prevent the elderly from entering the homeless category." (Bauer's title would have delighted Nikolai Gogol. She is Executive Assistant to the Deputy Assistant Secretary for Policy, Financial Management and Administration.)

In fact, the range of housing choices available to the poor of all ages has been steadily shrinking for the better part of two decades, thanks mainly to intensive redevelopment of low-income neighborhoods. During the 1970s, to cite some discouraging statistics compiled by HUD's Low Income Housing Information Service, the number of moderate-rental units nationwide fell from an estimated 5.1 million to 1.2 million. At the same time, median rents for low-income households rose by 148 per cent, from $72 to $179 a month. At the higher rent a family with an annual income of $3,000 is left only $72 each month to meet other expenses.

"The bottom line," says Cushing N. Dolbeare, founder of the National Low Income Housing Coalition, "is that there are 4 million more renter households with incomes below $7,000 than there are units renting for $146 per month or less, including utilities, which is what a household with a $7,000 income can afford to pay [one-fourth of its income]."

Displacement, in short, has been one major consequence of gentrification. Roberta Youmans, an attorney with the National Housing Law Project, has estimated that 2.5 million households are displaced each year, "some through publicly or privately financed redevelopment, others through abandonment." If older residents have suffered disproportionately, it may be because they frequently occupy precisely those sites deemed ripest for demolition.

Single room occupancy hotels are a case in point. "The majority of SRO tenants," Youmans notes, "are elderly and they represent the poorest of the poor. . . . Yet this valuable, often preferred type of housing is disappearing in record numbers." She goes on to offer some telling examples: "In San Francisco, 4,000 SRO units were demolished to make way for a convention center as part of the Federally funded Yerba Buena urban renewal project. In Denver, the Skyline Urban Renewal project caused a large loss of SROs. Since 1960 Seattle has lost one half of its downtown housing stock, including SROs. Portland lost 1,055 [SROs] since 1970 and New York City is close to losing its entire stock. Chicago has lost 3,000 SROs in the last decade, whereas in Hartford the last SRO has just been sold."

Lessons from all this are not hard to draw. They have less to do with our shelter programs, inadequate as these have been, than with our development programs, which must bear much of the blame for the homelessness epidemic. Especially as regards the aged poor—the group least able to withstand the cruel exactions of the private housing market—our public policies have strayed disastrously wide of the mark. The upshot has been not only widespread homelessness but equally widespread neglect of dwellings still occupied by older and poorer Americans. A recent University of Michigan study places the number of substandard dwelling units occupied by older Americans at 1.3 million, and predicts that by the year 2000 it will have increased to nearly 2 million.

It seems clear that the nation will continue to be haunted by homelessness so long as it fails to provide adequate, affordable housing for the poor of all ages. Every shack and tenement is an invitation to social catastrophe; every slum-dweller is a candidate for the streets.

THE HOMELESSNESS PROBLEM[3]

More Americans were homeless last winter than at any time since the Great Depression. Estimates of the size of the vagrant

[3]Reprint of an article by Ellen L. Bassuk, sociologist and author. Reprinted with permission from *Scientific American*, July 1984. Copyright © 1984 by Scientific American, Inc. All rights reserved.

population vary widely. The National Coalition for the Homeless puts the figure at 2.5 million for 1983, an increase of 500,000 over the preceding year. The Federal Department of Housing and Urban Development (HUD) estimates that only 250,000 to 350,000 are homeless nationwide. Whatever the number is, everyone agrees it is growing.

Particularly in the past five years government officials and private groups in cities around the country have responded by opening emergency shelters to try to meet the immediate needs of the homeless. Beds in these shelters fill as soon as they become available, and still only a fraction of those in need are provided for. Some of the rest seek temporary refuge elsewhere, for example in hospitals, but most probably fend for themselves on the streets, huddling in doorways or over subway ventilation grates. When the weather turns cold, some die.

At night in New York City 18 public shelters house some of the thousands of men and women who roam the streets during the day; 16 of these shelters did not exist before 1980. Private groups in New York have also stepped up their efforts. In 1982, 10 churches offered a total of 113 beds to homeless people; by the end of 1983, 172 churches and synagogues were providing a total of 650 beds in 60 shelters. In Boston two large shelters recently doubled their capacity. Nevertheless, on a snowy night in January, Boston's largest shelter, the Pine Street Inn, reported a record number of "guests": the 350 beds were filled, as always, and 267 people crowded onto the Inn's bare cement floors.

Who are these people? Unfortunately there are no reliable national data on the homeless, even though they have always been numerous in American cities. Anecdotal evidence suggests that in the decades before 1970 most of the homeless were unattached, middle-aged, alcoholic men—the denizens of Skid Row. Since about 1970 the population appears to have been getting progressively younger. Moreover, the sparse literature on the subject and my own experience as a psychiatrist working with homeless people in Boston lead me to believe a more important change has taken place: an increasing number—I would say a large majority—of the homeless suffer from mental illness, ranging from schizophrenia to severe personality disorders.

At a time when the accepted solution to the homelessness problem is to establish more shelters, this finding has disturbing implications. Shelters are invaluable: they save lives. The trouble is that many shelters do little more, and the mentally ill need more than just a meal and protection from the elements. Those whose disorders are treatable or at least manageable require appropriate psychiatric care, which they do not get at shelters. The chronically disabled people who will never be able to care for themselves deserve better than to spend their lives begging on the streets and sleeping on army cots in gymnasiums. Shelters have been saddled with the impossible task of replacing not only the almshouses of the past but also the large state mental institutions. At this task they must inevitably fail, and thus American society has failed in its moral responsibility to care for its weakest members.

The statement that a majority of the homeless are mentally ill does not in itself explain why their number is growing or why a particular individual joins their ranks. Without reliable data it is difficult to answer the first question, but several factors may have contributed to the recent swelling of the homeless population. The most obvious one is the recession. Unemployment reached a peak of 10.7 percent in November, 1982, its highest level since the 1930's. Some of those who lost their jobs and incomes undoubtedly lost their homes as well.

The effects of unemployment are intensified by another problem: the dearth of low-cost housing. According to an analysis of the Federal Government's Annual Housing Survey by the Low Income Housing Information Service, the number of renter households with incomes below $3,000 per year dropped by about 46 percent, from 5.8 to 2.7 million, between 1970 and 1980; at the same time, however, the number of rental units available to these households at 30 percent of their income fell by 70 percent, from an estimated 5.1 to about 1.2 million (excluding dwellings for which no cash rent was paid). As the "housing gap" widened, the median rent paid by households in the lowest income bracket rose from $72 a month in 1970 to $179 a month in 1980. That works out to 72 percent of an annual income of $3,000 and leaves $71 a month to cover all other household needs. A family devoting such a large fraction of its income to rent is in a precarious position: it may easily be dislodged by a drop in its income or by a further rise in its expenses. Unemployment and the lack of low-cost housing help to account for the increasing number of homeless families (as opposed to individuals), which once were rare.

Recent cuts in government benefit payments may also have thrown some people onto the streets, although the evidence is inferential. One of the Federal Government's most controversial measures in this area has been its effort to reform the Social Security Disability Insurance program, which in 1983 provided monthly benefits to a total of 3.8 million disabled workers and their dependents. To receive payments a worker must be physically or mentally unable to perform any kind of "substantial gainful work" for which he is qualified, regardless of whether such work is available where he lives. Following a report by the General Accounting Office that as many as 20 percent of the beneficiaries might be ineligible under the law, the Reagan Administration launched a "crackdown on ineligibility" in March, 1981. Between 150,000 and 200,000 people lost their benefits before the Administration halted its review of the beneficiary rolls in April, 1984, amid charges that truly disabled people, including some who were too mentally disabled to respond to termination notices, had been stricken from the rolls. Again, a lack of data makes it impossible to draw definite conclusions, but it seems not unreasonable to infer that the loss of disability benefits reduced some people to not being able to pay for their housing.

Far more important, however, in its impact on the homeless population has been the long-term change in the national policy for dealing with the mentally ill. A little more than 20 years ago state and county mental institutions began releasing large numbers of patients, many of whom suffered from severe illnesses. The "deinstitutionalization" movement followed the widespread introduction in the 1950's of psychoactive drugs, which seemed to offer the possibility of rehabilitating psychotic people within a community setting, under better living conditions and with greater respect for their civil rights. It was also thought the "community mental health" approach would be cheaper than operating large state hospitals. The movement was launched in 1963 when Congress passed a law promising Federal funding for the construction of community mental health centers.

Deinstitutionalization was a well-intentioned and perhaps even enlightened reform, but it has not proceeded according to the original plan. The first step has been accomplished: the patient population at state and county mental hospitals is now less than one-fourth of its 1955 peak level of 559,000. By and large, however, the various levels of government have not taken the second step: they have not provided enough places, such as halfway houses or group homes, for discharged patients to go. Other factors contributing to the problems of the system include the fact that fewer than half of the community mental health centers needed to cover the entire U.S. population have been built; moreover, existing centers often do not coordinate their activities with those of the institutions that are discharging their patients.

The inadequacy of the care available to deinstitutionalized patients is suggested by the large increases since the early 1960's in the rate of admissions to state mental hospitals and by the fact that a growing majority of admitted patients have been hospitalized before. The drop in the resident population of the institutions is accounted for by shorter average stays. Younger ill people who might have been institutionalized 15 years ago now receive only brief and episodic care; one major reason is that the courts have decided only those among the mentally ill who are dangerous to themselves or to others may be committed involuntarily. In the absence of alternatives to the institutions, respect for the civil rights of the disturbed sometimes conflicts with the goal of providing them with humane treatment and asylum. Chronically disturbed people are sent out into the community, often to empty lives in single-room-occupancy hotels and Skid Row rooming houses. With the growing unavailability of even these housing options many of the people end up on the streets.

Thus it should not be surprising to find that a significant fraction of shelter residents are mentally ill. In fact, a clinical study I designed and implemented last year found at a shelter in Boston a 90 percent incidence of diagnosable mental illness: psychoses, chronic alcoholism and character disorders. The shelter selected for the study, which was under the direction of Alison Lauriat of the Massachusetts Association for Mental Health and Paul McGerigle of the United Community Planning Corporation, was considered demographically representative of Boston-area shelters.

The demographic data are themselves interesting. Men outnumbered women by four to one, although the number of women at Boston shelters seems to be increasing. The median age was 34 and apparently decreasing. One-third of the guests were either recent arrivals or only occasional users of the shelter, whereas the other two-thirds had been staying in shelters for more than six months. Some 20 percent had been on the streets and in shelters for more than two years.

My colleagues (eight psychiatrists, psychologists and social workers) and I interviewed 78 guests at the shelter over the course of five nights. We diagnosed 40 percent as suffering from some form of psychosis: a generic term for major mental illnesses whose victims have difficulty distinguishing external reality from their own thoughts and feelings. The psychoses include some manic and depressive states and some organic brain syndromes, but most of the psychotics at the shelter wwere schizophrenic. Often subject to delusions and hallucinations, they have trouble coping with the demands of daily life.

A 42-year-old man, at one time a talented artist, in an extreme example. When he was 24, he killed his wife with a baseball bat because she had been unfaithful to him. At the time he believed he was Raskolnikoff, the protagonist in Dostoevski's *Crime and Punishment.* The court psychiatrist diagnosed him as schizophrenic, and he was hospitalized in an institution for the criminally insane for the next 16 years. Since being discharged more than two years ago, he has lived both in shelters and on the streets; not long before we saw him he had been arrested for trespassing in a cemetery, where he was living in a tomb he has hollowed out. He says he received messages from spirits who speak to him through spiders.

The story of an 18-year-old shelter guest is less striking but no less tragic. Until he became psychotic he was enrolled in an Ivy League college. He was hospitalized briefly in a state institution, where he was given antipsychotic medication, but when we saw him, he was receiving no treatment. For a while after his discharge his mother cared for him; eventually, however, she became too depressed to continue. Frightened and too confused to care for himself, he now wanders the streets by day, muttering incoherently and responding to voices he alone hears. At night he goes to a shelter where the staff are too busy feeding and clothing people to devote themselves to individual problems.

Many of the people we interviewed—we estimated 29 percent—were chronic alcoholics. One 33-year-old man had lived on the streets of Boston for 20 years and like many homeless alcoholics had been in and out of hospitals, detoxification centers and various treatment programs. In the past year he had made several suicide attempts, and he had recently been treated for pulmonary tuberculosis. (About 45 percent of the study group reported serious physical problems, including heart disease and cancer, in addition to their psychological difficulties.) Finally, about 21 percent suffered from personality disorders that made it hard for them to form and maintain relationships or to hold a job.

Chronic mental illness, even when it is severe enough to impair the ability to function in society, does not by itself cause homelessness, any more than unemployment does. For the great majority of shelter guests lack of a home is symptomatic of total disconnection from supportive people and institutions. Consider for a moment what would happen if a crisis were to strike your life—if you were to lose your job, say, or contract a serious illness. Most likely you are surrounded by family and friends, by co-workers and even by professional caretakers at various social agencies whose help you could call on to prevent a downward slide. You are insured, both in the literal sense of having coverage against financial loss and in the figurative sense of having a reliable support network.

To talk with homeless people is to be struck by how alone most of them are. The isolation is most severe for the mentally ill. Family and friends grow exhausted or lack the ability to help; overburdened social workers may be less responsive; the homeless themselves may be unwilling or unable to communicate their needs and to make use of the support available. Some 74 percent of the shelter residents we interviewed said they had no family relationships, and 73 percent said they had no friends, even within the shelter community. Those who had been hospitalized before for psychiatric reasons (about one-third of the group) reported even less social contact: more than 90 percent of them had neither friends nor family. About 40 percent of all the guests said they had no relationship with anyone or with any social institution; although only 6 percent worked steadily, only 22 percent received any financial assistance.

There is usually no single, simple reason for an individual's becoming homeless; rather, homelessness is often the final stage in a lifelong series of crises and missed opportunities, the culmination of a gradual disengagement from supportive relationships and institutions. A final example illustrates the point. A 45-year-old man whom I shall call Johnny M. has lived on the streets and in the shelters of Boston for four years. The youngest of four siblings in a lower-middle-class family, Johnny spent most of his adolescent years in an institution for the mentally retarded. He remembers washing dishes, going to classes and looking forward to the visits of his mother and older sister. When he turned 16, he moved back home and spent time watching television and puttering in the garden. Ten years later his older sister died suddenly and Johnny had a "nervous breakdown." He became terrified of dying, he cried constantly and his thoughts became confused. Because he was unable to care for himself, he was involuntarily committed to a state hospital, where he remained for the next eight years. He became very attached to a social worker whom he saw twice a week for therapy.

Although the hospital had become Johnny's home, he was discharged at the height of deinstitutionalization into a single-room-occupancy hotel. His father had died, his mother was in a nursing home and neither his remaining sister nor his brother could afford to support him. Within six months he had lost contact with the hospital. Johnny was forced out of the hotel when it was converted into condominiums; unable to find a room he could afford, he roamed the streets for several months until an elderly woman and her daughter took him into their rooming house.

When the daughter died unexpectedly of a stroke, Johnny became depressed, thought the other residents were trying to harm him and grew increasingly belligerent. His landlady evicted him. Without resources or supports and with an incipient psychosis, he ended up homeless. Resigned to street life, he now spends his days walking endlessly, foraging in dumpsters. Occasionally he collects bottles, sells his blood for transfusion or takes part in medical experiments to make pocket money. Itching from lice, wearing tattered clothes and suffering from cellulitis of one leg, he feels lucky that he can depend on an evening meal at the shelter and that on most nights he has access to a bed.

Shelters help to keep Johnny M. and his companions in misfortune alive. That is a shelter's function: to provide food, clothing and a bed. At a typical shelter guests line up outside until the doors open in the early evening. A security guard checks each person for alcohol, drugs and weapons. New guests are also checked for lice. At some shelters volunteers cook hot meals; at others dinner consists of soup, sandwiches and coffee. Some guests spend the evening socializing and playing cards, but most are too weary or too detached and go directly to sleep. The dormitory is typically a barren auditorium-size room with rows of cots or beds and one or two cribs. Sometimes groups of six or more beds are separated by partitions. Shelter guests usually have few opportunities to wash during the day, and so at night the bathrooms at the shelter are generally overcrowded. By 10:00 P.M. the lights are turned out, and the next morning the guests are awakened early, given coffee and a doughnut and sent out, even if the temperature is below zero.

The atmosphere in a shelter is sometimes volatile, and occasionally violent fights erupt that have to be broken up by the staff or the police. On the other hand, the anonymity and invisibility fostered by shelters is comforting to many of the guests, who spend their days as highly visible social outcasts. Shelter providers try to treat their guests with dignity and respect, asking no questions and attaching no strings to the help they offer.

Do they offer enough? In my view they do not. Shelters would be the appropriate solution if the homeless were simply the victims of unemployment, or of disasters such as floods or fires. Although these factors undoubtedly contribute to the problem, the overriding fact about the homeless is that most are mentally disabled and isolated from the support that might help to reintegrate them into society. Moreover, many are chronically, permanently ill and will never be able to live independently.

Although various innovative model programs exist, including one sponsored by St. Vincent's Hospital in New York City, shelters as a rule offer only minimal medical, psychological and social services. They are generally understaffed and have few personnel specifically trained to care for the severely disabled. Because they are open only at night, they cannot offer the continuing support and supervision that many chronically ill people need. People whose condition might improve with properly supervised treatment (for example the 18-year-old student I mentioned above) do not get it at the shelters. And it hardly needs saying that shelters are not a humane solution to the problem of providing a place to live for those who suffer from permanent mental disabilities.

The precise extent to which mental illnesses are prevalent among the homeless remains a matter of controversy. Recent clinical studies at shelters in Los Angeles, New York and Philadel-

phia support my contention that a majority of the homeless suffer
from psychiatric disorders, but other estimates have put the incidence of mental illness among shelter populations as low as 20
percent. All these studies, including our own, have been largely
descriptive and have been plagued by methodological problems.
Differences in results can be attributed to the different theoreti-
cal biases of the various investigators, to the use of different stan-
dardized scales as the basis for psychiatric evaluation and most of
all to the difficulty of obtaining a representative sample of a constantly shifting population. In addition, there is no reason to expect the characteristics of the homeless population to be constant
throughout the country when mental health policies and economic conditions vary regionally.

The public debate on homelessness would undoubtedly be enlightened by more rigorous research into the causes of the problem. It can already be said, however, that at the very least a
significant fraction of the people who frequent shelters have
diagnosable mental disturbances. Public servants of all ideologies
have failed to recognize the implications of this fact. Many political conservatives seem to believe the Government has little obligation to care for the homeless; this attitude is perhaps best
exemplified by President Reagan's often quoted remark that "the
homeless are homeless, you might say, by choice." For political
liberals the plight of the homeless serves as ammunition in their
attack on the Administration's economic policies, but the solution
they tend to support is the expansion of emergency shelters: simply putting a temporary dressing on what has become a large, festering wound in the social body.

There is no mystery about the nature of a more appropriate
solution. Essentially it would call for carrying out the aborted
plans of the 1963 community mental health law by providing a
spectrum of housing options and related health-care and social
services for the mentally ill. These would entail living arrangements with varying degrees of supervision, from 24-hour care at
therapeutic residences for patients with severe psychoses to more
independent living at halfway houses for patients with less severe
disorders. Some patients would receive counseling and therapy
with the goal of rehabilitating them and even getting them jobs
in the community. The one major change needed in the community mental health program, however, is a greater recognition of

the limitations of psychiatry: given the current state of the art many chronically disturbed people simply cannot be rehabilitated, and the goal in these cases would be to provide the patient with comfortable and friendly asylum.

The community mental health movement failed primarily because the Federal and state governments never allocated the money needed to fulfill its promise. American society is currently trying to solve the problem cheaply, giving the mentally ill homeless at best emergency refuse and at worst no refuge at all. The question raised by the increasing number of homeless people is a very basic one: Are Americans willing to consign a broad class of disabled people to a life of degradation, or will they make the commitment to give such people the care they need? In a civilized society the answer should be clear.

DISTANCING THE HOMELESS[4]

It is commonly believed by many journalists and politicians that the homeless of America are, in large part, former patients of large mental hospitals who were deinstitutionalized in the 1970s—the consequence, it is sometimes said, of misguided liberal opinion which favored the treatment of such persons in community-based centers. It is argued that this policy, and the subsequent failure of society to build such centers or to provide them in sufficient number, is the primary cause of homelessness in the United States.

Those who work among the homeless do not find that explanation satisfactory. While conceding that a certain number of the homeless are, or have been, mentally unwell, they believe that, in the case of most unsheltered people, the primary reason is economic rather than clinical. The cause of homelessness, they say with disarming logic, is the lack of homes and of income with which to rent or acquire them.

They point to the loss of traditional jobs in industry (two million every year since 1980) and to the fact that half of those who

[4]Reprint of an article by Jonathan Kozol, author. Reprinted by permission from the *Yale Review*, pp. 153–67. Winter '88. Copyright © 1988 by Jonathan Kozol.

are laid off end up in work that pays a poverty-level wage. They point to the parallel growth of poverty in families with children, noting that children, who represent one quarter of our population, make up forty percent of the poor: since 1968, the number of children in poverty has grown by three million, while welfare benefits to families with children have declined by thirty-five percent.

And they note, too, that these developments have coincided with a time in which the shortage of low-income housing has intensified as the gentrification of our major cities has accelerated. Half a million units of low-income housing have been lost each year to condominium conversion as well as to arson, demolition, or abandonment. Between 1978 and 1980, median rents climbed thirty percent for people in the lowest income sector, driving many of these families into the streets. After 1980, rents rose at even faster rates. In Boston, between 1982 and 1984, over eighty percent of the housing units renting below three hundred dollars disappeared, while the number of units renting above six hundred dollars nearly tripled.

Hard numbers, in this instance, would appear to be of greater help than psychiatric labels in telling us why so many people become homeless. Eight million American families now pay half or more of their income for rent or a mortgage. Six million more, unable to pay rent at all, live doubled up with others. At the same time, federal support for low-income housing dropped from $30 billion (1980) to $9 billion (1986). Under Presidents Ford and Carter, five hundred thousand subsidized private housing units were constructed. By President Reagan's second term, the number had dropped to twenty-five thousand. "We're getting out of the housing business, period," said a deputy assistant secretary of the Department of Housing and Urban Development in 1985.

One year later, the *Washington Post* reported that the number of homeless families in Washington, D.C., had grown by five hundred percent over the previous twelve months. In New York City, the waiting list for public housing now contains two hundred thousand names. The waiting time is eighteen years.

Why, in the face of these statistics, are we impelled to find a psychiatric explanation for the growth of homelessness in the United States?

A misconception, once it is implanted in the popular imagination, is not easy to uproot, particularly when it serves a useful social role. The notion that the homeless are largely psychotics who belong in institutions, rather than victims of displacement at the hands of enterprising realtors, spares us from the need to offer realistic solutions to the fact of deep and widening extremes of wealth and poverty in the United States. It also enables us to tell ourselves that the despair of homeless people bears no intimate connection to the privileged existence we enjoy—when, for example, we rent or purchase one of those restored townhouses that once provided shelter for people now huddled in the street.

But there may be another reason to assign labels to the destitute. Terming economic victims "psychotic" or "disordered" helps to place them at a distance. It says that they aren't quite like us—and, more important, that we could not be like them. The plight of homeless families is a nightmare. It may not seem natural to try to banish human beings from our midst, but it *is* natural to try to banish nightmares from our minds.

So the rituals of clinical contamination proceed uninterrupted by the economic facts described above. Research that addresses homelessness as an *injustice* rather than as a medical *misfortune* does not win the funding of foundations. And the research which *is* funded, defining the narrowed borders of permissible debate, diverts our attention from the antecedent to the secondary cause of homelessness. Thus it is that perfectly ordinary women whom I know in New York City—people whose depression or anxiety is a realistic consequence of months and even years in crowded shelters or the streets—are interrogated by invasive research scholars in an effort to decode their poverty, to find clinical categories for their despair and terror, to identify the secret failing that lies hidden in their psyche.

Many pregnant women without homes are denied prenatal care because they constantly travel from one shelter to another. Many are anemic. Many are denied essential dietary supplements by recent federal cuts. As a consequence, some of their children do not live to see their second year of life. Do these mothers sometimes show signs of stress? Do they appear disorganized, depressed, disordered? Frequently. They are immobilized by pain, traumatized by fear. So it is no surprise that when researchers enter the scene to ask them how they "feel," the resulting reports tell us that the homeless are emotionally unwell. The reports do not tell us we have *made* these people ill. They do not tell us that illness is a natural response to intolerable conditions. Nor do they tell us of the strength and the resilience that so many of these people still retain despite the miseries they must endure. They set these men and women apart in capsules labeled "personality disorder" or "psychotic," where they no longer threaten our complacence.

I visited Haiti not many years ago, when the Duvalier family was still in power. If an American scholar were to have made a psychological study of the homeless families living in the streets of Port-au-Prince—sleeping amidst rotten garbage, bathing in open sewers—and if he were to return to the United States to tell us that the reasons for their destitution were "behavioral problems" or "a lack of mental health," we would be properly suspicious. Knowledgeable Haitians would not merely be suspicious. They would be enraged. Even to initiate such research when economic and political explanations present themselves so starkly would appear grotesque. It is no less so in the United States.

One of the more influential studies of this nature was carried out in 1985 by Ellen Bassuk, a psychiatrist at Harvard University. Drawing upon interviews with eighty homeless parents, Dr. Bassuk contends, according to the *Boston Globe*, that "90 percent [of these people] have problems other than housing and poverty that are so acute they would be unable to live successfully on their own." She also precludes the possibility that illness, where it does exist, may be provoked by destitution. "Our data," she writes, "suggest that mental illness tends to precede homelessness." She concedes that living in the streets can make a homeless person's mental illness worse; but she insists upon the fact of prior illness.

The Executive Director of the Massachusetts Commission on Children and Youth believes that Dr. Bassuk's estimate is far too high. The staff of Massachusetts Human Services Secretary Phillip Johnston believes the appropriate number is closer to ten percent.

In defending her research, Bassuk challenges such critics by claiming that they do not have data to refute her. This may be true. Advocates for the homeless do not receive funds to defend the sanity of the people they represent. In placing the burden of proof upon them, Dr. Bassuk has created an extraordinary dialectic: How does one prove that people aren't unwell? What home-less mother would consent to enter a procedure that might "prove" her mental health? What overburdened shelter operator would divert scarce funds to such an exercise? It is an unnatural, offensive, and dehumanizing challenge.

Dr. Bassuk's work, however, isn't the issue I want to raise here; the issue is the use or misuse of that work by critics of the poor. For example, in a widely syndicated essay published in 1986, the newspaper columnist Charles Krauthammer argued that the homeless are essentially a deranged segment of the popu-lation and that we must find the "political will" to isolate them from society. We must do this, he said, "whether they like it or not." Arguing even against the marginal benefits of homeless shelters, Krauthammer wrote: "There is a better alternative, however, though no one dares speak its name." Krauthammer dares: that better alternative, he said, is "asylum."

One of Mr. Krauthammer's colleagues at the *Washington Post*, the columnist George Will, perceives the homeless as a threat to public cleanliness and argues that they ought to be consigned to places where we need not see them. "It is," he says, "simply a mat-ter of public hygiene" to put them out of sight. Another journal-ist, Charles Murray, writing from the vantage point of a social Darwinist, recommends the restoration of the almshouses of the 1800s. "Granted Dickensian horror stories about almshouses," he begins, there were nonetheless "good almshouses"; he proposes "a good correctional 'halfway house'" as a proper shelter for a mother and child with no means of self-support.

In the face of such declarations, the voices of those who work with and know the poor are harder to hear.

Manhattan Borough President David Dinkins made the fol-lowing observation on the basis of a study commissioned in 1986: "No facts support the belief that addiction or behavioral prob-lems occur with more frequency in the homeless family popula-tion than in a similar socioeconomic population. Homeless families are not demographically different from other public as-sistance families when they enter the shelter system. . . . Family homelessness is typically a housing and income problem: the un-availability of affordable housing and the inadequacy of public as-sistance income."

In a "hypothetical world," write James Wright and Julie Lam of the University of Massachusetts, "where there were no

alcoholics, no drug addicts, no mentally ill, no deinstitutionalization, . . . indeed, no personal social pathologies at all, there
would still be a formidable homelessness problem, simply because
at this stage in American history, there is not enough low-income
housing" to accommodate the poor.

New York State's respected Commissioner of Social Services,
Cesar Perales, makes the point in fewer words: "Homelessness is
less and less a result of personal failure, and more and more is
caused by larger forces. There is no longer affordable housing in
New York City for people of poor and modest means."

Even the words of medical practitioners who care for homeless people have been curiously ignored. A study published by the
Massachusetts Medical Society, for instance, has noted that the
most frequent illnesses among a sample of the homeless population, after alcohol and drug use, are trauma (31 percent), upper
respiratory disorders (28 percent), limb disorders (19 percent),
mental illness (16 percent), skin diseases (15 percent), hypertension (14 percent), and neurological illnesses (12 percent). (Excluded from this tabulation are lead poisoning, malnutrition, acute
diarrhea, and other illnesses especially common among homeless
infants and small children.) Why, we may ask, of all these calami-
ties, does mental illness command so much political and press attention? The answer may be that the label of mental illness places
the destitute outside the sphere of ordinary life. It personalizes
an anguish that is public in its genesis; it individualizes a misery
that is both general in cause and general in application.

The rate of tuberculosis among the homeless is believed to be
ten times that of the general population. Asthma, I have learned
in countless interviews, is one of the most common causes of dis-
comfort in the shelters. Compulsive smoking, exacerbated by the
crowding and the tension, is more common in the shelters than
in any place that I have visited except prison. Infected and untreated sores, scabies, diarrhea, poorly set limbs, protruding el-
bows, awkwardly distorted wrists, bleeding gums, impacted teeth,
and other untreated dental problems are so common among children in the shelters that one rapidly forgets their presence. Hunger and emaciation are everywhere. Children as well as adults can
bring to mind the photographs of people found in camps for refugees of war in 1945. But these miseries bear no stigma, and mental illness does. It conveys a stigma in the Soviet Union. It conveys
a stigma in the United States. In both nations the label is used,

whether as a matter of deliberate policy or not, to isolate and treat as special cases those who, by deed or word or by sheer presence, represent a threat to national complacence. The two situations are obviously not identical, but they are enough alike to give Americans reason for concern.

Last summer, some twenty-eight thousand homeless people were afforded shelter by the city of New York. Of this number, twelve thousand were children and six thousand were parents living together in families. The average child was six years old, the average parent twenty-seven. A typical homeless family included a mother with two or three children, but in about one-fifth of these families two parents were present. Roughly ten thousand single persons, then, made up the remainder of the population of the city's shelters.

These proportions vary somewhat from one area of the nation to another. In all areas, however, families are the fastest-growing sector of the homeless population, and in the Northeast they are by far the largest sector already. In Massachusetts, three-fourths of the homeless now are families with children; in certain parts of Massachusetts—Attleboro and Northhampton, for example—the proportion reaches ninety percent. Two-thirds of the homeless children studied recently in Boston were less than five years old.

Of an estimated two to three million homeless people nationwide, about 500,000 are dependent children, according to Robert Hayes, counsel to the National Coalition for the Homeless. Including their parents, at least 750,000 homeless people in America are family members.

What is to be made, then, of the supposition that the homeless are primarily the former residents of mental hospitals, persons who were carelessly released during the 1970s? Many of them are, to be sure. Among the older men and women in the streets and shelters, as many as one-third (some believe as many as one-half) may be chronically disturbed, and a number of these people were deinstitutionalized during the 1970s. But in a city like New York, where nearly half the homeless are small children with an average age of six, to operate on the basis of such a supposition makes no sense. Their parents, with an average age of twenty-seven, are not likely to have been hospitalized in the 1970s, either.

Nor is it easy to assume, as was once the case, that single men—those who come closer to fitting the stereotype of the homeless vagrant, the drifting alcoholic of an earlier age—are the former residents of mental hospitals. The age of homeless men has dropped in recent years; many of them are only twenty-one to twenty-eight years old. Fifty percent of homeless men in New York City shelters in 1984 were there for the first time. Most had previously had homes and jobs. Many had never before needed public aid.

A frequently cited set of figures tells us that in 1955, the average daily census of nonfederal psychiatric institutions was 677,000, and that by 1984, the number had dropped to 151,000. Subtract the second number from the first, conventional logic tells us, and we have an explanation for the homelessness of half a million people. A closer look at the same numbers offers us a different lesson.

The sharpest decline in the average daily census of these institutions occurred prior to 1978, and the largest part of that decline, in fact, appeared at least a decade earlier. From 677,000 in 1955, the census dropped to 378,000 in 1972. The 1974 census was 307,000. In 1976 it was 230,000; in 1977 it was 211,000; and in 1978 it was 190,000. In no year since 1978 has the average daily census dropped by more than 9,000 persons, and in the six-year period from 1978 to 1984, the total decline was 39,000 persons. Compared with a decline of 300,000 from 1955 to 1972, and of nearly 200,000 more from 1972 to 1978, the number is small. But the years since 1980 are the period in which the present homeless crisis surfaced. Only since 1983 have homeless individuals overflowed the shelters.

If the large numbers of the homeless lived in hospitals before they reappeared in subway stations and in public shelters, we need to ask where they were and what they had been doing from 1972 to 1980. Were they living under bridges? Were they waiting out the decade in the basements of deserted buildings?

No. The bulk of those who had been psychiatric patients and were released from hospitals during the 1960s and early 1970s had been living in the meantime in low-income housing, many in skid-row hotels or boarding houses. Such housing—commonly known as SRO (single-room occupancy) units—was drastically diminished by the gentrification of our cities that began in 1970. Almost fifty percent of SRO housing was replaced by luxury apartments or by office buildings between 1970 and 1980, and the remaining units have been disappearing at even faster rates. As recently as 1986, after New York City had issued a prohibition against conversion of such housing, a well-known developer hired a demolition team to destroy a building in Times Square that had previously been home to indigent people. The demolition took place in the middle of the night. In order to avoid imprisonment, the developer was allowed to make a philanthropic gift to homeless people as a token of atonement. This incident, bizarre as it appears, remind us that the profit motive for displacement of the poor is very great in every major city. It also indicates a more realistic explanation for the growth of homelessness during the 1980s.

Even for those persons who are ill and were deinstitutionalized during the decades before 1980, the precipitating cause of homelessness in 1987 is not illness but loss of housing. SRO housing, unattractive as it may have been, offered low-cost sanctuaries for the homeless, providing a degree of safety and mutual support for those who lived within them. They were a demeaning version of the community health centers that society had promised; they were the de facto "halfway houses" of the 1970s. For these people too, then—at most half of the homeless single persons in America—the cause of homelessness is lack of housing.

A writer in the *New York Times* describes a homeless woman standing on a traffic island in Manhattan. "She was evicted from her small room in the hotel just across the street," and she is determined to get revenge. Until she does, "nothing will move her from that spot. . . . Her argumentativeness and her angry fixation on revenge, along with the apparent absence of hallucinations, mark her as a paranoid." Most physicians, I imagine, would be more reserved in passing judgment with so little evidence, but this author makes his diagnosis without hesitation. "The paranoids of the street," he says, "are among the most difficult to help."

Perhaps so. But does it depend on who is offering the help? Is anyone offering to help this woman get back her home? Is it crazy to seek vengeance for being thrown into the street? The absence of anger, some psychiatrists believe, might indicate much greater illness.

The same observer sees additional symptoms of pathology ("negative symptoms," he calls them) in the fact that many homeless persons demonstrate a "gross deterioration in their personal hygiene" and grooming, leading to "indifference" and "apathy." Having just identified one woman as unhealthy because she is so far from being "indifferent" as to seek revenge, he now sees apathy as evidence of illness; so consistency is not what we are looking for in this account. But how much less indifferent might the homeless be if those who decide their fate were less indifferent themselves? How might their grooming and hygiene be improved if they were permitted access to a public toilet?

In New York City, as in many cities, homeless people are denied the right to wash in public bathrooms, to store their few belongings in a public locker, or, in certain cases, to make use of public toilets altogether. Shaving, cleaning of clothes, and other forms of hygiene are prohibited in the men's room of Grand Central Station. The terminal's three hundred lockers, used in former times by homeless people to secure their goods, were removed in 1986 as "a threat to public safety," according to a study made by the New York City Council.

At one-thirty every morning, homeless people are ejected from the station. Many once attempted to take refuge on the ramp that leads to Forty-second Street because it was protected from the street by wooden doors and thus provided some degree of warmth. But the station management responded to this challenge in two ways. The ramp was mopped with a strong mixture of ammonia to produce a noxious smell, and when the people sleeping there brought cardboard boxes and newspapers to protect them from the fumes, the entrance doors were chained wide open. Temperatures dropped some nights to ten degrees. Having driven these people to the streets, city officials subsequently determined that their willingness to risk exposure to cold weather could be taken as further evidence of mental illness.

At Pennsylvannia Station in New York, homeless women are denied the use of toilets. Amtrak police come by and herd them off each hour on the hour. In June 1985, Amtrak officials issued this directive to police: "It is the policy of Amtrak to not allow the homeless and undesirables to remain. . . . Officers are encouraged to eject all undesirables. . . . Now is the time to train and educate them that their presence will not be tolerated as cold weather sets in." In an internal memo, according to CBS, an Amtrak official asked flatly: "Can't we get rid of this trash?"

I have spent many nights in conversation with the women who are huddled in the corridors and near the doorway of the public toilets in Penn Station. Many are young. Most are cogent. Few are dressed in the familiar rags suggested by the term *bag ladies*. Unable to bathe or use the toilets in the station, almost all are in conditions of intolerable physical distress. The sight of clusters of police officers, mostly male, guarding a toilet from use by homeless women speaks volumes about the public conscience of New York.

Where do these women defecate? How do they bathe? What will we do when, in her physical distress, a woman finally disrobes in public and begins to urinate right on the floor? "Gross deterioration," someone will call it, evidence of mental illness. In the course of an impromptu survey in the streets last September, Mayor Koch observed a homeless woman who had soiled her own clothes. Not only was the woman crazy, said the mayor, but those who differed with him on his diagnosis must be crazy, too. "I am the Number One social worker in this town—with sanity," said he.

It may be that this woman was psychotic, but the mayor's comment says a great deal more about his sense of revulsion and the moral climate of a decade in which words like these may be applauded than about her mental state.

A young man who had lost his job, then his family, then his home, all in the summer of 1986, spoke with me for several hours in Grand Central Station on the weekend following Thanksgiving. "A year ago," he said, "I never thought that somebody like me would end up in a shelter. Nothing you've ever undergone prepares you. You walk into the place [a shelter on the Bowery]—the smell of sweat and urine hits you like a wall. Unwashed bodies and the look of absolute despair on many, many faces there would make you think you were in Dante's Hell. . . . What you fear is that you will be here forever. You do not know if it is ever going to end. You think to yourself: It is a dream and I will awake. Sometimes I think: It's an experiment. They are watching you to find out how much you can take. . . . I was a pretty stable man. Now I tremble when I meet somebody in the ordinary world. I'm trembling right now. . . . For me, the loss of work and loss of wife had left me rocking. Then the welfare regulations hit me. I began to feel that I would be reduced to trash. . . . Half the people that I know are suffering from chest infections and sleep deprivation. The lack of sleep leaves you debilitated, shaky. You exaggerate your fears. If a psychiatrist came along he'd say that I was crazy. But I was an ordinary man. There was nothing wrong with me. I lost my kids. I lost my home. Now would you say that I was crazy if I told you I was feeling sad?"

"If the plight of homeless adults is the shame of America," writes Fred Hechinger in the *New York Times*, "the lives of homeless children are the nation's crime."

In November 1984, a fact already known to advocates for the homeless was given brief attention by the press. Homeless families, the *New York Times* reported, "mostly mothers and young children, have been sleeping on chairs, counters and floors of the city's emergency welfare offices." Reacting to such reports, the mayor declared: "This woman is sitting on a chair or on a floor. It is not because we didn't offer her a bed. We provide a shelter for every single person who knocks on our door." On the same day, however, the city reported that in the previous eleven weeks it had been unable to give shelter to 153 families, and in the subsequent year, 1985, the city later reported that about two thousand children slept in welfare offices because of lack of shelter space.

Some eight hundred homeless infants in New York City, reported the National Coalition for the Homeless, "routinely go without sufficient food, cribs, health care and diapers." The lives of these children "are put at risk," while "high-risk pregnant women" are repeatedly forced to sleep in unsafe "barracks shelters" or welfare offices called Emergency Assistance Units (EAUs). "Coalition monitors, making sporadic random checks, found eight women in their *ninth* month of pregnancy sleeping in EAUs. . . . In one instance, the Legal Aid Society was forced to go to court after a woman lost her child by miscarriage while lying on the floor of a communal bathroom in a shelter which the courts had already declared unfit to house pregnant women.

The coalition also reported numerous cases in which homeless mothers were obliged to choose between purchasing food or diapers for their infants. Federal guidelines issued in 1986 deepened the nutrition crisis faced by mothers in the welfare shelters by counting the high rent paid to the owners of these buildings as a part of family income, rendering their residents ineligible for food stamps. Families I interviewed who had received as much as $150 in food stamps monthly in June 1986 were cut back to $33 before Christmas.

"Now you're hearing all kinds of horror stories," said President Reagan, "about the people that are going to be thrown out in the snow to hunger and [to] die of cold and so forth. . . . We haven't cut a single budget." But in the four years leading up to 1985, according to the *New Republic*, Aid to Families with Dependent Children had been cut by $4.8 billion, child nutrition programs by $5.2 billion, food stamps by $6.8 billion. The federal government's authority to help low-income families with housing assistance was cut from $30 billion to $11 billion in Reagan's first term. In his fiscal 1986 budget, the president proposed to cut that by an additional ninety-five percent.

"If even one American child is forced to go to bed hungry at night," the president said on another occasion, "that is a national tragedy. We are too generous a people to allow this." But in the years since the president spoke these words, thousands of poor children in New York alone have gone to bed too sick to sleep and far too weak to rise the next morning to attend a public school. Thousands more have been unable to attend school at all because their homeless status compels them to move repeatedly from one temporary shelter to another. Even in the affluent suburbs outside New York City, hundreds of homeless children are obliged to ride as far as sixty miles twice a day in order to obtain an education in the public schools to which they were originally assigned before their families were displaced. Many of these children get to school too late to eat their breakfast; others are denied lunch at school because of federal cuts in feeding programs.

Many homeless children die—and others suffer brain damage—as a direct consequence of federal cutbacks in prenatal programs, maternal nutrition, and other feeding programs. The parents of one such child shared with me the story of the year in which their child was delivered, lived, and died. The child, weighing just over four pounds at birth, grew deaf and blind soon after, and for these reasons had to stay in the hospital for several months. When he was released on Christmas Eve of 1984, his mother and father had no home. He lived with his parents in the shelters, subways, streets, and welfare offices of New York City for four winter months, and was readmitted to the hospital in time to die in May 1985.

When we met and spoke the following year, the father told me that his wife had contemplated and even attempted suicide after the child's death, while he had entertained the thought of blowing up the welfare offices of New York City. I would tell him that to do so would be illegal and unwise. I would never tell him it was crazy.

"No one will be turned away," says the mayor of New York City, as hundreds of young mothers with their infants are turned from the doors of shelters season after season. That may sound to some like denial of reality. "Now you're hearing all these stories," says the President of the United States as he denies that anyone is cold or hungry or unhoused. On another occasion he says that the unsheltered "are homeless, you might say, by choice." That sounds every bit as self-deceiving.

The woman standing on the traffic island screaming for revenge until her room has been restored to her sounds relatively healthy by comparison. If three million homeless people did the same, and all at the same time, we might finally be forced to listen.

WHAT WE KNOW ABOUT THE HOMELESS[5]

In April 1986, Joyce Brown, a former New Jersey secretary (who also calls herself Billie Boggs), had a fight with her sisters with whom she was then living—and hopped on a bus to New York City. Something happened, and she ended up living near the hot-air vent of Swensen's restaurant at Second Avenue and 65th Street. She stayed there for a year, during which time her hair became tangled and matted; she insulted passers-by (especially black men, at whom she hurled racial epithets, although she herself is black), she burned the money she was given by sympathetic observers, and she relieved herself on the streets.

[5]Reprint of an article by Thomas J. Main, contributor of articles on homelessness to journals and presently at the Kennedy School of Government, Harvard University. Reprinted from *Commentary*, May 1988, by permission; all rights reserved.

Eventually she came to the attention of Project Help, a mobile psychiatric unit that monitors mentally-ill homeless people in lower Manhattan. Until recently, Project Help would not involuntarily transport a "street person" to a hospital unless he was an immediate danger to himself or others, and it interpreted that criterion strictly. When the Koch administration decided to apply a less strict interpretation—on the ground that living on the street is dangerous for the mentally ill even if not immediately so—Joyce Brown became the first person removed from the streets to Bellevue Hospital for psychiatric evaluation. She was diagnosed as a chronic schizophrenic, and the city held her in the hospital for twelve weeks, during which time her doctors attempted to obtain permission to have her medicated. But with the aid of Robert Levey, a lawyer from the New York Civil Liberties Union (NYCLU), Miss Brown not only avoided medication but successfully litigated for her release.

At this point, under the guidance of Levey and NYCLU president Norman Siegel, Miss Brown declared that she had been "appointed the homeless spokesperson." After shopping trips to Saks Fifth Avenue, Lord & Taylor, and Bloomingdale's, and dinner at Windows on the World, Miss Brown and her lawyers hit the lecture circuit. She spoke at New York University Law School and at the Cardoza Law School, she was interviewed on *60 Minutes* and *Donahue*, and she received half-a-dozen book and film proposals. Then, on February 18, 1988, Miss Brown, Levey, and Siegel all participated in the Harvard Law School Forum on "The Homeless Crisis: A Street View."

Levey (describing himself as a kind of "warm-up act . . . at a rock concert") spoke first. He wanted, he said, only to raise some questions, of which the key one was why our society had decided to make Joyce Brown into a celebrity. Was it because we wanted to sweep the problem under the rug by focusing on the fate of a single individual who had successfully challenged the city and gotten off the streets? This seemed an odd question and a still odder answer since it was precisely Levey and his colleagues at the NYCLU who had made Joyce Brown a celebrity; and the last thing in the world they had in mind was to sweep the problem of homelessness under the rug.

At length, Miss Brown herself spoke. Her speech was slurred, and she dropped a few lines from her prepared statement, but she certainly gave a creditable performance. The first part of her talk

sounded very much as if it had been stitched together out of slo-
gans made familiar by advocates for the homeless: homelessness
is caused by policies that help the rich and not the poor; it will be
solved only by building low-income public housing; etc. Of her
stay in the hospital she said, "I was a political prisoner."

Much more interesting was what Miss Brown called "my street
view" of homeless life. She said nothing about her history either
of heroin and cocaine abuse or of mental illness. According to
her, she had had only two problems in being homeless. The first
was police harassment. She claimed that at some point she had
been beaten with night sticks and kicked by several police officers. Project Help also had degraded and humiliated her and had
denied her what she called "my right to live on the street." Never,
she said, had Project Help been of any use, except to offer her
a sandwich.

Her second problem was that, obviously, she had been unable
to find an apartment, which was why she had ended up on the
streets. With no place of her own and since there are no public
toilets, she had to use the streets as a bathroom. She did not explain why she did not return to live with her sisters in New Jersey,
who had been looking for her during the year she was living on
the streets. Moreover, if she had been eager all along to come in-
doors, what was the point of fighting tooth and nail for the right
to live on the streets?

Joyce Brown's claim that she had been beaten by the police
also presented difficulties. She provided no details of the event.
When she was asked during the question period if she intended
to press charges against the police for their abuse, her response
was, "Everyone knows New York City cops are killers."

Another difficulty was her complaint of being degraded by
Project Help. It is true that for most of the time she was on the
streets, outreach workers only offered her sandwiches. The reason for this was that Miss Brown spurned all other help. Project
Help workers kept regular tabs on her, they coaxed her to accept
further services, such as transportation to washroom facilities and
a women's shelter. Miss Brown refused every time.

In other words, until the city decided to bring her inside
against her will, Project Help was following exactly the policy that
her lawyers told the Harvard audience ought to be followed in
these cases: the city kept an eye on her, offered whatever services
she would accept, and tried to win her confidence. It was only af-

ter months of such attempts that this approach was abandoned.

Joyce Brown ended her talk, received applause, and sat down. Norman Siegel then rose to speak. He too claimed that homelessness was essentially a housing problem, or rather that it was an issue of economic justice and equality and in no sense a mental-health issue, still less a matter of public order or law enforcement. The main cause of homelessness was the construction of high-rise developments for the rich and the destruction of the single-room-occupancy hotels (SROs) that many poor people once lived in. Allowing landlords to warehouse apartments, failing to require developers to build low-income housing, and the unwillingness of the city to redevelop the abandoned apartments it had seized— these were the real problems.

As Siegel saw it, the only way to deal with these problems was by radical political action. Just as law students from Harvard had gone to the South during the 1960's to organize and register blacks as part of a progressive political movement, so in the late 1980's lawyers should go to the bus terminals and park benches of America's cities and organize for economic justice. Homeless people needed "guerrilla legal tactics" in order to win, though "non-legal solutions," pressed forward "in a harassing way," were also important.

Whatever else one may say of the approach that Siegel and Levey put forward at the Harvard Law School Forum, it is very close to the position taken by most advocates and researchers on the homeless. Writers like Jonathan Kozol in his new book, *Rachel and Her Children: Homeless Families in America*; activists like Mitch Snyder of Communities for Creative Non-Violence (CCNV) and Robert Hayes of Coalition for the Homeless; and research centers like New York's Community Service Society all agree with Joyce Brown's lawyers in their general analysis of the problem.

The thrust of this analysis is as follows:

1. Homelessness is a huge problem and it is getting worse. The size of the homeless population is at least two to three million (a figure originally advanced by CCNV in 1982), perhaps as large as four million, and growing.

2. Homelessness is simply or primarily a housing issue. As Kozol puts it, "The cause of homelessness is lack of housing" due to federal cutbacks and urban redevelopment.

3. Mental illness and other disabilities, such as alcoholism, while frequent among the homeless, have been greatly exaggerated. About one-third of the homeless are members of homeless families, who are neither mentally ill nor otherwise disabled.

4. Radical tactics and objectives are necessary if the problem is ever to be solved. Homelessness is a systemic problem, caused by the structure of the economy and society in general. As such it cannot be effectively addressed either by the charity of the welfare state or by benefits conferred at the whim of legislatures. What is needed is the enactment of a constitutional "right to shelter" that would be enforceable through the courts.

Let us take up these claims one by one, especially as they relate to the Joyce Brown case.

First, as to the size of the homeless population. The CCNV estimate of two to three million as of 1982 was based on an unsystematic telephone survey of shelter providers and advocates. It was never clear just how CCNV went from these local to its national estimates, or even exactly how CCNV defined homelessness.

To try to get things straight, the Department of Housing and Urban Development (HUD) conducted its own survey, released in 1984, which concluded that, as of 1983, there were about 250,000 to 350,000 homeless people in America.

The HUD report was widely attacked. Mitch Snyder of CCNV declared that the officials who had inspired it reminded him "of nothing so much as a school of piranha, circling, waiting to tear the last ounce of flesh." Various methodological critiques were also brought against the report, but their validity remained uncertain in the absence of an independent cross-check on its methods.

Such an independent cross-check was finally completed in 1986 by Richard B. Freeman and Brian Hall of Harvard University in their Report of the National Bureau of Economic Research, "Permanent Homelessness in America?" The bottom line of the Freeman-Hall study was that "the much-maligned" HUD figure of 250,000–350,000 was "roughly correct." Freeman and Hall's exact estimate for 1983 was 279,000 (and Freeman estimates that as of 1988 the number has jumped to about 400,000). Further, the key data on which they based their numbers were confirmed by surveys of homeless people done by other researchers using several different methods in Boston, Chicago, Nashville, Washington, D.C., Phoenix, Pittsburgh, and Los Angeles. I myself have also confirmed these findings in a survey of homeless people in San Diego.

To cite only the example of Chicago: CCNV had reported one estimate of 250,000; later, Coalition for the Homeless cut this by a factor of ten, to 25,000. Neither of these estimates was based on systematic scientific research, nor was either organization willing to say exactly how they were arrived at. Then after two surveys of his own, Peter Rossi of the University of Massachusetts released his conclusions: in the winter of 1986 there were about 2,020 homeless people in Chicago (give or take about 275).

These studies, all independent of one another, using various methodologies, and all arriving at approximately the same conclusions, reinforce one basic point: the estimate circulated by advocacy groups of between two and three (and even up to four) million homeless people is about ten times too high.

When confronted with this evidence, Jonathan Kozol and the others frequently argue (although without ever withdrawing their own claims) that, in Kozol's words, "Whether the number is one million or four million or the administration's estimate of less than a million, there are too many homeless people in America." Or as Chester Hartman, a housing analyst at the Institute for Policy Studies, testified before Congress during its hearings on the HUD report, " . . . the real issue is that in a society with the wealth of the United States, there should not be a single involuntary homeless person."

Now, it is undoubtedly true that homelessness is a tragedy no matter how few or how many people it touches, and it is also true that 400,000 is a large number. But such statements as Kozol's and Hartman's will not do. It is as though someone were to claim that the unemployment rate is 60 percent and then, upon being informed that the real rate is closer to 6 percent, were to respond: "No matter whether the rate is 60 percent or 6 percent, too many people are unemployed. The real issue is that in a society this wealthy not a single person should be involuntarily unemployed."

One final point on the size of the homeless population. Surveys done in Nashville and Boston, and shelter counts in New York, suggest that the growth of the homeless population has leveled off. One should therefore be very skeptical about recent claims by the National Coalition for the Homeless and the U.S.

Conference of Mayors that the number of people on the streets
has grown by 25 percent over the last year. Homelessness undoubtedly did increase throughout the early 1980's, but it may
by now have reached its peak.

What about the cause of homelessness? Is it, as Kozol says,
lack of housing? Before we can evaluate this claim, we have to re-
acquaint ourselves with a few basic facts.

First, it is indeed true that New York (to take a city with an
especially large homeless population, and which is the subject of
Kozol's recent book) faces serious housing problems. Between
1981 and 1984 the number of apartments renting for under $200
a month dropped from 437,000 to 256,000. As single-room-
occupancy hotels have been torn down for development, thousands of dwelling units for the poor have vanished.

Yet the fact is that, as in most other cities, the housing stock
in New York is so large (about 1.8 million rental units), and the
number of homeless families is so "small" (about 5,000 at any giv-
en point and about 12,000 in the course of a year) relative to that
stock, that a simple "lack" of housing cannot be the trouble. The
real trouble is that the current housing market is prevented from
making a rational allocation of such housing as exists. For the
housing market could easily meet the demand that a few thousand homeless families impose on it if it were allowed to, and it
could do so in a manner consistent with current standards of decency and fairness.

Again, the Freeman and Hall study throws light on the subject. They report that for the U.S. as a whole there was no dramatic decline in the number of "affordable" units (i.e., those
renting for under $200 in real terms) during the recent increase
in homelessness between 1979 and 1983. In central cities, as the
case of New York shows, the number of such units did decline
during this period (by about 5.4 percent according to Freeman
and Hall), but this decline is in itself too small to have caused
homelessness. Nor is it correct that the number of public-housing
units declined during this same period. In fact, public housing
units actually increased from 1,178,000 in 1979 to 1,250,000 in
1983.

What did happen, however, was a sharp rise in the number
of people looking for such units. Between 1979 and 1983 the
number of poor unattached individuals increased by about 21
percent and the number of poor families by 45 percent.

Yet this increase need not, in itself, have led to homelessness. In an open market, landlords and perhaps some developers would have responded to the new demand by providing more cheap housing. Through some combination of dividing up old units, renovating abandoned buildings, renting out space formerly used as garages and basements and the like, these newly-poor renters could have had their demand met. Admittedly such accommodations would have been of inferior quality, but they would have prevented homelessness.

This demand was never met because housing regulations in New York (and some other cities) made it difficult for the market to adjust. For example, New York offered a bonus of $6,000 to landlords who would put up homeless families. There were few takers, even when the bonus was raised to $9,700. One reason seems to be that participating landlords would have had to spend more than the bonus to bring their buildings up to the required standard.

That homelessness is not due to a lack of housing is also shown by the fact that most homeless families in New York *do* manage to find a place to stay fairly soon after they enter the shelter system. Half leave the system within two to five months, and two-thirds leave within a year. Writers like Kozol who think that most families in welfare hotels are in effect permanently homeless are focusing on the long-term stayers and missing the majority who do leave after several months. In other words, homeless families simply need more assistance in finding housing more quickly in the stock that already exists.

Since advocates for the homeless claim that homelessness is entirely or primarily caused by a housing shortage, they typically deemphasize the role that disabilities like mental illness, alcoholism, and drug abuse play in the plight of the homeless. This is the theme sounded by Peter Marcuse, a professor of urban affairs at Columbia University. Marcuse cautions against "blaming the victim," a tendency which (according to him) holds that "The homeless are not like you and me. There is something wrong with them or they wouldn't be homeless." We should, as Louisa Stark, president of Coalition for the Homeless puts it, "Blame the System, Not Its Victims."

To get a sense of how valid such claims are, we have to distinguish for the moment between homeless individuals and homeless families. This approach is controversial. Indeed, one reason that disability among the homeless is sometimes thought to be less of a factor than it popularly supposed is that many of the homeless are members of homeless families. Since these families—especially the children—have much lower rates of mental illness and other disabilities than homeless individuals do, amalgamating the two groups brings the disability rate down. At the same time, however, it conceals the true dimension of disability among homeless individuals. The best way to proceed, therefore, is first to consider individuals and families separately and then to reaggregate them for the total picture.

In some journalistic accounts of homelessness during the mid- to late-1970's, all homeless individuals were assumed to be mentally ill. It was thought that most such mentally-ill homeless individuals had once been patients in mental hospitals before they were "deinstitutionalized."

It is clear, however, that deinstitutionalization—if by this is meant the policy of reducing the number of patients in mental hospitals with an eye to having them cared for by community mental-health centers—cannot explain the plight of *today's* homeless, because this policy was implemented mostly during the 1960's. Very few homeless people today came to the streets or shelters *directly* from mental hospitals. (In the Freeman and Hall study the number of such people was only 1 percent of the sample.)

On the other hand, while few of the homeless are direct victims of deinstitutionalization, we learn from Freeman and Hall that more than 90,000 of the people on the streets today would have been in mental hospitals in the days before the policy of deinstitutionalization came into being. Almost all surveys indicate that between a quarter and a third of the homeless are indeed mentally ill. For example, the Freeman and Hall study found 33 percent of its sample to be mentally ill. Rossi, in a survey of eighteen studies of homeless individuals, found that the average rateof chronic mental illness was 36.5 percent.

According to some writers, these findings demonstrate that the perception of the homeless as being mentally ill is merely a stereotype. Thus Louisa Stark tells us that "Although only one-third of homeless people nationwide are mentally disabled, since the early 1980's homelessness has become synonymous in the public mind with mental illness. What we have done, then, is taken one stigmatized illness, alcoholism, and replaced it with another, mental illness, as a stereotype for the homeless." Peter Marcuse presents the other side of this observation when he remarks that "most of the mentally ill are not homeless. More mentally ill are housed than homeless."

But neither of these superficially correct observations can break the link between mental illness and homelessness. For a rate of mental illness of 33 percent is very high. In the general population, according to Freeman and Hall, the rate is less than 2 percent, and it is not much more than that even among the dependent poor: Rossi has found that among individuals receiving General Relief in Chicago the rate of previous hospitalization for mental illness is between 3 and 4 percent.

Further, to say that the majority of the mentally ill are housed and that therefore mental illness is not a key factor in the current homeless problem is like saying that during the 1930's the majority of Americans were employed and that therefore the Depression had nothing to do with unemployment.

Yet those researchers who stress that the majority of the homeless are not mentally ill are making an important point. Just as it is misleading to assume that homelessness is *simply* a housing problem (although it is partly that), so too is it misleading to assume that homelessness is *entirely* a problem of mental illness (although it is partly that, too). There are several other groups among homeless individuals with different problems of their own.

The most obvious are alcoholics and hard-drug abusers. Freeman and Hall report that 29 percent of their sample suffered from alcohol abuse (the rate for the general population is 13 percent), and they found a rate of hard-drug abuse of 14 percent (the rate for the general population is less than 1 percent). My own guess is that something like a fifth to a third of homeless individuals suffer from some combination of these disabilities.

Mental illness, alcoholism, and drug abuse are all regarded as quasi-medical problems. But of course straightforward medical or physical problems can be disabling, too. Indeed, such disabilities turn out to be characteristic of significant percentages of homeless individuals. For example, 36 percent of Rossi's Chicago sample reported "fair" or "poor" health (a level of self-reported ill health roughly twice that of the general population); 28 percent reported a hospital stay of more than twenty-four hours in the last year; and 28 percent were unable to work for health reasons. Also, a survey of over 8,000 clients in New York City's shelters for individuals (conducted in 1984 by Stephen Crystal and Mervyn Goldstein, then of New York City's Human Resources Administration) found almost two-fifths had a current medical problem.

It is difficult to extrapolate from these numbers to a hard estimate of physical disability among the homeless. But a safe guess is that about 25 to 30 percent of homeless individuals suffer from such problems.

In addition to such strictly or quasi-medical difficulties, there are problems of a qualitatively different type that can be contributing factors to a spell of homelessness. Thus 41 percent of Rossi's sample had been in jail for periods of longer than forty-eight hours, 28 percent had at some point been convicted by a court and given probation, and 17 percent had felony convictions behind them. And Freeman and Hall found 39 percent of their sample had at some point been in jail.

One objection to regarding a criminal record as a disability characteristic of a subpopulation of the homeless is that such a history might be considered a result rather than a precipitating. or contributing cause of homelessness. My experience in San Diego suggests that many homeless people are frequently convicted of misdemeanors like jay-walking or littering as a form of harassment by police. Yet Freeman and Hall found that 61 percent of the time spent in jail by their sample was before the subjects became homeless. This indicates that being convicted of a crime can indeed be a contributing cause of homelessness. Moreover, it is unlikely that minor police harassment can account for a felony conviction rate of 17 percent.

What, then, is the overall picture of disability among homeless individuals? First, these data—dramatic as they are—do not support the idea that homelessness is some "special" problem quite unlike any other social problem. The disabilities involved are not unique to the homeless; they are found among the extremely poor and the underclass in general. In this sense, those who caution against "stereotyping" the homeless have a point.

However, a point which these data highlight with at least equal force is that homeless individuals are much more disabled than the general population or even than the poor in general.

Somewhere between 70 and 80 percent of homeless individuals suffer from one or more major disability. Thus Rossi found that 82 percent of his survey had *at least one* of the following disabilities: poor or fair health; previous mental hospitalization; previous stay in a detoxification unit; clinically high scores on psychological tests for depression or psychotic thinking; sentence(s) by a court.

Similarly, the Crystal and Goldstein study of New York's shelters for singles found that 74.9 percent of the men and 70.4 percent of the women suffered from *at least one* of the following disabilities: hard-drug abuse; alcoholism; jail record; less than an 8th-grade education; never employed; physical/medical problems; psychiatric problems; over sixty-five years old.

The homeless, then, are *not* "just like you and me" and most of them *do* have "something wrong with them" which contributes to their being homeless. (We should also keep in mind, however, the approximately 20 to 30 percent of the homeless who are relatively able and who have been described in other studies by Crystal as "economic-only" clients.)

When advocates for the homeless are confronted with figures like the above, they often choose to shift attention away from homeless individuals to homeless families. For example, a recent publication of the National Coalition for the Homeless argues:

. . . not only is homelessness increasing in numbers, it is also broadening in reach. The old stereotype of the single, male alcoholic—the so-called "skid-row derelict"—no longer applies. Increasingly, the ranks of the homeless poor are comprised of families, children, ethnic and racial minorities, the elderly, and the disabled. The face of America's homeless now mirrors the face of America's poor: skid row has become more democratic. Perhaps the starkest indication of this diversity is the fact that, today, the fastest growing segment of the homeless population consists of families with children. In some areas, families with children comprise the majority of the homeless . . . families with children now account for about 30 percent of the homeless population.

Kozol and other advocates also claim that the rate of disabilities like drug abuse and mental illness among such families is very low. Although "Many homeless *individuals* may have been residents of such [mental] institutions," writes Kozol, "in cities like New York, . . . where nearly half the homeless are small children, with an average age of six, such suppositions [of former mental hospitalization] obviously make little sense."

There are two questions here: (1) Just how many homeless family members are there and what percentage of the total homeless population do they represent? (2) What are the rates of disability among homeless family members?

As to the question of numbers, the Freeman and Hall study again provides the best source. They estimate that in 1983 there were 32,000 homeless family members, and that in 1985 there were 46,000 such people.

Right away, we can see from the Freeman-Hall data that Kozol is exaggerating wildly when he tells us that 500,000 children are currently homeless. Since only 46,000 members of families were homeless in 1985 (this includes *both* adults and children), homeless families would have had to grow by more than ten times in three years for Kozol's figure even to approach reality—not to mention that there are in fact no more than a *total* of 400,000 homeless people in 1988. The truth is that the widely circulated estimate that families with children represent 30 percent of the total homeless population is more than twice too high.

So far as the question of disability goes, we know roughly what the rates are among homeless individuals, but at this point we do not know enough to conclude either that homeless families suffer from no more disabilities than do other poor families, or that in fact they do have special problems which contribute to their being homeless. Such studies as we do have suggest that the rate of disabilities among such families may be significant. But until better information is available on this subject, we have to regard the confident pronouncements of advocates that homeless families are simply victims of a tight housing market as being largely conjectural.

What are we to make of the advocates' interpretation of the politics of homelessness? It is important to understand that they see homelessness not as an aberration or a failing but as a natural outcome of the ordinary workings of social policy and the economy in general. As Mitch Snyder of CCNV writes (in collaboration with Mary Ellen Hombs):

We live in a disposable society, a throwaway culture. The homeless are our human refuse, remnants of a culture that assigns a pathologically high value to independence and productivity. America is a land where you *are* what you consume and produce. The homeless are simply surplus souls in a system firmly rooted in competition and self-interest, in which only the "strongest" (i.e., those who fit most snugly within the confines of a purely arbitrary norm) will survive.

Similar sentiments are expressed by Robert Hayes of Coalition for the Homeless ("the homeless are indeed the most egregious symbol of a cruel economy, an unresponsive government, a festering value system") and by Peter Marcuse of Columbia ("homelessness in the midst of plenty may shock people into the realization that homelessness exists not because the system is failing to work as it should, but because the system *is* working as it must").

Yet it ought to be obvious that homelessness cannot be the result of "a festering value system," or "free-market capitalism," or "a system firmly rooted in competition and self-interest," or any other long-term systemic feature of American society, for the simple reason that all these have remained more or less what they always have been, and so cannot explain the rise of homelessness *now*.

Advocates seem to recognize this at some level, since, after having made sweeping pronouncements against American society in general, they usually concentrate their fire on the Reagan administration's social and economic policies. But while poverty did increase during the Reagan years, the Reagan administration can hardly be blamed either for deinstitutionalization or for the housing policies—such as rent control and byzantine regulations—which in cities like New York have undoubtedly exacerbated the situation.

To sum up: homelessness is a much *smaller* problem, in terms of the number of people affected by it, than is commonly thought, but it is also much more *intractable* than advocates understand. This intractability stems from the fact that the great majority of homeless individuals, and possibly some significant proportion of homeless families, are afflicted with behavioral or medical disabilities or both. Dealing with such problems requires a willingness to assert *authority*—for example, in refusing to allow people like Joyce Brown to live on the streets—as much as it requires an expenditure of resources. Nonetheless, an important part of the problem is economic, and can best be addressed not by building more public housing but by raising the income of the extremely poor and by removing regulations which block the allocation of housing to them.

In short, a reformist agenda—one aimed at enabling our mental-health system to treat people who need treatment, at re-

ducing extreme poverty through income supports, and at allowing housing markets to function—can go a long way toward the
elimination of homelessness.

This agenda is a far cry from the radical systemic measures
such as a constitutional "right to shelter," or the "guerrilla legal
tactics" and the "harassing" techniques recommended by Joyce
Brown's lawyers and other activists in the field. But it has the vir-
tue of being based on a truthful diagnosis rather than on wild and
tendentious analyses which, by simultaneously exaggerating the
dimensions of the problem and underplaying its difficulties, make
it harder rather than easier to help the homeless at all. In taking
up the case of Joyce Brown, and in securing her release, the NY-
CLU lawyers may have furthered the "delegitimation" (as Peter
Marcuse calls it) of a social system they consider evil. But as for
Joyce Brown herself, only a short time after her appearance at
Harvard, she was found begging on the streets and hurling abuse
at passers-by who refused to give her money.

TOWARD A NATIONAL POLICY
TO END HOMELESSNESS[6]

The deaths of homeless people are reported routinely in
newspapers, on television, on the radio. The television evening
news reports that three persons died in the first freezing temperatures of the season in the North. In Dallas, a penniless shelter resident, a woman of 60, is found dead, her head bashed by a brick.
In Washington, D.C., on a dark morning, a truck driver inadvertently drives over and kills a homeless man huddled at the entrance of a public garage.

The harshest aspects of our society have been cruelly apparent in hearings and site visits conducted by the Select Committee
on Hunger during the past two years. The fortunate within the
growing and vulnerable homeless population are in shelters.
With my colleagues, I have talked with homeless folks—parents,

[6]Reprint of an article by Mickey Leland, chairman of the House Select Committee on Hunger. Reprinted by permission from *America*, V. 156: 69-71. Ja. 31, '87.
Copyright © 1987 by *America*.

children, teen-agers, single adults—at the Star of Hope Mission in Houston, and in shelters and soup kitchens in Washington, New York City and San Francisco.

As we studied the deprivation in our society, two things became apparent. First, the number of homeless persons is growing, and the resources of cities and private agencies are stretched to the limit. Second, the population is becoming more diverse; there are more families and younger single persons. A core group of mentally ill persons and others who are drug addicts remain, but even these difficult and sometimes self-destructive persons fared better several decades ago.

That this situation existed for years without an adequate national response is appalling. Using the committee's findings and working with the National Coalition for the Homeless, I introduced the Homeless Persons' Survival Act (H.R. 5140) last June. Senator Albert Gore Jr. (D., Tenn.) introduced a companion bill in the Senate. This omnibus bill covered the multiple needs of the homeless: mental health assistance, nutrition, guarantee of access to Federal benefit programs without a fixed address. The largest and most costly component of the bill was, of course, housing.

Including all the needs of homeless persons in this one bill is appropriate, because every source of income and resource for the poor has been systematically eaten away by the restrictive policies of the Reagan Administration and by changes in the economy during the 1980's. Because of the bill's comprehensive approach, it was necessary to break it into seven smaller bills, which were referred to the proper committees of jurisdiction.

The legislative climate for H.R. 5140 was not auspicious. In a year of stringent Gramm-Rudman-Hollings budget targets and massive deficits, introducing late in the session a bill with a $4-billion price tag seemed foolhardy. But beyond the Washington Beltway, people were showing they cared. Those who took part in Hands Across America last May were typical. It was time to take a belated first step in creating a national policy to address homelessness. Fortunately, portions of the bill passed in October—record time for a busy pre-election Congress. With bipartisan support, specifically the leadership of Senator Peter V. Domenici (R., N.M.), "no cost" provisions were attached to the politically popular drug bill. Although President Reagan has regularly dismissed hunger and homelessness as national problems, the majority in Congress acted to ameliorate this visible sign of national failure.

The provisions that passed assure that benefits under Aid for Families with Dependent Children (A.F.D.C.), Supplemental Security Income (S.S.I.) and Medicaid may no longer be denied because of a lack of a permanent address. The same requirement applies to benefits for veterans, who make up 15 percent of the homeless population.

During committee visits, we consistently heard of the barriers faced by the homeless in getting food stamps and other Federal benefits—problems caused by the lack of fixed address and proper documentation. Without Social Security cards and photo identification cards, benefits can be delayed for weeks.

Under the new law, the Secretaries of Health and Human Services and Agriculture must come up with a single application for S.S.I. and food stamps as part of prerelease procedures in mental health and penal institutions, which will assure that individuals will not be put on the streets without regular support. This type of coordination between Federal departments has always been possible. Unfortunately, it must be brought about by Congressional fiat rather than executive leadership.

The new law allows nonprofit homeless shelters and soup kitchens to accept food stamps when presented voluntarily by the homeless persons. This provision has not been endorsed by some nutrition advocates who feel that it may invite abuse. However, similar legislation has been successfully implemented at congregate feeding-sites for the elderly and shelters for battered women. Don Johnson of Houston's Star of Hope Mission points out that food stamps are of little use to people with no place to cook. The funds will allow shelters to improve the quantity and quality of their meals while giving recipients the dignity of making a contribution.

Two other pieces of legislation that will aid the homeless were included in the continuing resolution that passed at the end of the 99th Congress. The Emergency Food and Shelter Program was again funded at $70 million. Since 1982, these monies have been the only Federal response to the homeless crisis, which has been growing, and they have proved grossly inadequate. Comparatively small grants have been used well by the private sector. Individual churches have put in kitchens and now serve meals; shelters are able to make up food packages for residents. But local agencies say the grants are Band-Aids applied to a gaping social wound.

A new program of grants for emergency and transitional shelters to be administered by state and local governments and nonprofit organizations was established. It provides $10 million in direct funding for the emergency shelters and $5 million in noninterest-bearing loans (which can become grants in 10 years) for transitional shelters with supportive services. These shelters are desperately needed.

Every penny that goes to help homeless persons is well spent, but we must get beyond the emergencies. Families and individuals cannot leave shelters and make it on their own until there is an adequate supply of affordable housing and until jobs and income-support programs are sufficient to meet their basic needs.

Since 1981, there has been a 71-percent reduction in budget authority for low-income housing programs assisted by the Department of Housing and Urban Development. In the same period, the number of assisted rental units has fallen from 220,500 in 1981 to less than 98,000. Where will people go when they leave shelters? Gentrification and condominium conversions have reduced the supply of low-cost private housing. With 7-percent unemployment and a minimum wage that has remained at $3.35 an hour since 1981, how can people make it?

The remaining provisions of the Homeless Persons Survival Act were reintroduced as H.R. 286 on Jan. 7. The big-ticket item is housing. This includes both conventional public housing and rental assistance as well as more innovative approaches, such as conveyance of tax-foreclosed housing to nonprofit agencies for rental development, and funding for rehabilitation of housing and community residences for mentally ill persons.

This legislation is cost effective. Funds invested in long-term solutions will decrease the expanding and often wasteful expenditures for emergency housing. President Reagan recently noted the high cost of welfare hotel accommodations in New York City ($27,600 per year). By comparison, the cost for rental assistance for existing Section 8 public housing units is $4,100 per year.

Substantial aid for children who suffer from the disruptive effects of homelessness during the developmental years and grants for shelters for families with babies are included in the bill. To encourage young parents to remain in the family home, the bill would repeal A.F.D.C. rules that require counting grandparents' and step-parents' income in determining the eligibility and grant level of a child.

The legislation also takes into account the health needs of homeless persons. The high incidence of hypertension and heart disease among homeless adults and chronic infections among the homeless of all ages places them at particular health risk if they are undernourished for even short periods. Many soup kitchens and shelter operators, aware of the poor physical condition of homeless persons, arrange for them to visit clinics or medical volunteers, but these efforts reach far too few.

Congressional concern is evident. On Dec. 15, 1986, in the hiatus between sessions, the Health and Environment Subcommittee of the Energy and Commerce Committee held a hearing on the health and mental health portions of the bill. In addition, Majority Leader Thomas S. Foley (D., Wash.) is sponsoring a $500-million Urgent Relief for the Homeless bill to supplement 1987 funding. This responds to the surge in demand for emergency shelter this winter, which, according to the U.S. Conference of Mayors, is up 20 percent.

The 100th Congress must find the political will to end the hunger and homelessness among us. The destitution, indignities and hazards to life itself suffered by homeless persons are an affront to the majority in our nation. The time has come to bind up this wound in our society, which, as it grows, becomes ever more costly to cure.

[Editor's note: The Leland bill was killed in committee in June 1988.]

BIBLIOGRAPHY

An asterisk (*) preceding a reference indicates an excerpt from the work has been reprinted in this compilation.

BOOKS AND PAMPHLETS

Abramovitz, Mimi. Regulating the lives of women, social welfare policy from colonial times to the present. South End Press. '88.

Austin, David M. The political economy of human service programs. Jai Press. '88.

Axinn, June and Stern, Mark J. Dependency in a new world. Lexington Books. '88.

Bailey, Thelma and Bailey, Walter. Child welfare practice. Jossey-Bassius. '83.

Bell, Winifred. Contemporary social welfare. Macmillan. '87.

Berkowitz, Edward D. and McQuaid, Kim. Creating the welfare state. Praeger. '88.

Beverly, David D. and McSweeney, Edward P. Social welfare and social justice. Prentice-Hall. '87.

Bingham, Richard, Green, Roy, and White, Sammis, eds. The homeless in contemporary society. Sage. '87.

Birch, Eugenie Ladner, ed. The unsheltered woman. Rutgers University Center for Urban Policy Research. '85.

Block, Fred L. The mean season: the attack on the welfare state. Pantheon. '87.

Brickner, Philip W., ed. Health care for homeless people. Springer. '85.

Brock, William. Welfare, democracy, and the New Deal. Cambridge University Press. '88.

Brown, Michael K. Remaking the welfare state. Temple University Press. '88.

Burghardt, Stephen and Fabricant, Michael. Working under the safety net. Sage. '87.

Bush, Malcolm. Families in distress. University of California Press. '88.

Butler, Stuart M. and Kondratas, Anna. Out of the poverty trap. Free Press. '87.

Carroll, Barry J., Conant, Ralph W., and Easton, Thomas A. Private mean–public ends: private business in social service delivery. Praeger. '87.

Champagne, Anthony and Harpham, Edward, eds. The attack on the welfare state. Waveland. '84.

Cibulski, Ann and Hoch, Charles. Homelessness: an annotated bibliography. CPL Bibliographies. '86.

Clode, Drew, Parker, Christopher, and Etherington, Stuart. Towards the sensitive bureaucracy. Gower. '87.

Cogswell, James A. No place left called home. Friendship Press. '83.

Colby, Ira C. Social welfare policy. Dorsey Press. '88.

Costein, Lela B. Toward a feminist approach to child welfare. Child Welfare League of America. '87.

Cottingham, Phoebe H. and Ellwood, David. Welfare policy for the 1990's. Harvard University Press. '89.

Coughlin, Richard M. Reforming welfare. University of New Mexico. '89.

Critchlow, David T. and Hawley, Ellis. Poverty and public policy in modern America. Dorsey. '89.

Dale, Jennifer and Foster, Peggy. Feminists and state welfare. Routledge & Kegan Paul. '86.

Day, Phyllis J. A new history of social welfare. Prentice-Hall. '89.

Dear, M. J. and Welch, Jennifer. Landscapes of despair. Princeton University Press. '87.

Denton, James S. Welfare reform. University Press of America. '88.

DiNitto, Diana M. and Dye, Thomas R. Social welfare. Prentice-Hall. '87.

Dudley, William. Poverty. Greenhaven Press. '88.

Dunbar, Leslie. The common interest. Pantheon. '88.

Erickson, Jon and Wilhelm, Charles, eds. Housing the Homeless. Rutgers University Center for Urban Policy. '86.

Evers, Adalbert, Nowotny, Helga, and Wintersberger, Iy. The changing face of welfare. Gower. '87.

Fanning, Beverly J. Workfare vs. welfare. G. E. McCuen. '89.

Friedmann, Robert, Gilbert, Neil, and Sherer, Moshe. International study group on modern welfare states in transition. Wheatsheaf. '87.

Gaylord, Catherine and Schaefer, David. General relief-medical. Center for Public Representation. '89.

Gibelman, Margaret. Services for sale: purchasing health and human services. Rutgers University Press. '88.

Glazer, Nathan. The limits of social policy. Harvard University Press. '88.

Glennerster, Howard. Paying for welfare. Blackwell. '85.

Gould, Arthur. Conflict and control in welfare policy. Longman. '88.

Gueron, Judith M. Reforming welfare with work. Ford Foundation. '87.

Gutman, Amy. Democracy and the welfare state. Princeton University Press. '88.

Harrington, Michael. The new American poverty. Holt, Rinehart & Winston. '84.

Harris, David. Justifying state welfare. Blackwell. '87.

Hope, Marjorie and Young, James. The faces of homelessness. Lexington. '86.

Ismael, Jacqueline S. The Canadian welfare state. University of Alberta Press. '87.

Jansson, Bruce S. The reluctant welfare state. Wadsworth. '88.

Joe, Tom and Rogers, Cheryl. By the few, for the few: the Reagan welfare legacy. Lexington. '85.

Johnson, Judith M. The welfare state in transition. University of Massachusetts Press. '87.

Johnson, Louise C. and Schwartz, Charles L. Social welfare. Allyn and Bacon. '88.

Jordan, Bill. Rethinking welfare. Blackwell. '87.

Kadushin, Alfred and Martin, Judith A. Child welfare services. Macmillan. '88.

Katz, Michael B. In the shadow of the poorhouse. Basic Books. '86.

Kosof, Anna. Homeless in America. Watts. '88.

Kozol, Jonathan. Rachel and her children. Crown. '88.

Lamb, Richard H. The homeless mentally ill. American Psychiatric Association. '84.

Landau, Elaine. The homeless. Messner. '87.

Landon, John W. The development of social welfare. Human Services Press. '86.

Levine, Daniel. Poverty and society. Rutgers University Press. '88.

Levitan, Sar A. Progress in aid of the poor. Johns Hopkins University Press. '85.

Loney, Martin and Bocock, Robert. The state of the market: politics and welfare in contemporary Britain. Sage. '87.

McGerigle, Paul and Lauriat, Alison S. More than shelter: a community response to homelessness. United Community Planning Corp. '84.

McGovern, Brenda G. and Meezan, William, eds. Child welfare, current dilemmas—future directions. Peacock. '83.

Meyer, Philippe. The child and the state: the intervention of the state in family life. Cambridge University Press. '83.

Miringoff, Marc L. and Opdycke, Sandra. American social welfare policy. Prentice-Hall. '86.

Mishra, Ramesh. The welfare state in crisis. St. Martin's Press. '84.

Morris, Robert. Social policy in the American welfare state. Longman. '85.

Newman, Sandra J. and Schnare, Ann Burnet. Subsidizing shelter. Urban Institute Press. '88.

Novak, Michael. The new consensus on family and welfare. Marquette University. '87.

Novak, Tony. Poverty and the state. Open University Press. '88.

Papadakis, Elim and Taylor-Gooby, Peter. The private provision of public welfare. Wheatsheaf. '87.

Prigmore, Charles S. and Atherton, Charles R. Social welfare policy. Heath. '86.

Redburn, F. Stevens, and Buss, Terry F. Responding to America's homeless. Praeger. '86.

Reich, Robert B. Tales of a new America. Times Books. '87.

Resener, Carl. Crisis in the streets. Broadman. '88.

Riemer, David R. The prisoners of welfare. Praeger. '88.

Rochefort, David A. Americal social welfare policy. Westview Press. '86.

Segalman, Ralph and Marsland, David. Cradle to grave. St. Martin's Press. '88.

Sidel, Ruth. Women and children last. Penguin. '87.

Singer, Greta, Rachlin, Marcia, and Cassidy, Maybeth, eds. Child welfare problems. University Press of America. '83.

Spicker, Paul. Principles of social welfare. Routledge. '88.

Spicuzza, Frank J. Aid to families with dependent children: a bibliography. Vance. '87.

Sullivan, Michael. Sociology and social welfare. Allen & Unwin. '87.

Titmuss, Richard and Abel-Smith, Brian. The philosophy of welfare. Allen & Unwin. '87.

Tomaskovic-Devey, Donald. Poverty and social welfare in the United States. Westview Press. '88.

Torrey, E. Fuller. Nowhere to go. Harper & Row. '88.

Tropman, John E. American values and social welfare. Prentice-Hall. '89.

Undy, Harry. Children need homes. Wayland. '88.

Watson, Sophie and Austerberry, Helen. Housing and homelessness. Routledge & Kegan Paul. '86.

Weir, Margaret, Orloff, Ann, and Skocpol, Theda. The politics of social policy in the United States. Princeton University Press. '88.

Zuckerman, Erva. Child welfare. Free Press. '83.

For those who wish to read more widely on the subject of the welfare debate, this section contains abstracts of additional articles that bear on the topic. Readers who require a comprehensive list of materials are advised to consult the *Readers' Guide to Periodical Literature* and other Wilson indexes.

WELFARE REFORM

The culture of poverty. Nicholas Lemann *The Atlantic* 254:26-7+ S '84

Poverty in America is a disease for which there is plenty of treatment, but no known cure. President Reagan claims that cuts in federal poverty programs lower government spending without burdening the poor. His administration clearly has no desire to foster independence in the disadvantaged, but only to minimally feed, clothe, and shelter them. When Reagan restricted the allowable gains a welfare mother could take from the earned-income disregard without shorting her welfare payment, experts predicted that working mothers would abandon their jobs in favor of total welfare reliance. In fact, this did not happen and no solid reasoning can explain why low-salaried jobs and longer working hours are attractive to this population. However, despite regular salaries, former welfare clients still live in the midst of poverty. Congress has reinstated some programs, but poverty is still claiming victims.

Blinded by metaphor: churches and welfare reform. Robert S. Bachelder. *The Christian Century* 105:1147-9 D 14 '88

The church must change its habit of automatically responding to welfare issues with an unreformed liberal approach. Earlier attempts at welfare reform through workfare were more like slavefare, but new workfare legislation, such as the Family Security Act of 1988, deserve examination. The bill combines the conservative emphasis on demanding something in return for welfare with the increased spending for education and job training that liberals have always supported as a means of breaking the cycle of poverty. The bill's rules mandating work are fair and contain such provisions as guaranteed day care assistance for single parents. Christian Faith and Economic Life, the United Church of Christ's version of the Roman Catholic bishops' pastoral letter on the economy, exemplifies the unreformed liberal approach. In the letter, the authors reject the arguments for welfare reform and workfare before giving them a fair hearing.

What came in like a lion (welfare reform). Nancy Amidei. *Commonweal* 115:551-2 O 21 '88

The welfare reform bill recently passed by Congress and hailed by sponsors as the most significant revision of welfare reform in 53 years contains no major benefits for low-income parents. Consequently, it has been opposed by virtually every church, labor, low-income, and social-advocacy group interested in welfare reform. The bill will not enable families currently on welfare to climb out of poverty, nor will it help most poor people who are not already eligible for welfare. It contains no national welfare benefit floor, no help for poor states with extremely low benefits, and only six months' aid for children in two-parent families in the 23 states that still require fathers to leave home. It will also reduce benefits for women who want to supplement welfare with work.

What does the government owe the poor? (views of C. Murray and J. L. Jackson). *Harper's* 272:35-9+ Ap '86

Americans' distrust of welfare is not surprising. Public assistance threatens the very core of capitalism, which is premised on the notion that the urge to possess fuels the desire to work. The past three or four years have witnessed a resurgence of charges that government efforts to ease poverty have largely been failures. Welfare, claim the new critics, has destroyed families, encouraged out-of-wedlock births, and demeaned the value of work. In his influential book *Losing Ground*, Charles Murray argues that the government best serves the poor by letting them fare for themselves. Civil rights activist Jesse Jackson is known for his sympathetic defense of poor people's interests. A transcript of a conversation between Jackson and Murray about welfare, government, and poverty is provided.

Reality and welfare reform. George P. Brockway. *The New Leader* 71:14-16 N 28 '88

The Family Security Act contains two faulty provisions. A workfare provision, supported by President Reagan and conservative Republicans, is expected to reduce expenditures for public housing, food stamps, Medicaid, and Aid to Families with Dependent Children by cracking down on fathers who must pay child support and by emphasizing job training for welfare recipients. The child support aspect is certainly praiseworthy, but the puny budget allocation for workfare will not help much in fostering vocational education for the unemployed. Moreover, the scarcity of jobs defeats the purpose of vocational training. The JOBS program provision has the laudable aim of getting people off the welfare rolls and into steady employment. It assumes that workers are to blame for economic friction, however, when in fact the fault lies with the present price system and its tendency to widen the chasm between rich and poor.

Gaining ground (Family Security Act). *The New Republic* 199:7-9 Jl 11 '88

The much-touted Family Security Act, sponsored by Sen. Daniel Moynihan and overwhelmingly approved by the Senate, will not significantly al-ter the barriers and perverse incentives inherent in the welfare system. Nevertheless, the relatively inexpensive bill is valuable as a statement of principle. By sanctioning the idea that able-bodied adults should work for their welfare checks, it lays the groundwork for more substantial legislation based on a similar philosophy. Moynihan balked at a real workfare program, partly because it would be expensive, and no one expects that the new JOBS program will find employment for more than 1 in 50 people a year. If workfare is ever to become a reality, a lot of money will be required for day care, and politicians will have to accept the necessity of forcing women to juggle motherhood and a job. In five years, the nation may be ready for the harsher and more expensive measures that are needed to change the culture of poverty.

New efforts to help America's poor (special issue). *Scholastic Update* (Teachers' edition) 119:3-10+ Mr 23 '87

An issue on efforts to help America's poor examines the new breed of poor people, the economics of poverty, historical attempts to deal with the poor, U.S. antipoverty programs, Western European public welfare, and promising aid programs in Massachusetts, California, Texas, and Wisconsin. Charts illustrate the nation's wins and losses in the fight against poverty and demonstrate the effects of poverty on different demographic groups. A map portrays where the poor live by region, and a glossary defines words relating to poverty.

Safety nets and welfare ceilings (special section). *Society* 23:4-27 Ja/F '86

A special section features a debate on the welfare system. An essay by Sar A. Levitan defends the welfare system. Blanche Bernstein, Lawrence M. Mead, John Pencavel, Morgan O. Reynolds, Simon Rottenberg, Gordon Tullock, and Walter E. Williams offer opposing views. Levitan responds with a final rebuttal.

Human service corporations and the welfare state. David Stoesz. *Society* 25:53-8 Jl/Ag '88

The proliferation of for-profit human-services corporations in health care, child care, and other areas indicates that the American welfare state is undergoing a fundamental reorganization. As the corporate sector continues to make inroads into the human-services market, it may begin shaping welfare policy toward its own ends. In addition, the competitive practices of for-profit firms are influencing the activities of nonprofit social welfare organizations. Most important, the voluntary sector, which has historically played a crucial role in American culture, may be reduced to a marginal role in the welfare system.

Liberal heretics back off the dole (D. T. Ellwood proposes end of welfare). David Whitman. *U.S. News & World Report* 104:27 My 23 '88

In his book *Poor Support*, noted liberal scholar David Ellwood advocates scrapping the present U. S. welfare system. Ellwood, a young Harvard professor and the welfare system's patron saint for the last five years, now claims that cash relief for the poor doesn't work because it isolates struggling families from working families and does little to help recipients gain independence. Neo–New Dealers recommend replacing the welfare system with nonwelfare reforms, such as a higher minimum wage, a childcare tax credit for poor families, and a broader child-support-collection system aimed at absent parents. These proposals put Ellwood and other liberal converts to the anti-welfare cause at odds with leading Democratic politicians like Daniel Patrick Moynihan and Michael Dukakis, who support pending federal bills that would keep the welfare system while increasing child-care and job-training opportunities for welfare recipients.

Did Congress slay the welfare giant? *U. S. News & World Report* 105:9+ O 10 '88

A new welfare-reform package passed by Congress last week was touted by Sen. Daniel Moynihan, who sponsored the bill, as a redefinition and overhaul of the current system. The new bill, which has a conservative bent, aims to shift financial responsibility for welfare families from the taxpayer to the absent father. The bill also provides for the expansion of a jobs-and-training program aimed at chronic welfare recipients. The Congressional Budget Office predicts that the new work program will remove 80,000 families from welfare assistance over the next five years, but one expert predicts that in five years there will still be millions on welfare.

Children in shelters (special section). *Children Today* 15:6–25 Mr/Ap '86

A cover story discusses the effects of family violence on children. The status of research and intervention programs is reviewed. Since mothers and children generally first seek and find help in shelters for battered women, many intervention programs are shelter-based.

Massachusetts spotlights day care. *Children Today* 16:2–3 Mr/Ap '87

In January 1985, Massachusetts launched the Day Care Partnership Initiative to help parents in the state locate quality child care at an affordable price. The program involves business, schools, labor and community leaders, early childhood and day-care experts, local government officials, and parents. Two funds for day care were created, including the nation's first publicly sponsored loan fund designed to stimulate employer investment in day-care facilities. Another part of the program is a statewide network of community-based Child Care Resource and Referral centers designed to provide information for parents, recruit new child-care providers, and enhance the quality of existing services.

Playing politics with children (presidential campaign issue).
Mickey Kaus. *Newsweek* 111:26-7 Je 13 '88

Concern for the welfare of children could become a significant presidential campaign issue, but the politics of children consists largely of rhetorical distortion, if not outright deception. Some Democrats, including Mario Cuomo and Albert Gore, have tried to trumpet the kids issue, but Michael Dukakis has not given the child theme a major role in his campaign, stressing adult economic concerns instead. The media have also downplayed the issue, concentrating on trade and drugs. Perhaps voters sense that many kids issues are merely repackaged liberal spending programs. The Child Welfare League and the Children's Defense Fund both use this trick. Voters may also sense that money targeted for welfare and institutional day care benefits adults more than children. The kids issue may be moot for most voters, but George Bush plans to make it a major theme of his fall campaign, possibly forcing Dukakis into a bidding war over who will do more for children.

Where Christmas never comes (children in New York shelters and hotels). Michael Small *People Weekly* 28:50-60 D 14 '87

Descriptions of the lives of children who live in New York City's hotels and shelters for the homeless.

Caring for children (special section). *Society* 24:5-52 Mr/Ap '87

A special section on caring for children includes articles on welfare reform, ways to prevent abuse of children by teenage mothers, family dependency, and services appropriate for the postmodern family.

In Illinois: victims of Grand Boulevard (infant mortality rate).
Richard Conniff *Time* 127:11-12 Ja 13 '86

Chicago's Grand Boulevard neighborhood, formerly elegant and fashionable, has become a slum. First settled in the 1870s by white urbanites, it developed a busy nightclub scene between the world wars, but the whites and later the blacks who could afford it left the area. Today, the neighborhood has a population of 54,000, most of them black and poor. One in every thirty-eight babies there dies before the age of one. Even if saved by sophisticated medical technology and intensive care, children of the Boulevard may later succumb to the slum itself. The destructive life-style that results from fatalism and hopelessness does not stress child care. Moreover, the society that provides the medical care that initially saves the children later withdraws the programs that could keep them healthy.

A father's place in the welfare state. David Whitman *U. S. News & World Report* 105:41+ O 17 '88

Studies show that unmarried teen fathers often help care for or support their children, but policymakers rarely pass laws that take this into account. The recently passed welfare-reform bill, for instance, provides virtually no training and few jobs for the fathers of children on public assistance. In an effort to correct the imbalance, some federal, state, and local officials have introduced experimental programs that encourage young men to be responsible for contraception and for their children. Among these are programs to distribute condoms, recruit young men to appear on videos warning about the evils of teen pregnancy, and provide unwed fathers with training, family counseling, or wage supplements.

The children's hour. Merrill McLoughlin *U. S. News & World Report* 105:34–7+ N 7 '88

A cover story examines the welfare of children in the United States. Articles examine the schools visited by Michael Dukakis, George Bush, and Dan and Marilyn Quayle and discuss the barriers faced by the government when it comes to helping children. Sidebars discuss several children who have suffered, three national programs for children, and the child-welfare promises made by the two candidates for president.

Our children: the hungry Americans (views of D. P. Moynihan). Maureen Orth *Vogue* 175:164+ N '85

Hunger in America is at epidemic levels and the most vulnerable victims are children, who as a group are now the poorest members of the population. The Reagan administration's reductions in social services for children and the nation's economic slowdown have also affected the status of children. The Association of Junior Leagues has taken a leadership role in providing programs and lobbying for children. But despite even these efforts, many more children fall between the cracks than is necessary. In the black community, especially, poverty is part of the fabric of daily life, and it is the children who suffer most. New York Senator Daniel Patrick Moynihan is working to aid the nation's needy children, but his Family Economic Security Act, along with a bill proposed by Connecticut senator Chirstopher Dodd have been opposed by the White House as too costly. Private efforts will have to continue to provide the care the federal government no longer makes available.

HOMELESSNESS

Homelessness: the policy failure haunting America. Elizabeth Ehrlich *Business Week* 132–4+ Ap 25 '88

The growing problem of homelessness is exacerbated by the deinstitutionalization of the mentally ill, welfare programs that offer subsistence rather than opportunities, or incentives, and social spending cuts during the Reagan administration. Federal expenditures for public and private low-cost housing have been cut from $30 billion in 1981 to $7 billion in 1987. Only about 4 million of 10 million eligible households receive federal rental assistance of any kind. Most federal money for the homeless is spent on shelters, health care, and other emergency services. Advocates for the homeless fear that shelters merely keep the poorest out of sight and create a permanent underclass. The failure of social policy does not mean that homelessness is inevitable but that social policy toward the homeless must be redesigned.

The chronic calamity. Kai Erikson *The Nation* 246:465–6 Ap 2 '88

Part of a special section offering reactions to Jonathan Kozol's book about homelessness, *Rachel and Her Children*. Homeless families are among a new wave of Americans who have been cast adrift by society. Often these families were evicted from their homes and lacked sufficient funds for another dwelling. As Kozol argues, the effects of homelessness are overwhelming to these families; they are drained of self-respect and confidence and left feeling bewildered, afraid, and disoriented. Homeless people are to a large extent victims of trauma. Society is unnecessarily running the risk of crippling great masses of people, especially children, and it will eventually face the consequences.

Give them shelters. Theresa Funiciello *The Nation* 246:469–72 Ap 2 '88

Part of a special section offering reactions to Jonathan Kozol's book about homelessness, *Rachel and Her Children*. Kozol effectively incorporates firsthand accounts of homelessness into his book, but he fails to listen to the homeless, choosing instead to listen to their professional advocates. In doing so, he overlooks the alarming problem of the siphoning of funds by shelter developers. Housing codes and space requirements have been ignored, while funds have been conveniently misappropriated.

Practical solutions to the housing problem include the redirection of funds from temporary to permanent dwellings, the restoration of responsibility to public housing authorities, and improvement of the welfare department's income maintenance program. Such progress will not be made, however, until people start listening to the homeless rather than to their so-called advocates.

Who's who among the homeless. David Whitman *The New Republic* 198:18–20 Je 6 '88

In their effort to make the homeless more palatable to the public, journalists have created a distorted impression of how mothers and children end up on the street. Most of the recent media reports on the issue portray homelessness as a problem that afflicts people who suddenly find themselves poor and unable to pay for housing. Recent studies show that only a small fraction of the poor end up homeless and suggest that two-thirds are either mentally ill or substance abusers. By fostering the myth that most of the homeless are families needing apartments, journalists are misleading the public about what kind of help families need in order to get homes of their own. Advocates and politicians also do the homeless a disservice by focusing on the shortage of affordable housing. Although more low-income housing is needed, many homeless mothers will require drug and psychiatric treatment and assistance in matters like budgeting, child care, and jobs in order to become self-sufficient.

Help for the homeless (single room occupancy hotels). Patricia King *Newsweek* 111:58-9 Ap 11 '88

In response to the worsening plight of homeless Americans, many cities and private investors are battling to preserve the single-room-occupancy hotel (SRO). These actions come as the result of a severe depletion of SROs between 1974 and 1983, when an incredible 896,000 units were torn down or upgraded to luxury apartments. As the demand for cheap rentals and the cost of rents have risen, cities have been forced to deal with the SRO drought. Los Angeles, for example, has prohibited the demolition or conversion of skid-row hotels without city approval. Some private investors have also joined the fight, maintaining their consciences as well as their balance sheets with respectable profits. These actions, however, will not solve the homelessness problem. According to city officials, only the federal government can find a solution. Although some progress has been made, federal funding has so far been inadequate.

The homeless and their children (II) (families at the Martinique Hotel in New York City). Jonathan Kozol *The New Yorker* 63:36-8+ F 1 '88

Although the plight of the homeless has been well documented, authorities avoid taking corrective action by appointing investigative task forces and announcing long-term plans that do not address the immediate problem. As homelessness worsens, our concern turns to exhaustion, then to indifference, and, eventually, to mistrust and hatred. The writer describes meetings he had with homeless people at one of the largest hotels for the homeless in New York City and at the city's central emergency-assistance unit in lower Manhattan, discusses the psychological effects of institutional living, reviews public attitudes on homelessness, outlines the restrictive shelter provisions of the New York City Council, and discusses the tendency of the public to make a specious distinction between the deserving and the undeserving poor.

Homeless families: how they got that way (study by Kay Young McChesney). *Society* 25:4 N/D '87

Kay Young McChesney, director of the Homeless Families Project at the University of Southern California, notes that families are the fastest-growing segment of the homeless population and that single women head most of these families. Based on interviews of women with children in five Los Angeles County shelters, McChesney notes that these homeless mothers are neither crazy nor substance abusers. Some 40 percent of the women became homeless because of legal eviction or the threat of eviction. About 33 percent of them had been robbed or had run out of money after moving to Los Angeles, and about 25 percent became homeless when male partners left them or threw them out. McChesney's research indicates that one factor that homeless families have in common is that they cannot turn to relatives for help, because of death, estrangement, or distance. She believes that the shortage of low-cost housing is at the root of the homelessness problem.

Homelessness and mental illness. E. Fuller Torrey *USA Today* 116:26-7 Mr '88

Homeless people fall into one of three distinct subgroups: those who suffer from mental illnesses such as schizophrenia and manic-depressive psychosis; those with problems such as alcohol or drug addiction, criminal behavior, marginal IQs, or personality disorders: and those who have been displaced from their homes and jobs through bad luck and social change. The approximately one-third of homeless people who fall into the first category should be temporarily hospitalized for treatment, involuntarily if necessary. Other homeless people should be given shelter and tools for advancement such as job training and basic education.